THE
AMERICAN
MIXED
BORDER

Beauty bush, Kolkwitzia amabilis, *pours in a cascade of soft pink behind a bronze* Cordyline australis *and a cluster of* Allium *'Purple Sensation' in my mixed border garden.*
Photo: Mark Lovejoy

Ann Lovejoy

THE
AMERICAN
MIXED
BORDER

GARDENS FOR ALL SEASONS

Macmillan Publishing Company   New York

Maxwell Macmillan Canada   Toronto

Maxwell Macmillan International
New York   Oxford   Singapore   Sydney

Macmillan Publishing Company
866 Third Avenue
New York, NY 10022

Maxwell Macmillan Canada, Inc.
1200 Eglinton Avenue East, Suite 200
Don Mills, Ontario M3C 3N1

Macmillan Publishing Company is part of the Maxwell Communication Group of Companies.

Library of Congress Cataloging-in-Publication Data

Livejoy, Ann, 1951-
The American mixed border : gardens for all seasons / Ann Lovejoy.
p.   cm.
Includes index.
ISBN 0-02-575580-3
1. Garden borders.   I. Title.   II. Title: Mixed border.
SB424.L67   1993
635.9′63—dc20   92-27309
CIP

Macmillan books are available at special discounts for bulk purchases for sales promotions, premiums,
fund-raising, or educational use. For details, contact:

Special Sales Director
Macmillan Publishing Company
866 Third Avenue
New York, NY 10022

Book design by Cora Lee Drew

10 9 8 7 6 5 4 3 2 1

Printed in the United States of America

Contents

Geof Beasley garden near Portland, Oregon, formally shaped shrubs and small trees preside over a comfortable melange of seasonal ephemerals. Designer: Mark Schultz. Photo: Mark Lovejoy

Introduction

A writer needs a pretty good reason to introduce yet another garden book into today's crowded market. Though there are many books about plants, and not a few about gardening, or garden design, or landscaping, there are precious few books about garden making. For many a frustrated gardener, the burning question is not, "What plants shall I use?" or even "Where shall I put them?" but rather, "How do I make a bunch of plants into a real garden?" *The American Mixed Border* offers the garden maker not templates but tools with which to implement the garden of the heart. Each chapter addresses a different plant category in terms of its place in the mixed border setting, examining the principles behind garden-making practices and techniques. You will discover why foolproof combinations work, and explore the mechanics of taste itself. *The American Mixed Border* combines practical advice and philosophical analysis to help you re-create favorite borders, learn how to develop lovely and long-lasting plant combinations, or implement original ideas of your own.

Mixed borders are not new, having been around in various forms for the better part of a century. Overshadowed by more popular garden styles, they have never gained the recognition they deserve, yet both practically and philosophically, mixed borders are excellently suited to the North American tempera-ment. In gardening, as with everything else, we tend to want it all: fabulous looks, easy care, no worries. That combination would seem to suggest plastic flowers and Astro Turf, for no living garden is truly carefree. However, mixed borders can fill the bill far better than most, combining the structural strength of evergreen landscaping with the colorful abundance of the herbaceous border. At their best, mixed borders remain attractive throughout the year, yet require no more upkeep (and less water) than the average suburban lawn.

In simple terms, a mixed border is one which holds both herbaceous and woody plants. Trees and shrubs, perennials and bulbs, vines and ground covers are mingled in artful yet soundly practical plantings designed to complement each component. The mixed border is based on a framework of woody plants, many of them evergreen, so its shape is preserved during the colder months. Ephemerals—perennials, biennials, and annuals—appear within this sturdy frame, bringing seasonal bursts and waves of color all through the gardening year. The varied plant palette helps to extend that garden year at both ends, while winter interest is assured by concentrating plants with off-season beauties in shrubby midborder islands or clusters. These islands serve in turn as backdrops against which the earliest bulbs and latest perennials may be displayed to uncommon advantage.

The concept behind mixed borders may best be explained in terms of the four tiers of nature, which roughly speaking are trees, shrubs, ephemerals, and ground covers. In a natural woodland, maples and pines might shelter kalmias and rhododendrons, the shrubs skirted in turn by wildflowers and shod with ferns and mosses. This is obviously a simplification of an enormously complex relationship, yet it holds true on every scale. In many gardens, the plants are segregated by kind, ranked by height, and confined in rows or stiff patterns. In the mixed border, plants are grouped in naturalistic clusters and casually graduated by size and proportion. The backbone planting encircles the border like an informal, living wall; within its confines, each larger plant is given an attendant circle of suitable companions. A delicate Japanese maple placed midborder might be flanked by a pair of daphnes, the small shrubs in turn underplanted with hellebores and spumy grasses. Nearby, a graceful little dogwood rises between stiff sheaves of Siberian iris, a trailing clematis dripping from its slim gray fingers, a sprawl of silvery ground cover at its feet. Sturdy mounds of catmint and carpets of burgundy bugleweed, punctuated in season with early and late bulbs, link the two clusters, each of which is similarly connected to other neighboring groups along the border.

Mixed borders hold more kinds of plants than are commonly seen in our gardens, giving them advantages secondary to a fuller plant palette. Rich textures derive from multiple contrasts of leaf form, size, and coloring, for foliage makes as important a contribution to mixed borders as flowers will. Placement designed to emphasize variety in plant habit, shape, and stature continually refreshes the eye and creates more stimulating topography than offered by a pigeon-breasted herbaceous border. Unexpected and piquant juxtapositions—a scented jasmine trickling through a ground cover of variegated ivy, shrub roses laced with ornamental oreganos and sheaves of lilies—encourage us to look again at plants we have long taken for granted.

Thanks to this diversity, plants in mixed borders tend to be healthy. The pests and diseases that plague monocultural ghettos like rose gardens and heather beds are rare, partly because roses and heathers grown in eclectic plant communities are less obvious to their predators than those grown enticingly en masse. Another important aspect of mixed borders is that their plants are grouped according to cultural needs as well as for artistic purposes, also helping to minimize problems. Ideally, each plant is further placed where its natural inclinations as to habit and form are assets. Thoughtfully combined plants require relatively little intervention as they grow, and such chores as pruning and shaping become aesthetic considerations rather than brutal necessities. Mulching keeps most weeds at bay, but certain members of the mixed border community are permitted to colonize freely (particularly those which do not abuse the privilege). Vines roam through shrubs and over the ground at will, though guidance is always available when needed. Plants tumble through and over and under each other, as they do in their native situations. Many are growing closer together than would be recommended in most garden books, but their eagerness is restrained only when it endangers health, since the abundant growth both shades the ground, conserving moisture and nutrients, and acts as a weed-suppressing barrier.

Philosophically, mixed border making implies paying attention to the reality of each site rather than imposing preconceived patterns or ideas on a given space. In style and content, each mixed border garden should be in harmony with its setting. Within the garden, plants are combined with an eye both to the present and to the future, arranged to give immediate and lasting pleasure, and remain in good health for years with little intervention. A mixed border is a far cry from a "natural" garden—gardening is by definition interference with nature—yet the idea is to arrange the plants so that they grow well and look comfortable, both individually and as a company, as plants do in natural settings. A tightly planted garden will certainly need revision as the individual plants mature. However, maintenance is less the issue than ongoing garden making, rearranging combinations and refining one's idea of garden beauty over the years. For most of us, this—the process—is the juice and the joy of the garden, as much or more important than the flowers and fruits of our labors.

INTRODUCTION

Mixed borders have earned their present popularity in England through their combination of practical strengths and artistic virtues. Healthy and relatively easy to maintain, they are in full beauty for much of the year, and offer significant off-season attractions as well. Mixed borders are wonderful for novice border makers, for they are flexible and forgiving, and their firm outlines disguise and soften a multitude of mistakes. They appeal to those who simply want to enjoy an established garden, as well as to those who prefer the process of garden making over any finished product. Collectors find in them the key to turning a group of plants into a coherent garden. Ardent gardeners appreciate the possibilities for indefinitely extending the gardening year. Beginning gardeners may find them most rewarding, since successful mixed border making depends chiefly upon time, thoughtful observation, and the will to experiment.

Carried to its logical extensions, mixed border making is a radical, even revolutionary way to garden. Plants that are growing in appropriate conditions require far less assistance or intervention. When plants are grouped intelligently as well as aesthetically, their innate qualities and characteristics are assets, making the gardener's role less one of control than of light-handed mastery, leaving us free to pursue the realization of a personal aesthetic. If we are looking for the path that will lead us to our own gardens, if we seek tools that equip us to bring to life the gardens of the inner eye, if we want to break free of tradition without discarding centuries of practical knowledge, we need look no further than to mixed borders.

Ann Lovejoy
Bainbridge Island, Washington
May 15, 1992

THE
AMERICAN
MIXED
BORDER

Mixed borders incorporate plant elements of all sorts and sizes. Here, a small tree, Laburnum × watereri, shelters rhododendrons and azaleas which supply a firm backdrop for a seasonal flow of perennials and bulbs. Woodyard garden, Portland, Oregon. Photo: Cynthia Woodyard

Chapter One

LOOKING

AT

MIXED BORDERS

*M*ixed borders all over the world are united in combining woody plants with seasonal ephemerals. All have perimeter plantings (often combined with walls or fences) to frame the garden. All have backbone plants, many of them evergreen, that shape the borders within those garden walls. All have a lively, seasonal flow of color, thanks to the presence of bulbs and perennials, flowering vines, and vivid annuals. However, there is no one pattern for making mixed borders, and in practice they vary enormously, reflecting the diversity and interests of their makers.

Mixed borders can be formal in design and planting style, as at Filoli in California, where spring bulbs and bedding annuals are ranked in symmetrical, echoing patterns and every bed is neatly outlined in clipped boxwood. They may be free-flowing in form and naturalistic in planting, like the wild garden at Wave Hill in the Bronx, New York. They may be formally laid out, yet have their rigid, geometrical lines softened by generous plantings, as at Tintinhull and Barnsley, both famous English gardens. At North Hill in Vermont, the mixed borders flow in seemingly effortless arrangements that mask the structural quality of the garden's living framework. Existing forest trees and shrubs are intermingled with garden varieties, tying the house and garden securely into their setting. In my own island garden in the Pacific Northwest, towering Douglas

firs, aging fruit trees, and mature shrubs weave into wide borders which encircle our old farmhouse in a colorful, scented embrace all through the year.

Mixed borders can be made to suit any site or style of architecture. Even using a similar palette of plants, a flexible designer could create mixed borders which would faithfully reflect the architectural values of a funky old farmhouse or a sleek new construction gleaming with glass and exposed steel. Using a similar design, but different plants, an ornamental mixed border could look equally appropriate surrounding suburban homes in Santa Fe or Savannah. Their essence is not the exuberant abundance of the English cottage border, nor is it the sculptural austerity of the American grass and daisy border. It lies rather in sensitivity to site and local conditions, as well as to the plants' cultural requirements. More than any other school of garden making, mixed borders are adaptable to situational reality. For proof, we can look at examples of mixed borders in very different parts of the world. Some of these are long-established gardens, others are quite new. Some are famous and highly influential, others private and personal. One or two are horticultural museums, dedicated to preserving the memory of a garden long gone. Others are still forming, and a few are in constant, deliberate flux. Though varied in style and atmosphere, all are true to the underlying principles of mixed border making.

HIDCOTE MANOR

GLOUCESTERSHIRE, ENGLAND

The garden at Hidcote Manor was laid out during the earliest years of the twentieth century by an expatriate American, Lawrence Johnston. In it, Johnston explored several contemporary design theories, fleshing out the concepts with startling innovation. His ten-acre garden was laid out as a series of outdoor rooms, each with its own theme or character. Each room is framed with living walls, and in Johnston's day, their borders held a treasure trove of uncommon plants that was the envy of plantsmen everywhere. The borders were equally unusual in the artful and intelligent arrangement of their contents. Trees and shrubs framed, and in many cases entered, beds which held a profusion of hardy plants, decorative vines, bulbs for all seasons, and tender or half-hardy exotics grouped in handsome and sometimes provocative combinations. One of Johnston's interests was in developing the color themes proposed in the late 1800s by the redoubtable Gertrude Jekyll. His smoldering Red Border, still a tour de force of mixed planting, set a trend amongst the avant gardeners of his day, influencing Vita Sackville-West to make her famed White Border at Sissinghurst.

Johnston was an avid plantsman, famous for the depth and breadth of his collections, yet he had a keen sense of design which precluded the usual plantsman's hodgepodge garden. Instead of limiting his plant palette, as a design oriented garden maker might recommend, he divided his plants into subgroups, giving each its own domain. There were shady walks for woodlanders, banked, raised beds for exotic plants which craved drought and drainage, boggy streamside beds for aquatics. The many plants which tolerate average conditions were arrayed and interplanted to produce successive seasonal displays, often based on remarkable color runs which altered and developed over time. Because most of his budget was dedicated to plant acquisition, Johnston built his garden framework with trees and shrubs, rather than traditional architectural ele-

In one of Hidcote's woodland walks, formally shaped evergreens are linked in sculptural repeats between deciduous shrubs. This informal tapestry hedge both frames and enters the border below it. Photo: Cynthia Woodyard

ments. Walls are woven of beech and yew, arches are made of intertwined shrubs, fastigiate small trees act as pillar and post. The many paths are paved with local materials, often smooth pebbles or rough cobbles. Living, verdant topiary stood in for statuary, marking niche and gateway.

The core of Hidcote is a long, straight walk walled in yew, off which runs an interlinking series of smaller gardens. These garden compartments held thousands of plants, many of them exceedingly rare. The late Peter Healing, himself a noted plantsman and the owner of the wonderful hot-colored mixed borders at The Priory in Kemerton, Worcestershire, spoke with great pleasure of visiting Hidcote in its heyday. "There would be something astonishing 'round every corner," he recalled. "It was literally full of treasures, which Major Johnston shared quite generously." Plants from his garden enriched the private collections and public nurseries of England for many years. Johnston had a keen eye for good form, and many of his selections, such as the lovely spotted lungwort *Pulmonaria* 'Hidcote Pink' and the sturdy rose 'Lawrence Johnston' are still unsurpassed.

Hidcote's garden walls are chiefly hedges, often made of the usual plants—yew, holly, and beech—yet in several cases the species are intermingled in a novel way. Ink green slabs of sheared yew give way here and there to mixed hedges in which beech and holly are regularly alternated. These mixed hedges are sheared like the plain ones, retaining the essential formality of the enclosures they frame. However, the mixtures produce a handsome tapestry effect when in leaf and retain considerable interest in winter, when the combination of skeleton and solid evergreen makes lovely patterns. In the wilder parts of the garden, trimmed hedges give way to looser frames of interwoven shrubs and trees, forerunners of the informally mixed and often unsheared hedges which characterize contemporary American mixed borders. Although Hidcote was made to be a summer garden, the structural evergreens give the garden year-round presence.

Johnston was one of the first to exploit the contrast between tightly sheared hedging and the luxurious abundance of the romantic style of border planting that was replacing the geometric simplicity of Victorian bedding-out at the turn of the century. He liked, too, the contrasts offered by the juxtaposition of the formal central walk and the wild gardens on either side; a few steps through an arched entrance transports you from a landscape of classical, controlled purity to gardens made with an almost anarchistic freedom. Furthering the pattern of contrasts, Johnston organized his garden rooms so that the areas nearest to the house were formally laid out and planted, but the farther the observer wanders afield, the less structured the plantings become. The tidy symmetry of Mrs. Winthrop's garden (a tribute to his mother), gives way to a small natural stream lushly planted with ferns and waterside plants. The

Baroque magnificence of the Red Border is heightened by a nearby rambling walk which leads to a tree-lined meadow full of black faced Jacob's sheep.

Johnston took advantage of the range of settings by placing plants according to their character. In Mrs. Winthrop's garden, elegant white lily-flowered tulips sway amid silver spotted pulmonarias, while the nearby stream runs blue with naturalized scilla and forget-me-nots. Flowering vines decorate arches and drape walls, then escape to pour over hedges, scale trees, and scramble through the borders. Statuesque hardy perennials preside over stiff wheels of fan palms and spiky New Zealand flax, half-hardy exotics which winter over in greenhouses or cold frames.

Now, after years of National Trust guardianship (careful though it is), Hidcote has lost much of its impellingly personal quality. However, the garden continues to present a splendid study in form and contrasts. The framework of the garden holds its own all through the year. In any season, the eye is captured by lovely details—the bronzed, silken foliage of a tree peony shimmers against a matte sheet of clipped yew, spiky bronze cordylines spill from oversize terra-cotta pots against a ruddy terrace of old brick, the joyous warmth of the Red Border after the cautiously tasteful pastels of more typical English gardens.

Covering some ten acres, and serviced by a large and hard-working staff, Hidcote might seem worlds removed from the average American backyard. Nonetheless, this garden offers vital lessons to mixed border builders everywhere, no matter what the scale of their own garden. Hidcote demonstrates the positive value of enclosure, of clearly defining the shape and extent of the garden with boundary hedges, walls, and fences. We see how the style and kind of enclosing material—whether vegetable or manmade—influence the ambience of the space within. We see, too, the worth of borrowed views, learning how to expand the garden's visual limit by framing distant trees or mountains or rolling meadows. In some of the smaller garden rooms, where the captured object might be a singular tree, we recognize that this concept can apply just as well to a tiny urban lot.

The Red Border at Hidcote gains a good deal of its sumptuous color by coupling tender bedding plants like this spiky Cordyline australis 'Atropurpurea' with small shrub roses and hot colored annuals. Photo: Peter Ray

In Hidcote's mixed borders, we find that grouping plants by their cultural proclivities reduces the need for the controlling hand or frequent cosseting. There is no denying the visual boost given to seasonally flowering plants by their evergreen background, which sets off floral incidents much as an appropriate frame can lend a minor drawing importance. Theme gardens based on colors or color families illustrate the strength such limitations offer to a simple border design. Further themes are everywhere to be found, whether based on seasonal display, a habitat, or an emotional atmosphere. Hidcote embodies the concept of the outdoor garden room and utilizes the contrasts between garden styles as well as materials. For mixed border makers, it represents a mother lode of information and ideas.

TINTINHULL HOUSE
SOMSERSET, ENGLAND

The garden at Tintinhull was made in the 1930s by Mrs. Phyllis Reiss, a friend of Johnston's and a great admirer of his garden. The Tintinhull garden is intimate in scale, covering only three quarters of an acre, yet it ably demonstrates the same principles seen at Hidcote. Reiss was a passionate plantswoman who wanted to give her plant collections the sound setting they deserved. Like Hidcote, Tintinhull is divided into compartments and courts, each with its theme of color or style. Here, the inner walls are often made of brick or stone, frequently festooned

Tintinhull is an architectural garden, gaining much of its character from hedge and arch and wall. Its geometrical borders are moderated by abundant plantings, generous yet controlled, which spill softly over the clean edges. Photo: Cynthia Woodyard

with flowering vines and climbing plants. The hedges are mostly formal in shape and shearing, though where the kitchen garden borders the orchard, a line of slim trees makes a natural barrier which successfully ties the garden to the more open landscape of meadows and orchards beyond. Within the garden, repeats of shaped evergreens, bold foliage, and character plants unify the generously varied border plantings.

Though its lines are geometric rather than fluid, and its character owes much to the regularity of its architecture, Tintinhull is in essence a flower garden.

Expansive, intricately constructed border plantings temper the strict geometry of its design and give a personal flavor to each of its courts and small gardens. The color borders which dominate the larger pool garden and the cedar court remain similar to those arranged by Mrs. Reiss half a century ago. However, Penelope Hobhouse, the garden's caretaker for the National Trust, has refined and improved the color combinations and transitions over the years of her tenure. Now they are considered to be among the premier examples of English colorist borders.

Although flowers are a primary feature of Tintinhull, they are made important and substantial by the firm, evergreen structure which envelops them. Indeed, Hobhouse feels that this concept is a key one for amateurs, who so often struggle without success to make their gardens come together into a coherent whole.

"Very often, when gardens disappoint, it is because they lack firm structure," she notes. "Flower gardens, especially, need a structural background to succeed and be at their best."

Disenchanted American garden makers are sometimes heard to grumble that it's easy enough to make a marvelous garden where gorgeous supportive architecture is a given. They may even go so far as to apply the guidebook test to this or that famous border, thereby exposing any innate weakness. (This litmus test involves surreptitiously masking off the background of a border or bed with one's guidebook, then evaluating the plantings when stripped of their architectural trappings. It's fascinating to see how many borders owe an enormous debt to the walls and turrets and whatnot which frame them.) At Tintinhull, the borders read with or without their frames, except when the frames are integral to their design. Structural shrubs and powerful foliage plants give strength and coherence to the perennial tapestries, which in turn bring the more static woody plantings to life. Even in winter, the beautiful old walls and trim hedges, the shaped evergreens and graceful, naked trees, the paths and flagged terraces have a definite presence of their own, keeping the garden space vital and alive all year.

Americans, who are traditionally loath to enclose their yards, often misunderstand the nature of this element of garden design. Our open, unstructured gardens lack privacy as well as enclosure, and rarely develop a distinctive or positive ambience. Exposed to all influences of weather, screening nothing of the local architecture, open to anybody's view, they remain a part of the greater landscape, thus never fully becoming places in their own right. People who build walls and solid fences are considered snobs, if not reclusive weirdos with something to hide. The result, however, is masses of wasted space, empty, sterile yards that are neat as a pin, yet never used. Indeed, these yards do not invite our presence, and offer us nothing if we should venture in them. Take that same space—the average suburban front yard—

and hedge it round with lilac and shrub roses, pyracantha and winter jasmine, hawthorne and dwarf apple trees, and it is suddenly someplace, an outdoor room. Close it off with a lacy iron gate, hooped over with a rose-covered arch, and, presto, the place has charm. Put in a flagstone patio, add a table and a few chairs, and the former dead space becomes alive and inviting. However, it it surprisingly easy to incorporate structural elements into our gardens without persuading them to work together. We may have the hedge along the driveway, an arch over the back gate, a patio and table in the side yard behind the gargage, yet there is nothing to connect these things or set them off from the surrounding neighborhood. It becomes easier to use structural elements coherently when we clarify their purpose:

Penelope Hobhouse has refined Tintinhull's famous color theme borders, making them among the most highly regarded examples of colorist gardening in the world. Here, harsh whites have been exchanged for gentling cream, while the strong reds and coppers are linked with intermediate golds and yellows. Photo: Cynthia Woodyard

they are to provide enclosure for the garden and a framework for its softer plantings. It further helps to think of this structural frame as an entity or a team, its individual parts related both visually and practically. At Tintinhull, for instance, wall and gate give way almost imperceptibly to hedge and arch, and by the time we reach the kitchen garden, we readily accept the implicit barrier of the slim line of trees that divides garden and orchard.

At Tintinhull, we can also see classic color theory put to practice, learn how to balance lesser plants with greater ones, follow sequences of color events leading each into the next, watch foliage patterns and textures carry their weight over many months. We become aware as well of the primary importance of two precepts. First of all, flowers need a setting if they are to be fully appreciated. Secondly, if they are to be experienced as unique places, our gardens must have both enclosure and a discernible form. At Tintinhull, we see how shapeless gardens might gain definition from strategically placed visual barriers of shrubs and small trees. Within the garden, we see that dwarf hedges and paths of any kind guide both eyes and feet, and could similarly give direction and flow to formless garden spaces. Gardens without walls can be given backbone plantings like those of Tintinhull, using fast-growing shrubs and small trees which will provide significant shelter and enclosure within about five years. Existing open fences of chain mesh or widely spaced posts and beams can be covered with trelliswork screens or clothed in living greenery of vines and climbing shrubs. This is an excellent and relatively inexpensive alternative to erecting masonry walls or solid fences, and beats waiting a few centuries for young yew hedges to mature.

BARNSLEY HOUSE
GLOUCESTERSHIRE, ENGLAND

At Barnsley, Rosemary Verey has made a masterpiece of a garden that works in harmony with its house, enfolding it in intimate embrace.

Again, the lessons of Hidcote are telescoped, here to a scale and interpretation readily adaptable to small American gardens. At Barnsley, many features common to the older great English gardens are reproduced, if not quite in miniature, at least on a modest scale which demonstates their flexibility. Barnsley's laburnum walk would not be out of place in an undersized urban plot, brightening the narrow walkway between garage and back entry. Dripping with floral gold in May, glowing with clematis or roses all summer, an openwork tracery of stem and branch in winter, this could be the backbone of a tiny mixed border, filled, as Verey has filled hers, with a lively assortment of blossoms. The fat tulips that blow in spring are followed by rosy ornamental onions, the frowsy bulb foliage soon hidden by spreading hostas. Each laburnum tree, carefully shaped and clipped, has a demure ruff of ivy around its ankles, a lovely detail for winter pleasure.

The larger borders within the garden offer similarly adaptable possibilities, embodying principles that hold true on any scale, from the grandest park down to a dish of bonsai. The Barnsley garden is encircled by the sheltering green of farmyard and countryside, and its mixed borders echo that pattern of frame and filling. The shrubs and small trees that make up the backbone plantings often merge into the borders themselves. A delicate clematis threads through sturdy ivy to surround a doorway or gate with bloom. Golden variegated euonymus insinuates itself up a gnarled old pear tree. Each plant is placed to support specific interactions; a large, solid shrub fills the space behind a delicate filigree of flowers, lending substance and a setting to their floral fluff. Curls of ground cover lick the edges of the borders, dashing in deeper here and there, pulling the eye toward a charming minor effect or echoing colors and textures from the main border.

During the warmer months, flowering plants take center stage, supported by shrubs and foliage plants. When the year grows cold and floral incidents are few, skeletons and evergreenery take on new importance. Snow and frost rime reveal the strength of line and solidity of form that underlie summer's floral tapestry. The garden gains mass and substance from shrubs of all sizes, while character trees anchor

At Barnsley, house and garden unite in a flowing whole, gracious and welcoming in effect.
Plants clothe the house walls and lap the doorstep, encircling windows with color and scent.
Photo: Cynthia Woodyard

flurries of fine textured details. Evergreen shrubs that rise like rocks in a foamy sea of spring bulbs or summer perennials reveal in winter unsuspected sculptural qualities of their own.

Like Tintinhull, Barnsley is a gracious and livable garden, one which welcomes people, not just as visitors, but as inhabitants. The garden is full of places where one can sit with teacup and notebook, enjoy an evening drink by the plashing pool, or absorb the uncanny atmosphere of the garden by night from the steps of the stone memorial.

Verey is adept at balancing design with softening details, knowing where one can afford to let things go and where to be ruthless. A little self-sowing adds charm and spontaneity to a border, while the wrong plant in the wrong place can make for jarring discord. Barnsley is inclusive rather than imposing, its design orderly yet free spirited. Though rich in both vegetable and architectural structure, the scale of the garden transforms the stiffness of formality into an enchanting artifice.

From the house windows, one learns that the garden as a whole holds textures as intriguing as those within the borders. Here is a little quilted herb garden, crisscrossed with boxwood ribbons; over there, a smooth lawn. A straight-edged border is filled with informal drifts of perennials and mature shrubs. Nearby sits an Elizabethan knot garden, latticed like an openwork pie crust with box and germander. Sculpture may be hand-smoothed stone or carven topiary. A double row of portly sentinel yews flanks a flagged path that leads to a beckoning gate. Through it, on a soft spring evening, I once heard a cowman broadly calling home his charges as he stumped down the adjacent lane; "Poppy, Buttercup, Clover, Daisy, come along naow, do!"

Across this lane lies Verey's *potager*, a vegetable garden made in the French manner. This, too, is a mixed border, hedged with lavender and roses, its lovely vegetables arrayed in neat, box-edged beds. Rows of ruffled cabbages and frilled lettuces are presided over by graceful, arching apple trees trained over frames. It is a highly attractive garden and, as Verey is quick to point out, it is highly demanding in return.

"Visitors often tell me how much they love Barnsley, and how lucky I am to have such a lovely garden. I must say, it is not luck which makes the garden lovely. It takes a tremendous lot of work—my staff of three or four people work very hard to keep it in excellent trim, and I am in it every day. When a garden is so much visited, one's standards simply can't relax. Gardens don't make themselves, and they certainly don't keep themselves."

WAVE HILL

NEW YORK USDA ZONE 5

The Bronx, New York, does not immediately suggest a setting for one of America's foremost public gardens, yet it is home to Wave Hill, an extraordinary garden on a twenty-eight-acre estate just a short train ride from the heart of Manhattan. Nearly half the property is wooded, in thick ribbons of trees that screen the garden from the suburban neighborhood around it. The estate is open to the west, allowing expansive views over the Hudson to the rough cliffs of the New Jersey Palisades. Though the estate holds a number of gardens and plant collections, the Wild Garden and the Flower Garden are of most direct interest to mixed border builders. Though quite different in style and atmosphere, both gardens contain plants of all sorts in great variety. Each presents its plants in a setting and manner that suit the character of the plants themselves. The first is informal in design and planting, and holds chiefly wildflowers, stressing species rather than hy-

Adventurous color runs are a Wave Hill trademark, where saturated oranges, purple blacks, and murky reds are lightened by plenty of gray, silver, and lavender. Photo: Marco Polo Stufano

brids. The second is rather formal in design, though adventurous in planting, and showcases garden flowers, including uncommon older hybrids.

The Wild Garden runs over and along a ridge of high ground, its rambling paths meeting at the rustic gazebo that overlooks the river from the ridge's peak. Naturalistic in form and planting, the Wild Garden overflows with a succession of native and exotic plants. Evanescent annuals seed themselves into the gravel of the paths. Colonies of woodland perennials are punctuated with small bulbs. The shadbush and elderly maples are laced with vines. Feathery, upright chamaecyparis flicker like flames in the river breezes, echoed on a smaller scale by towering, silvery verbascums and stands of species lilies. At the garden's heart stands a graceful, multi-trunked staghorn sumac, its velvety branches spreading in benediction over its lesser neighbors. Here is haven for plants too flopsy in form or too casual in style for life in the formal border. Native or imported, true species or not, these plants have the simple habit and careless grace of wild things. Their flowers are fleeting, the successions of color ebbing and flowing with the seasons. Like the woods and fields of New England, the Wild Garden is quietly delightful in spring, handsome in summer, glorious in autumn, serene in winter. Its cycles are those of the earth, rather than the social calendar, its harmonies subtle rather than brash.

Many of the shrubs and trees in this garden are relics of older plantings, absorbed into the design of the Wild Garden as it grew up around them. Some are now out of scale, and will be replaced over the next few years with younger plants. "Gardens of this kind are not static," explains Marco Stufano, Wave Hill's Director of Horticulture. "When we made the Wild Garden, it was wonderful to have some mature things to work with it; it gave a feeling of permanence right away. However, you've got to keep your eyes honest when you look the garden over. If a plant is wrong, or has grown to be wrong for its setting, you've got to be tough and do something about it."

The Wild Garden is artfully laid out to give the illusion that its plants are growing as they might in nature. Meandering paths divide the garden into a series of irregularly shaped beds, each with a shrubby spine that acts as foil and frame to the plants on either side, and makes visual walls between the several parts of the garden. The occasional fallen log, mats of rotting leaves (carefully removed where they might prove lethal to the plants beneath), and self-sown colonies of annual wildflowers add realism to its atmosphere. Narrow paths allow only one or two people to walk abreast, directing attention to the garden and its plants rather than to human companions. The plants themselves are close at hand, near enough that leaves and flowers may be examined closely, their textures felt, their scents appreciated. This proximity, the winding paths which create pockets of privacy, and the carefully human scale of the plantings create together an impression

of intimacy unheard of in public gardens and sadly uncommon even in private ones. After a few moments alone in this garden, social tensions are forgotten. The ear is caught by bird song, the eye by sun-dappled bark, a shimmering fountain of purple fennel, the thick velours of a club moss, the green fingers of an arching fern.

The mixture of evergreen and deciduous shrubs and the changing terrain within the Wild Garden offer a multitude of conditions and ecological niches for its plants. In some places, full sun, silty soil, and the sloping banks of the ridge provide the summer heat and good drainage demanded by native perennials like butterfly weed (*Asclepias tuberosa*), as well as species tulips and many other small bulbs. In other spots, the leaves of many years have composted into the crumbling forest duff beloved of true woodlanders. In late winter, leafless shrubs are belted about with spangled snowdrops, starry anemones, and snow crocus, which dream dormant beneath leafy branches come summer. In summer, the same shrubs spread protective arms over shade-loving wildflowers and ferns. Here grow hepaticas and hostas, nodding trilliums, and blankets of bloodroot that run heedless into the sun they are supposed to detest. Whether native or not, the plants are initially placed in like minded communities where their needs will be complementary. As they spread and compete, their progress is judiciously directed to preserve the health and survival of the community members as well as the natural appearance of the garden as a whole. If plants seem to alter their preferences after a bit, they are not hindered by Wave Hill's gardeners, who are taught to learn from the plants, and to control them with the lightest of hands.

Though utterly different in style and appearance, Wave Hill's Flower Garden is governed by the same philosophy. Plants and setting are well matched, each complementary to the other, and controlled abundance is again the keynote. Geometric in layout, the wide, intersecting slate paths, and ample seating make this a convivial garden, evocative of the glamorous garden parties of the golden twenties. Once a formal rose garden, the Flower Garden now holds a connoisseur's collection of classic garden flowers, including many hybrids and forms popular in the early decades of the century. In May, the beds overflow with great, blowsy peonies, the stiff fans and ruffled flowers of iris providing counterbalancing contrast of form. Clematis drape the silvered wood of arch, bower, and fence. Roses still abound, but small shrub and climbing roses have replaced the fussy, disease-prone hybrid teas that filled the previous garden. Rivers of constant color run through intermingled plantings of bedding annuals, perennials, and summer-blooming bulbs. Each bed has a shrubby backbone to support the floral abundance. Butterfly bushes (*Buddleia*) and hydrangeas, dwarf lilac, and purple-leaved sand cherry (*Prunus* × *cistena*) provide both seasonal flowers and interesting foliage. The dusky smoke bush, *Cotinus coggygria* 'Royal Purple' and a red honey locust, *Robinia pseudoacacia* 'Rubylace', offer lovely leaves all season, then burst into flame at summer's end. Indeed, autumn may be the most visually sumptuous season at Wave Hill, for both the Wild Garden and the Flower Garden hold treasure troves of late-blooming flowers as well as vibrant fall foliage plants.

Stufano, along with the late John Nally, former Curator of Plants at Wave Hill, deliberately shaped both of these gardens to have an intimate, personal atmosphere. Unlike most public gardens, these are planted both to please and to provoke. "I get tired of safe plantings of pale blue, silver, and white," Stufano explains cheerfully. "Though people bristle at orange, gold, or scarlet, they all have a place, and a good place, in our gardens. No color is impossible to work with, and sometimes the most unlikely ones—like orange, or magenta—make the most exciting effects. One of the best gardens I've seen in a long time is the new purple and orange border that Doug Ruhren and Nancy Goodwin are making at Montrose Nursery in North Carolina. As Americans get more liberated, we can be bolder in the use of color, and finally escape the traditional formulas to find our own way."

At Wave Hill, tasteful runs of pewter and pastels are enriched with royal reds and murky purples, making an excitingly successful place to put the more violent magentas. Orange, perhaps the next most difficult color to use well, is paired here with copper and bronze, muted purples and smudgy reds to waken its clarion tones while subduing the shrill. When they come off, such plantings are triumphs indeed. When they fail, they are equally spectacular in their wrongness, yet this bothers Stufano not at all.

"Making mistakes is one of the most important tools in garden making," he declares roundly. "If we want to do something different, to get beyond the safe and obvious, we have to be willing to be wrong sometimes. The trick is to know that mistakes don't matter, they're part of the learning process. Daring to be wrong is how great gardens get made." Stufano and his staff no longer wait to find the perfect solution before implementing changes. "These gardens are very much in the public eye, and it is part of our policy to show our visitors how gardens come into being. We let them see everything—process, development, failure, and success."

Stufano also believes, with Hobhouse, in the primacy of form. "Architecture—the woody and evergreen plants, the bones, and the hardscape—is the most important part of the garden. Once you have that right, you can play around, making changes and just letting things happen until the plants start to fall into place. Even then, to keep a garden vital, it has to keep changing. Some of that happens anyway; plants get too big, or die, or maybe we just lose interest in them. But we have to go beyond that, take risks, try really new things, if we want to break out of old patterns and formulas to make gardens that are genuinely our own."

BAINBRIDGE ISLAND

WASHINGTON USDA ZONE 8

Like the National Forests, my present garden is a multiple use facility. This garden is mixed in every sense of the word; not only are the borders full of all manner of plants, but the garden itself is the hub of our active family. It is as apt to host a horde of Cub Scouts as staid horticulturists, and is embellished with plastic wading pools rather than stately fountains. The lawn is decidedly imperfect in visual terms, but more than adequate as a place to hold barbecues, birthday parties, and water balloon fights. Garden ornaments range from tasteful bunny planters to artful groups of model dinosaurs or abandoned swords and shields. Several dogs and an embarrassing number of cats consider it their turf as well as mine. The remarkable thing is that the garden often looks very nice despite all this, and that the heavy use results in surprisingly little damage to the garden or the gardener's temper. Because there is goodwill on all sides, the acre or so of garden satisfies most of its users most of the time.

Such peaceful coexistence is made possible in part by the fact that there are also six acres of untrammeled woods and meadows. However, in our previous garden on a tiny urban lot, kids and cats shared ground with my mingled beds for five years without serious difficulties. This point is worth underlining, for the conviviality of gardens is rarely held up as a virtue. Not all good gardens are shrines to good taste, but all are a place to be, welcoming the presence of people. A garden may be far from perfect in textbook terms, yet have a definite style and beauty of its own. In making and evaluating my own gardens. I have learned that it is important not to compare apples to oranges. If your inner eye is focused on Sissinghurst, it can be hard to see the quite different strengths and attractions of your own garden. If you feel overwhelmed and discouraged by the garden making process, it helps to ask yourself a few home questions. What needs must your space fulfill? How experienced is your staff, if you have one at all? Is your budget in thousands and millions, or in tens and hundreds? How many Elizabethan stone walls do you have to work with? If your garden is pleasant, or charming, or exciting, or comfortable despite your resources rather than because they are so vast, you have a good deal to be proud of. As always, compromises help. Accept that your yard isn't Sissinghurst, remember that garden making takes time and patience, aim to please yourself, and you will find enormous pleasures in the process.

Still very young, our present garden is nestled into the shell of a long neglected orchard. When we

Thai sheep and local cats wait for thirsty birds on the well cover in my kitchen garden. This is a multi-use garden, serving an active family, numerous pets, and native wildlife. Photo: Mark Lovejoy

arrived here some five years ago, the entire property could charitably have been described as a mess. The garden was a tangle of dog kennels, goat pens, and scores of closely planted trees and shrubs, all distinctly worse for wear. It was a bit daunting, but we immediately loved the ambience and knew that, once reawoken, it would be a wonderful garden. Rather than sweep the whole business away and start fresh (as every landscape architect and designer we knew strongly urged), we elected to take a year for assessment before making any major decisions on what was to go or stay. We learned where the sunny places are in each season, where the prevailing winds need blocking, where the ground stays soggy for months, and where it dries out in minutes. We studied our old trees, watching for hidden seasonal beauties. We passed the time by removing several miles

Year one in our island garden: a big job lies ahead. Photo: Mark Lovejoy

of barbed wire left over from the kennels, as well as dozens of dead or dying trees and shrubs. Anything that looked at all hopeful or occupied a strategic position was spared. We were cautious, reasoning that homely plants can always be removed later, but could never be put back. As the garden began to take shape, and our use patterns emerged, we developed a twenty-year plan for the property as a whole. The garden was among the first undertakings, but it, too, was conceived as a long-term project.

Today, many trees and shrubs have been removed, yet others that will eventually go are still in place, either because they screen the road, give privacy from neighbors, or are great climbing trees. Certain handsome but ailing trees are undergoing restorative treatment, their soil replenished, their broken limbs removed, their suckers carefully thinned over five or six years to avoid shock. The best of the old shrubs have been fed and cleaned out or, in a few cases, cut to the ground. Their established root systems will give us a larger renewed shrub in less time than it would take a replacement

to mature. The battered old hedges have been cleaned out and fed, the many gaps filled with fresh plantings. In some places, young plants have been placed close to the elderly ones they are to replace. Small, inexpensive trees and shrubs are growing on to full size in a nursery bed. Planted in tree bags, large sacks of permeable horticulture cloth, their maturing root systems are contained by the sides of the bag. When old plants must come out, we will have large, well-grown stock on hand that can be moved without shock or root damage.

During the first year, part of the decision process was finding out how we as a family would use the property. The sunniest, best drained spots went to the vegetable garden and chicken yard. Since the children seized immediate possession of the little stream, I content myself with introducing a few willows and shrubby dogwoods each year, and coaxing the skunk cabbages out of the boggy woods. A giant *Gunnera magellanica* has appeared on the far bank, and the boggy foreground has begun to fill up with candelabra primulas and water iris which I want to mass in the future bog borders. The big meadow

Four years later, the same area has become a garden. There is still much to do, yet our work and patience have already been rewarded. Photo: Mark Lovejoy

by the road has become a playing field, so I limit myself there to a wide roadside strip (our baseball border) where no plant is more valuable than my children's pleasure in active games. In both places, the patient shrubs and trees will grow on with minimal intervention or assistance. When the time comes to develop these areas further, the border backbones will already be in place.

The main garden surrounds the house and its attendant sheds on three sides. When we came here, the garden area was almost impenetrable, the unmown lawn chest high and full of stumps and sudden potholes. During our initial yard cleanup, we uncovered a section of informal hedge, mixed even more than the English tapestry hedges, and clearly

never pruned. Holly and camellia, rhododendrons and skimmias, barberries and viburnums were interwoven in a richly textured array. On either side were large gaps, but a number of deciduous shrubs indicated the line the entire hedge had once taken. This battered, informal hedgerow was repaired, its combinations continued to wrap the mixed borders in an angled ribbon some three hundred feet long. To avoid the repressive feeling of an unbroken evergreen hedge, we mixed in red-leaved sand cherries and purple smoke bush, marbled rose and cream barberries, shrub roses, and large hydrangeas. The original palette of evergreens was expanded to include silvery *Senecio greyi* and *Artemisia* 'Huntington', and several forms of variegated euonymus, some splashed silver, others gold.

Some ancient fruit trees set a few yards in front of the hedgerow became the centerpieces for the first borders. These were initially made very narrow and mulched heavily to keep them free of weeds. As we got each section under control, we widened the borders again, always mulching as we went. The first plantings were chiefly of shrubs and larger plants, but I always threw in lots of annuals and perennials just for the fun of having them. Last year, the borders reached their full size, and now the plantings are being rearranged properly. I am constitutionally incapable of following directions, even my own, so I have not found the careful planting charts I always make to be of much use. My favorite method for planting borders is to group all sorts of things that seem compatible. The main relationships are generally planned out ahead; I may have thought out a scheme for a silver weeping pear and a lot of *Hosta* 'Krossa Regal', for instance, or want to set off the lemon-lime variegated dogwood 'Cherokee Sunset' with white and yellow plants, throwing in a fair amount of red to echo the dogwood's wine red flowers and frosted burgundy twigs. Dozens of plants— far more than I will use—come up from the nursery bed and holding area to make the working palette for the bed in progress. The secondary and minor combinations suggest themselves from these, as do ground covers and transitional plants of various sorts that link the new arrangement to those on either side.

All is allowed to settle in for a season or two, then I begin to make frequent notes about the border's character and development. Later, these notes guide both the rearrangement of unsatisfactory groupings and the fine tuning of pleasing ones. Most plant-moving sessions take place in spring and late fall, whichever is best for the plant in question. However, spontaneous forays may occur at any time of year as something especially good or awful inspires action. The notes, compiled over many months, are especially helpful since, though background areas may be planted with extreme simplicity, the main borders are complex indeed. The concept or vision so clear in April is clouded by August, when a whole new set of problems may present itself. By comparing a year's worth of notes, it is easier to avoid solutions to one difficulty that may compound another. Through continual refinement, the beds may come in time to fulfill the challenge of year-round good looks. It is perfectly true that this goal requires constant tinkering from the gardener. I am often asked if this isn't a tremendous bother, but to me it is the soul of garden making, that which keeps the connection between garden and gardener alive.

Though the aim throughout this garden is to develop borders that remain attractive throughout the year, I am not looking for June in January. I do want harmonious plant communities that have character and presence every day. Winter gardens are usually strong on evergreens and architecture, but both of these elements can be overdone to the garden's detriment. Architectural gardens that do not derive their character from plants are often lifeless. Though invaluable for creating a visual frame, an excess of evergreens makes a garden feel gloomy and static. Too few leave a garden exposed and formless. When the proportions of decorative plants and structure are in balance, the garden has heart as well as body. The right proportions, however, cannot be reduced to a formula. What is right for one setting may be all wrong in another. Then, too, all garden plans are subject to sudden change, as our ever interesting climate goes through mood swings. Here in the Pacific Northwest, a few decades of mostly mild winters lulled many gardeners into planting all

sorts of tender evergreens that are only borderline hardy in Zone 8. The past few years have reminded us that we can expect single-digit temperatures hard on the heels of warm, wet weather that encourages active growth, leaving plants extremely vulnerable to frost damage. In some places, our perimeter hedges, as well as key border plants, have been winter-killed three times in four years. Each time, we replaced the lost with hardier plants, yet each time, a new combination of climate events proved fatal. This is discouraging, but rather than rely strictly on old standbys, we have kept on experimenting. Slowly, we are broadening the palette of winter-hardy plants by trying many species, many hybrids, and strains, and selections, seeking sturdy survivors which may succeed where so many have failed.

One of my main garden goals is to place each plant so that it is appreciated for itself. This is true even of structural plants, for I don't want to value any plant merely as part of a vegetable wall, divider, or screen. When we walk through the garden in November or January, I want to see the gloss on the holly, the blue haze on the spruce, the sunny splash of yellow on a 'Gold Band' yucca or variegated euonymus. I like my garden walls rough and irregular, with the appeal of homespun textiles. I also have a profound dislike for plants used like manmade architecture. Though I can appreciate how they function, and even see a certain beauty in them, it is offensive to me in the same way that watching trained bears in a circus rouses a deep distaste. It would be simplistic to say that I prefer plants to be natural, for nothing is less natural than a garden, and any plant, in any garden, might be considered as trapped as a zoo animal by natural plant purists. What I do strive for is an understanding and appreciation of the essential nature of each plant, so that they can be used in ways that make their true qualities working assets, and so that they will need minimal control or interference from me. Partly this is ethics, but partly too it is laziness, for it is far easier to care for plants that are well placed than those that are stressed.

Now that the garden is approaching its fifth year, it is like an adolescent, gawky but pleasing, and showing sure promise of future beauty. The quickest growing plants are already performing strongly, with intimations of maturity on every hand. By making wonderful soil everywhere, by double digging the beds (once and only once and never again) and supplying annual feeding mulches of compost and amendments, we have managed to speed up the gentle progress a bit, but it is still true, as Vita Sackville-West so often stated, that a garden takes between five and seven years to come together. In those first years, when the garden seems to be all sticks and mud, and visitors may fail to see what is so clear to your inner vision, it can seem a hopelessly long time. I have learned to soften the frustration of the waiting period by planting immediately decorative things—annuals, biennials, perennials, and bulbs—in great quantities. As the narrow borders deepened and the backbone shrubs enlarged, I was always shifting these ephemerals forward, reminded of a visitor's comment that perennials really ought to come with wheels. (My husband would like to see wheels on trees as well, for they become as unwieldy as pianos if one waits too long to find their permanent home.) Abundant planting is a terrific morale booster, while sparse planting, especially when the borders are young, has a most depressing appearance. Though you will certainly need to divide some of the plants within a few years to keep their proportions in bounds, it is well worth the extra bother to have well-filled borders right away. It is best to begin as you mean to go on, planting with bold generosity.

This credo serves as well in tiny urban gardens as in sprawling country ones. Our Seattle garden filled a thirty-five by sixty-foot lot, which also held a swing set and a sandbox, not to mention a house. Because there was so little room, we made mingled beds with dwarf and low-growing shrubs rather than mixed borders. The original modest plantings, based on Mediterranean subshrubs and evergreen herbs, rapidly expanded, spilling down our steep front hillside to fill the parking strip. Soon, nearby traffic circles held our overflow and, before long, we had the satisfaction of watching a greenbelt of small gardens appear along neighboring streets. City gardens, open as they often are to public view, can be highly influential, encouraging similar plantings

This old apple tree and the evergreen shrubs behind it were the inspiration for the informal tapestry hedge and mixed borders which the garden holds today. Photo: Mark Lovejoy

and giving hundreds of passersby a share in the floral abundance. Even though our house was on the edge of a rough neighborhood, each act of vandalism seemed to be balanced by one of anonymous generosity. Pots of lilies and spent florist's azaleas were left on the porch, and once we found several sacks of manure with an anonymous note reading, "For the roses." Complete strangers would stop by with favorite plants, explaining that, though they didn't have gardens themselves, they enjoyed ours and wanted to be part of it.

Even now, living on a relatively rural island, passersby stop in to ask about various plants and comment on the garden's progress. Much as we value our privacy, I also value this connection with other gardeners. At times, however, I have struggled with the burden of reputation, finding it hard to reconcile the expectations of others with my own

Existing evergreens like this young hemlock became the backdrop for year-round seasonal displays in our island garden. In May, powdery blue flowers of evergreen Ceanothus thyrsiflorus set off red Jupiter's beard, Centranthus ruber, along the driveway. Photo: Mark Lovejoy

desire to experiment and love of change. When the garden was just begun, I was showing a landscape architect around, explaining the developmental stages that were to follow this raw beginning. He shook his head sadly and said, "Ann, Ann, I could make you a garden that looked like something in a week." I forbore from the obvious retort, "Yes, but it would never look any different after that," and made instead a (vain) plea for process. For me, a garden is not something to have, but something to do. My relationship with my garden, like that with my husband and children, is ongoing. Gardens are never finished, but always in the making. Our twenty-year plan is just a way to break a huge amount of work into manageable pieces. When it is done—if, indeed, that plan is ever fully implemented—the garden will still be in flux, alive and ever changing.

Mixed borders may be summer or year-round gardens, formal or casual, but all contain a broad palette of woody and ephemeral plants. Elk Rock, Portland, Oregon. Photo: Cynthia Woodyard

Chapter Two

BORDER BUILDING

FRAMEWORK

When it comes down to practical details, the making of mixed borders and mingled beds is much like any other kind of garden making. In all parts of the country, indeed, in all parts of the world, the basics are the same. Soil and sun, rain and wind patterns should guide the arrangement of any garden, as will local conditions and site specifics. However, what most powerfully shapes a mixed border garden is its framework. This may mean trellis baffles or mirrored panels, stone walls or wooden fences, hedges sheared or shaggy, but whether mineral or vegetable, garden framework must be architectural. It must have both visual and physical strengths if it is to effectually define the garden space and enclose the private areas, marry the garden to its immediate surroundings and selectively filter out architectural elements we wish to ignore. It should simultaneously provide shelter for both people and plants, and create an ambience of welcome and privacy. Framework takes on a similar role and importance to house walls, yet we do not wish it to dominate or overshadow the garden itself.

This sounds daunting, yet it need not be, for both design and process may be relatively simple and still yield a complex result. My own definition of the mixed border garden is even more demanding than the original English version, which only has to be wonderful in high summer, yet mine can be realized by an amateur working alone in a tiny urban space just as well as on a rambling country estate crawling with garden help. My mixed borders are expected to have character and distinction all year round, and to house healthy communities of plants in rich variety. The success of such a garden depends heavily on its frame. In the lovely English and European gardens that fill glossy picture books, framework consists largely of mature, precisely clipped hedges and picturesque old walls punctuated with turrets and battlements. North American architectural styles are legion, but very few of them offer similar combinations, nor would they be in sympathy with walls and hedges of the European sort even if we could make convincing counterfeits. This doesn't mean that we can't learn from the Old World, only that we must adapt rather than copy their framing techniques. It is easy to develop an impression that framework must be some combination of walls and wide hedges, yet in fact, how the frame is made matters not at all, so long as the basic goals of definition, enclosure, privacy and shelter are appropriately met.

Having identified what framework should accomplish, we have a splendid opportunity for creative problem solving. Where traditional solutions are not workable, dozens of alternatives are waiting to be applied or discovered. The style of frame we choose must be compatible with what we are gardening around; split level ranch house, angular condo, and elderly farmhouse all suggest different treatments. In very small gardens, there may not be room for hedges, and even where space is not a limitation, there may be a number of screening options which seem more appealing. Any given site might require several kinds of visual barriers that vary in height and width as well as style. Often, only a portion of the garden will be truly enclosed, with less private areas receiving less visually exclusive demarcation. There are endless combinations of screens and baffles, fences and trellis that can fulfill the function of fat hedges and expensive walls, especially on a smaller scale. Fences in particular lend themselves to a wide range of treatments. Many are both functional and handsome, while any that fall aesthetically short but can support plant life are easily disguised. Even the lowly chain link fence can be given an entirely new appearance by threading it with cedar slats, perhaps running them in diagonal ribbons. A thick layer of climbing shrubs and decorative vines will further increase its effectiveness as a barrier to sight and sound. In our present garden, a rusty barbed wire fence has been transformed by the addition of straight apple prunings woven upright through the wire strands. Ivies and a pink-variegated kiwi creep between the sticks, making a handsome barrier that is less than an inch thick and cost nothing but time.

In narrow side gardens where there is no room to introduce an element of mystery with billowing plant veils or angled turns in a path, the magic can literally be worked with mirrors. Set at angles, mirrored panels mounted within arches or solid fence sections alter our perception of space. A fascinating illusion of spaciousness is produced when paired or multiple panels are set up to reflect the garden back and forth into infinity. (Do be sure, however, that the mirrors are set well behind the beds, so nobody tumbles Alice-like through them.) Where the neighborhood offers immediate or distant views you would like to enjoy, consider making a window in your hedge or fence. Privet or laburnum can be woven into a leafy arch through which a splendid tree or far off mountain is framed. Hedges may be punctuated by portholes or peepholes or cozy bolt-holes like deep, Victorian windowseats in which a person can hide from the world. Fences may have windows as well, round or rectangular, tiny or big as a picture window. These can be understated, as when deliberate gaps are left between rough, bark-covered boards, through which one glimpses the sea or a staggering cityscape as if by accident. Fence windows may be framed with sash and shutters or rimmed with seashells. They can be bold cutouts in strong geometrical shapes, stars and triangles splashed with bright paint for emphasis, or led up to with trompe l'oeil painting or trelliswork panels to suggest lengthy vistas.

There is no single right way to make garden framework, no formula or specific combination of elements that will yield the ideal garden. Implementation and techniques may vary enormously, depending on time, expense, and other factors. Short-term answers and shortcuts are usually frowned upon by traditionalists, yet the same end can often be achieved by a variety of means; which method is right for you depends on your current circumstances. In garden making, as in everything else, it always pays to question the shoulds and the givens, for many rules were developed in other times and other places, and few, if any, encompass the only version of truth. We frequently hear that structure is the single most important element in a garden, yet structure alone makes a sterile enclosure rather than a living garden. It is further said that structure is easiest to introduce into a young garden and much harder to add later, yet this is only partially true. Where permanent or solid barriers are impractical, the illusion of structure, whether worked by mirrors or by paper thin bamboo screens masquerading as fences, achieves the same ends as the real thing. Though such shortcuts are achieved by less than permanent means, why not? For better or worse, ours is not a society based on permanence. For every gardener who hopes to dig the same bit of earth for decades, there are many more who can't hope to, or don't even want to. Planting a young yew hedge is indeed a powerful and positive statement of hope

Mixed borders gain strength and definition from their woody framework, which provides enclosure for the garden, privacy for people, and creates a variety of habitats for plants. Author's garden. Photo: Mark Lovejoy

for the future. However, if you know you will have only a few years in a garden, forgo the yew in favor of more immediately gratifying choices. Perhaps they are not as elegant as traditional choices, but invention doesn't come cheap. Success is born of practice, time, and failure. Out of our experimentation will come new traditions that will stand on equal footing with those of other ages.

Where time and space permit, there are plenty of good reasons for defining the garden with hedges. The classic English and European models are not the only options. Hedges may be formal or informal, plain or mixed, imposing or welcoming. They can be classically severe or warmly personal, backing the borders with geometric precision, or melding almost indistinguishably into them. They can be

expensive or cheap, integrating stray shrubs you have somehow collected into an important contribution to the garden rather than an irrelevance. In densely populated aeas, hedges bring life to the concrete wilderness, while in rural places, they lend order to the chaos of nature. Hedges filter noise, dust, pollution, and visual distractions and, unlike a wall or fence, even an evergreen hedge will change through the seasons, emphasizing the natural cycles of the garden itself. Even on a small scale, their influence is greater than that of a similar mass of bedding annuals, for though hedging of any sort is innately structural rather than decorative, in essence it is alive. No matter what their size or style, perimeter hedges determine the character of the borders they enclose as inert walls and fences cannot.

THE FORMAL HEDGE

The formal hedge is the mainstay of both English and European gardens. Whether it entirely encloses a garden or links a series of buildings and standing walls, a formal hedge acts as a strong barrier to the outer world while wedding all that lies within. Invariably made of a single kind of plant, the formal hedge is distinguished by its artificial shape which often mimics that of an architectural wall. Though some hedge plants grow in uniform shapes by nature, in formal hedges, geometry is imposed on a regular basis by the gardener. Such hedges are indispensable in formal gardens, where they provide instant and utterly clear direction for eye and foot. They define the garden space, delineate borders and garden rooms, and direct the flow of movement, all at the same time. Their strength and uniformity can unite disparate or irregular plantings, or complement symmetrical planting patterns. While certain schools of design consider them a garden in themselves, formal hedges are the traditional backdrop for overflowing ornamental borders. Coupled with immaculate lawns, they give loose, romantic plantings instant definition, and are a powerful enough frame to make a mediocre border look dramatically better than it really is.

Formal hedges are generally quite broad (many are half as wide at the base as they are tall), which makes them excellent baffles for street pollution and traffic noise, and for eliminating unwanted views. With their massive, castlelike qualities, they make convincingly architectural arches, tunnels, and passageways within a garden, and are useful for marrying gardens and lawns to large houses and other imposing buildings. Very often, formal perimeter hedges are echoed within the borders on a smaller scale. Dwarf hedges, clipped into running rectangles, perhaps interrupted with topiary balls, may edge beds, line paths, or divide the garden space into rooms. The hedges may be more or less matching in color and texture, as in the classic coupling of yew and box, or made in contrasting pairs, as when ribbons of gray-green lavender offset rows of pyramidal, silvery spruce. Formal hedges are as often deciduous as evergreen, particularly in colder

climates where evergreen choices are limited; there, dense, twiggy shrubs and trees that tolerate frequent pruning are the hedge plants of choice. Yew, holly, privet, and beech are old favorites, as are laurel and box, hazel and hemlock.

Traditional formal hedges do offer some drawbacks, especially for North American gardeners. For one thing, they can take up a tremendous amount of room—a rare commodity in our small yards—for relatively little in return. At their best matched up with imposing architecture, formal hedges look far less appropriate beside a suburban ranch house, a seaside saltbox cottage, or a modest Craftsman bungalow. Though a safe and reliable choice beside mock-Tudor or mock-Tara, and quite suitable companions for sleek, modern constructions, formal hedges are hardly visually exciting. They are very expensive to install and maintain, and slow to de-

Formal hedges require a good deal of upkeep to look their best, and plant damage or imperfections can be hard to conceal. They make a magnificent canvas against which flowery pictures may be displayed, but mature very slowly, making them an investment in the future. Merton Garden, England. Photo: Cynthia Woodyard

velop and mature. Until a hedge is big enough to fulfill its assigned role, the garden will appear unfocused. In the meantime, the hedge must be assiduously tended if it is to develop properly. Few American garden helpers are skilled pruners (one wishes the majority of them would take up computer hacking and leave defenseless plants alone), yet good pruning, especially in the formative years, is crucial to the health and looks of a hedge. At every stage, formal hedges must be carefully clipped two or three times a year or they will lose their carefully produced shape. Then, too, any irregularity in growth or health destroys the value of a formal hedge, the uniformity of which is its definitive strength. Young hedges need frequent weeding to keep them clean of pernicious weeds (a fact that makes sharp-leaved holly and barberries seem less attractive), though a deep mulch will help here. Care and feeding must be carefully adjusted each season to balance the effects of each microclimate along the hedge site. Plants that are growing strongly might need a bit of reshaping, while any that falter would get appropriate action, whether it be a dose of fertilizer, extra mulch, or a drip line for extra summer irrigation. If all this is done, regularly and properly, a few decades down the road the hedge will have achieved its full height and bulk, and will look just like the picture books. If it doesn't look quite that great to you, perhaps it will to your grandchildren, for many of those splendid picture book hedges are not decades but centuries old.

THE INFORMAL HEDGE

In North America, where architectural styles vary enormously, informal hedges are often a visually appropriate option. Like formal hedges, they are made of one kind of plant, but because they are not sheared, and are often flowing in line as well, they present a less artificial appearance. Informal hedges are as often made with deciduous plants as with evergreens, and may offer the gardener a bonus of flower and fruit that would be lost to the secateurs on a sheared hedge. Though they look fine rowed out along straight boundary lines, informal hedges lend themselves just as well to the curving, irregular swoop favored by many contemporary garden makers. Depending on the kind of plants used, informal hedges fit nicely into almost any kind of garden scheme. A simple row of unclipped arborvitae may successfully screen off close neighbors, make an overture toward the nearby native woods, and play backdrop for a mixed border. A bushy band of flowering quince can divide a play yard from a driveway, while a curving line of shrub roses might keep dogs out of the vegetable garden. Sometimes, too, one can employ the appearance of unity while celebrating diversity (this technique especially appeals to collectors of certain species). A solid hedge of rhododendrons or camellias or quince might be revealed in spring as a ribbon of color, spilling in carefully graded tints from rich black-red through rose and pink to palest blush, or running from spectrum yellow to white, or presenting the whole range of purples.

Because they do not have to accept heavy annual pruning, informal hedges may be made of anything that will naturally achieve the height and bulk you are looking for. It also helps if they appreciate the local conditions. Skinny columnar junipers like 'Skyrocket' are excellent choices in tiny urban gardens, where they will never outgrow their position, and, once established, are quite tolerant of pollution and drought (though this is not intended as license for total neglect). Mountain laurel and dwarf rhododendron make handsome hedges in shady gardens, while shrubby dogwoods are an excellent choice in damp places. A row of dwarf apple trees may be espaliered into a fetching wall for an edible mixed border where many of the plants contribute to the kitchen as well as to the general aesthetic.

Though less labor intensive than formal hedges, informal ones are not entirely carefree. They too must be given a good start and kept free of weeds if they are to grow well. They too will benefit from a feeding mulch each year, and although uniformity of growth is less vital to the good appearance of an informal hedge, an annual light pruning to remove deadwood and keep new growth in balance will contribute greatly to its looks.

THE TAPESTRY HEDGE

Strictly speaking, the traditional tapestry hedge is but a slight variation on the formal hedge. As developed at Hidcote, tapestry hedges are symmetrically arranged and regularly clipped, but are made with two or three kinds of plants rather than just one. Some classic mixtures are beech and yew, holly and hornbeam, or Portuguese laurel and golden privet. Gold or silver variegated holly, purple or copper beech, blue and gray leaved conifers and other variations may be introduced for greater con-

Unclipped hedges are looser in texture than sheared ones, but offer similar structural support to garden plantings. Informal tapestries may be woven of several or many kinds of plants for added variety of color and form. Photo: Mark Lovejoy

trast. Most often, the shrubs are arranged in regular, alternating patterns, with evergreens employed as full stops at all ends. Arches or doorways are usually made of evergreen elements as well. Classic tapestry hedges lend themselves nicely to both thoroughly formal gardens and those with formal layout and relaxed plantings, but blend less easily into a garden with an informal layout and naturalistic plantings.

Informal tapestry hedges are similar combinations of a few kinds of plants in hedges that are not sheared, but only lightly pruned each year. These fit comfortably into large landscapes, and are an excellent means of relating mixed gardens to the native flora. Though less common in urban settings, informal hedges are sympathetic to the transitional architecture of suburb and countryside. In implementation, this style lends itself to less obvious patterns, with one ingredient taking precedence in one part of the garden and another coming to the fore elsewhere. This proves especially practical where site conditions alter a good deal, since the combination can include plants which favor each major condition while tolerating the other(s). The overall effect may be unified by making theme combinations of the several kinds of plants which are then repeated, either at regular intervals or at important focal points within the garden. Such a hedge requires the same initial care in planting and pruning as the others, but once its basic shape is established, it will need only light annual pruning and the routine care offered to all garden plants.

THE MIXED HEDGE

The mixed hedge is a more complex tapestry, woven of as many strands as the gardener cares to employ. There may be four or five kinds of evergreens, complementary in texture and color, mixed with as many sorts of deciduous shrubs to provide seasonal blossom and fruit. In a cottage garden, the hedge may be utterly mixed, with no plant duplicated. In an edible landscape, the hedge may be made entirely of fruiting trees and shrubs. One of my own mixed hedges is called the wreath hedge, my source for favorite holiday greenery. It combines long-needled pines with bristling blue Atlantic cedar, feathery gray Lawson cypress, and waxy-berried Irish juniper. Hollies and pyracanthas of several sorts complete the mixture, which offers a wealth of textures, leaves in multiple shapes and colors, and berries of yellow or terra-cotta or tawny orange as well as red and rust. Another mixed hedge alternates clusters of evergreen viburnums, rhododendrons, and holly with spring-blooming shrubs—Chinese lilac, spireas, deutzia—that color pleasantly in autumn. In yet a third, native willows and mountain ash are coupled with evergreen barberries and an assortment of ivies.

Most of my own hedges are very mixed indeed, partly in order to house a tremendous variety of plant material, but partly too because I get bored very easily. However well they work in other situations, in my own garden, I prize diversity over the monotony of formal hedges. Valuable as they are as unifiers (and often as I might use them in other people's gardens), formal hedges do not provide enough interest to earn them houseroom here. Fortunately, even a very mixed border defines the garden as a whole, simply by enclosing the overall space. Within the living walls, however, we must find other ways to create visual unity. In gardens where both borders and hedges are mixed, unity comes both from repeating important plants and groups of theme plants, and from reinforcing similarities of color, texture, and form. Even when space is very limited, it is quite possible to enjoy the benefits of variety without paying the penalty of visual hodgepodge.

Perhaps the simplest way to bring coherence to a very mixed garden is to repeat strong, architectural hedge elements. The eye tends to connect such shapes (though the camera may not), so a sprinkling of slim, upright junipers, broad, shaggy chamaecyparis, or glossy hollies throughout the hedges will often establish sufficient visual order. It may suit your interests to place such key plants formally within the informal mixture, perhaps as matched pairs at the ends of each border section, or where you might want to create a visual gateway to a borrowed view, announce the entrance to the garden proper, or make a strong frame for a border focal point. Such matched pairs can be insouciantly effective in nonsymmetrical arrangements, though it takes a good eye to avoid placement that suggests you aren't very good at geometry. If it doesn't quite work, try using odd numbers of key plants; this is the classic way to remove the implicit suggestion of formal pairing. Unity may also come through echoed form, for similarly narrow, spirelike shapes can also provide a continuing theme, even though the plants used may be quite different. Color and texture may equally perform this function, as when blue conifers of various sorts provide a running thread in a mixed garden, alike enough in hue and feel that the eye accepts them as links between various garden sections.

Yet another way to promote visual unity is to develop pronounced color themes for various parts of the borders, themes that carry over into the mixed hedges. A large collection of hollies might be used this way, with golden-leaved types ranged in one area, separated by plain greens of various values, while another area might be given over to silver and white, and yet a third to blues and grays. In the first section, the hollies might be joined by golden privet and golden yew, copper beech and rhododendrons with felty, cinnamon-backed foliage, muted with dull blues and murky reds to keep the gold from turning brassy. The others might be moderated with variegated and plain elders, bottle green conifers, shrubby artemisias and silver-backed Russian olive. The hollies, though various, are alike enough to make convincing connections between these disparate groups of plants.

Mixed hedges require the same care in planting as other hedges, but here, dissimilarity in plant size and shape presents no disadvantage. Indeed, mixed hedges can be planted piecemeal or in sections without harm, for where the eye is not expecting conformity, the lack of it does not tease the mind. Those who are not naturally prone to prune will find this attribute a boon, for with formal hedges, any neglect or irregularity stands out annoyingly. Like formal hedges, mixed ones will benefit from hard initial pruning to encourage dense, twiggy growth. After this, the longest side shoots of neighboring shrubs may be intertwined to form a solid wall much like the mixed hedgerows along rural English lanes. Even if you do nothing at all but prune out dead-wood and keep the hedge weeded and fed, a nicely arranged mixed hedge will reward benign neglect with healthy good looks.

Best suited to informal garden situations, mixed hedges lend themselves exceptionally well to native or wild gardens, where indigenous shrubs and small trees can make up the backbone plantings and relate the garden thoroughly to its larger setting. They are good solutions too where the gardener has inherited a few mature shrubs in an otherwise empty garden. By regrouping the original inhabitants instead of throwing them out (probably assisted by the addition of younger plants), you can make a mixed hedge that will give a very young garden a settled feeling in short order. This approach can also help to bridge the gap between a very old garden and a brand new one. In our present garden, the newly installed mixed hedges incorporate rather than displace the homely old fashioned farmyard plantings—lilacs and weigelas, forsythia and shrub roses—that seem so appropriate for this old house. The presence of these shrubs and small trees in our hedges mellows the raw edges of the new borders, and gives the garden as a whole a pleasant sense of continuity and connection with the gardeners long gone who first found the garden in this piece of land.

FENCES

Good fences make good neighbors, as the poet tells us, and the dictum has never been more true. Particularly where space is tight and neighbors are near, fences offer immediate peace and privacy. The right fence in the right place can turn an underused space that is overlooked by neighbors into a secluded garden spot. Unlike hedges, fences can be erected in a matter of days or even hours, and though they lack the life and bulk of a hedge, they can fulfill many of the same functions. Like hedges, fences can relate the garden to the very neighborhood it excludes. So often, however, a great opportunity for fun or flare is lost, for fencing is generally perfunctory when it could be carried off with panache. We seem to have

lost the inventiveness of our forefathers when it comes to designing fences, for there is very little variety to be found amongst modern examples, yet many of the moldering old fences found in urban alley or country lane go beyond the necessary, showing a charming spontaneity of design. Wonderful concoctions of wrought iron gingerbread surround Victorian houses in New England, while sprawling Western ranches boast aging rustic fences of sturdy unpeeled branches. Southern gardens may be enclosed by fancy fretwork looking like white wooden lace as well as rural fences decorated with delicate arches and feathers of bent ash and willow. The Midwest presents pickets in an infinity of forms, each more marvelous than the last. Our ancestors took the time to think such things through, and they liked to put their own stamp on what they made.

When fencing seems the best option for garden enclosure, it is worth doing a bit of investigation before settling for whatever the local lumberyard has in stock. Perhaps a minor modification would give the standard model more character, or perhaps you, too, might want to design a fence that expresses more than closure. What you choose will depend, naturally enough, on what atmosphere you want to create within your garden enclosure, as well as what lies beyond. Comfortable old houses wed well with informal fencing that evokes rural or even bucolic imagery, but hard-edged urban architecture requires sophisticated elegance. Sleek, angular buildings will be complemented by a fence or wall that doubles as art in its own right, functioning too as gallery walls against which the art of the garden is displayed. Modern suburban architecture is rather harder to work with, since it is indeterminate in character. Here, the neighborhood is better ignored than matched. A simple board fence will suffice to eliminate the surroundings, while the inner walls can be given all the richness you desire.

It is worth remembering that any sort of garden enclosure, fences included, need not be the same on both sides. If you live in a very tidy suburban neighborhood where a half-wild hedgerow would bring wrath (and possibly the intervention of the law) down upon you, you could compromise by shearing the outer half of your hedge or backing it with a tall street-side board fence. If your garden is already enclosed by a solid fence of unsurpassing ugliness that nonetheless suits the immediate environs, you can leave the outside untouched while working changes upon the inner surface. Screens of fingerling bamboo come in rolls up to fifteen feet long and as much as ten feet high. Though flimsy, they are amazingly long-lasting if not abused, and make highly effective screens when stretched between sturdy posts and supported by a top beam. Coupled with a solid fence, they become almost indestructible, and make a gorgeous backdrop for mixed borders and sunbathers alike. In a little suburban garden that sits high above the sidewalk, a delightful series of pleated picket fans runs in arches and semicircles down the hillside. The pickets are painted clean white, which shows up nicely against an inner sheath of cedar boards, graying with age and weather. The contrast is delightful, and the inner walls makes a sanctuary of the little garden within. Where covenants restrict color use, fences may be left plain on the streetside while their inner faces can be painted in primary brights or dreamy, painterly shades of slate and moss and lead.

WALLS

Many a fetching picture book border owes its impact to the gorgeous wall behind it. Faded Elizabethan brick and crumbling, moss-covered stone are highly picturesque, and lend themselves readily to garden making. Unfortunately, these must be considered natural attributes; they can't be faked, and you either have them or you don't. For one thing, walls are prohibitively expensive for most of us. New walls of brick and masonry have a radiant quality of rawness that makes them difficult in the garden setting. Even new walls made of old brick rarely achieve the desired appearance, because the regularity of shape and clean new mortar or pointing make the incredibly expensive old bricks look spandy new, which defeats the whole purpose. I suppose one could find a craftsperson who could build a crumbling, old-looking wall from elderly materials, but the expense would most certainly be astronomical, and the result

all too probably suggestive of the absurd follies, mock hermitages, and gothic ruins beloved of our Victorian ancestors.

That doesn't mean we have no good options; where local stone is plentiful, a hard-working amateur can make fieldstone walls of exceptional beauty and endurance. In adobe country, mudded walls make wonderful garden enclosures, often with dramatic, sculptural qualities. Prairie gardens might have thick sod walls topped with turves full of wildflowers and small bulbs. Stockade walls of rough, bark-covered logs would look right at home in much of the West, as would zigzags of solidly packed split rails. One tiny garden I know has one enclosed corner where roof and wall are made of matched pairs of rippled fiberglass panels, bound tightly together with wooden stripping. Water is cycled through the resulting tubes, making the restful noise of a rushing little brook while casting wonderful shadows over the ferns and woodland plants growing inside. In Seattle's UPS park, a great wall of rugged stone is brought to life by waterfalls and tumbling cascades that cycle endlessly through the small pools at the wall's feet. I suspect that there are dozens of interesting options yet unrecognized, regional styles just being born, materials and techniques that await discovery or more general application. The key to development lies in our own willingness to experiment, to try and fail and learn from our mistakes, to recognize and value the best qualities in both old and new.

DESIGN AND STYLE
DEVELOPING APPROPRIATE PLANS

The first step in designing a mixed border is the same as that for any garden. Always begin by gathering information on the specific site. Where will the sun be in summer, in winter? How much rainfall can you expect? Where does the rainwater linger,

Mixed borders hold plants of all sizes, from trees down to ground covers. This ancient apple tree in my front garden shelters a mutually supportive community of shrubs and perennials, vines and bulbs which provide an ongoing array of color through the year. Photo: Mark Lovejoy

where does water vanish in a flash? Which are the prevailing winds? Do you need shelter from them? What sort of soil(s) do you have to work with? What kinds of shade? Are there any plants already there worth saving? Are there any worthy of showcasing? Which plants need instant removal, and which could benefit from restorative treatment? Where will the meterman walk, the dog sleep, the kids play? Where are the sewer lines? What path will bulky loads like furniture and garbage need to follow? Are there borrowed views to frame or screen? Is there any privacy in the yard? Where might privacy be readily achieved? Where do you want to sit to savor the

garden, take coffee, enjoy an al fresco meal? Can you work in a water feature? Could a bird and butterfly garden be tucked into a corner? Can you find room for vegetables and fruits as well as ornamentals; might an edible landscape suit your desires? These and similar practical questions provide the physical parameters within which you must make your garden.

From there, ask yourself what you want from the garden. What do you want it to do for you? While that first planning step is rooted in reality, the second is born of dreams. Feet firmly on the ground, give your imagination wings and let it soar. With "garden" as your mantra, meditate upon the theme. Conjure up all the garden images you can, then look at them with an analytical eye. What unites them, what is important about them? Track down your associations to find out what "garden" means to your heart. What ingredients will bring that heart's garden to life? Do you need a bower of roses, a deep, trellised garden seat smothered in jasmine, a plashing fountain alive with birds? Do you see a picket fence, a white gate, a tall hedge of lilac? Would masses of flowers all summer long be enough? Must there be delphiniums, or just something deeply, magically blue? Look through picture books and mark pages with pictures that speak to you. By examining all these things, we assemble a lexicon of personal musts that shape the garden as much as the path of the mailman or the demands of the dogs.

The third step unites the first two. Make a pattern map of the actual site, indicating the position of the house and existing plants as well as nearby buildings and trees that could affect garden plantings. Run off dozens of copies and start experimenting with designs and themes. At this stage, it is useful to generate as many variations as possible, fitting the garden elements together playfully as well as purposefully. The map works best when its proportions are as accurate as possible, but don't worry about the quality of your design sketching; most designers use what are called "bubble diagrams" in this early stage, marking out different areas with rough circles and lines and blobs. It helps to show the direction of the sun as well as the location of important house doors and windows, for these will influence both planting and traffic flow patterns within the garden areas. For some people, this blank slate approach frees up the imagination better than walking through the real space. Others will do better to sketch on site. Try both ways, and see which is most productive for you.

This process is worth following even when the available space seems ludicrously small. The tiniest garden areas may hold a surprising amount if the available space is cleverly utilized. A bower can be rigged on a balcony, if need be, while a trickling wall-mounted fountain can ornament a narrow side yard, with mossy cobbles, ferns, and woodland flowers tucked in on all sides. Scaled down mixed borders made with dwarf shrubs, bonsai trees, and delicate flowers can be fitted into the smallest condo courtyard; all it takes is vision and a bit of planning. Where available space is unnervingly large, breaking it up into garden rooms makes planning more manageable and keeps each border section on the human rather than grand scale. Once the space is organized, you can play with color, plant, or architectural themes, choosing running motifs to unify the whole. In any case, the idea is not to create a plan which you will unswervingly follow, but to better acquaint yourself with the possibilities latent in your garden site. Once your ideas take shape on paper, take them back out to the garden and try to visualize them in place. When plans are right, you can see and feel the garden coming together. If nothing gels, and the place still feels formless or uncertain, a bit more research might be in order.

Any good design book can steer you through the basics of proportion and scale and debate the relative merits of formal and informal designs. (I highly recommend *The Book of Garden Design* by John Brookes.) Formal gardens are certainly easier to design well, simply by sticking to classic geometrical arrangements. Planting them is easier as well, since most bedding patterns are both simple and symmetrical. Less formal plantings tend to hold together visually in formal settings even when they are not intrinsically strong. Formal gardens hold their form in any season, because there are so many guides for the eye; every hedge and edging directs the attention as well as the foot. Informal gardens

are more challenging, if only because they present a greater possibility of failure, but they also offer greater opportunity for creativity. Mixed borders lend themselves to either style; the deciding factors must be personal taste as well as the architecture of one's home.

NATURAL GARDENS

Informal styles vary enormously, but the natural or wild garden seems increasingly appealing to American gardeners. How natural and wild the borders ought to be depends on one's taste, but it should be pointed out that control and maintenance are at least as much of an issue in this sort of garden as in a formal one. Formal gardens betray neglect very openly, but lend themselves to weekly tidying sessions that can be as routinized as house cleaning. In informal gardens, where loose, romantic plantings spill from free-form beds, it can be harder to know where and when to interfere. Many of us love the look of a garden that seems untrammeled, as if things "just happened." Since the effects of negligence can be less obvious, the untrained eye may not be able to pinpoint what's wrong, but the garden will look slovenly rather than casual, and the minor effects which should enrich the plantings are lost in the shuffle. If you opt for such a garden, you must be prepared to spend a good deal of time fine tuning it, for consistent garden keeping sharpens up all the details and keeps the big picture clearly in focus as well. Making the overall design bold and simple will help even more by making the garden read as a whole. Solid framework, whether provided by interwoven hedges or fences, also unifies the garden areas. Such structure calms a restless garden, for one's eye, no longer distracted by incoherence, is free to appreciate plant vignettes. The trick is to incorporate the principles of formal design without borrowing its stiffness or geometry.

Penelope Hobhouse, who has designed both formal and natural gardens in various parts of North America as well as in England, reminds us that, "A natural or 'wild' garden, where rounded graceful shapes and curving lines take the place of any obvious geometric detail, is most successful if integrated by some over-riding design themes. A repetition of plant shapes or of drifts of foliage or flower color should be purposeful, firmly adding nuances of recognizable control, linked together by flowing lawns, pathways or what you will." Even in country gardens, where real wilderness may lie a stone's throw from the garden, Hobhouse feels that, "Wild gardening does not mean bowing to nature, it means manipulating natural effects to create beautiful pictures, so arranged that they appear in a sequence."

Artful control creates the illusion of naturalness, but natural gardens are not so much an imitation of nature as artificial variations on nature's themes. The element of artifice is not to be despised; it is what divides a garden from an accident of nature. (It is as well to remember that the nature we are emulating is idealized; the real thing is "red in tooth and claw." Left to nature, gardens soon disintegrate, as Tennyson suggests, into chaos. Though romantics may find battered plants and fallen pillars picturesque, to a gardener, they are not a pretty sight.) This same idealized nature inspired generations of classical painters and, later on, lastingly influential landscapers like Capability Brown. Indeed, Hobhouse recommends that people who want to make natural gardens should first "Get their eye in by looking at landscape paintings and Impressionists." The first teach the value of scale, balance, and proportion, and demonstrate how plants can act as architectural elements. The second teach us to weigh the effects of light and shade, mass and form, as well as variations in color and texture. Both give validity to human interpretations of nature, recording not nature itself but the effects of the skilled hand and trained eye upon natural subjects. Gardens composed largely of native plants sometimes struggle for identity precisely because they walk an uneasy line between the garden and the woods. The most successful, whether deliberately or intuitively, are arranged as mixed borders; their perimeters are clearly defined by informal mixed hedges, the beds are shaped with strength and simplicity, while the plantings are varied and abundant.

REGIONALITY AND NATIVE PLANTS

The increasing interest in using native plants has begun to broaden the national garden palette. Every year, more native species are proven garden worthy by experimental gardeners like Edith Eddleman, whose enormous and stunningly beautiful mixed borders at the North Carolina State University at Raleigh rely heavily on native plants. Thoughtful amateurs often recognize and introduce fine garden forms of our native species, as do horticultural professionals who actively seek out unusual variants of native plants. Alert breeders have begun reevaluating popular species with an eye to raising good-looking, well-behaved hybrids. For years, ardent plantsmen have brought home named forms of American natives from England and Germany, where our native flora has long been respected and admired. Slowly these are passing from the hands of the few into the nursery trade for wider distribution. A few, like *Coreopsis verticillata* 'Moonbeam', have even achieved star status.

The popularity of native plants is welcomed by most garden designers, but with a few caveats. "When you work with unknown natives, you have to keep the possibility that they may turn out to be thugs firmly in mind," says Eddleman, who advises growing all unfamiliar species and not a few hybrids in nursery beds for a few seasons before letting them loose in a border. On the other hand, she reminds us, "Some will need coaxing and tender care, so you can't just assume they will be trouble free garden plants." Glenn Withey, a partner in the Seattle-based design firm of Withey/Price, agrees, adding, "Many people who are newer to gardening have picked up the idea that planting a garden of natives means it won't need water or regular maintenance, but this just isn't so. A garden is a garden; you can design it to be less wasteful of water, or to need less regular care, but you can't ignore it. People who want genuinely carefree gardens should stick to Astro Turf and plastic flowers."

The assumption that all plants native to a given region will automatically thrive in a garden setting can also lead to some sharp disappointments, Withey

Regional palettes are broadened by exotic plants which adapt well to their new home. Palm trees of several kinds are hardy well into Zone 8, bringing wonderful texture and a strong silhouette to the informal hedge. Photo: Mark Lovejoy

brownii, that grows in a number of western states is almost impossible to bring into cultivation, even where it occurs naturally. Terrestrial orchids like the charming *Calypso bulbosa* and ladies' slippers (*Cypripedium* species) almost never transplant successfully, and many are endangered, thanks to hopeful but ignorant gardeners convinced that they will succeed where so many have failed.

Like most designers, Withey and his partner, Charles Price, prefer to mix native plants with good border plants from all over the world. "If you want to use natives, choose the most attractive as well as the toughest," advises Price. "Always use the best form you can find of a given plant. Choice things are more expensive than common plants, and harder to find in large sizes, but they make a more valuable contribution to the garden over time. The best is worth waiting for." Price also encourages creative thinking when it comes to designing gardens using native plants. "The obvious thing is to make natural or wild gardens," he observes. "But there are many other possibilities well worth pursuing." Indeed, he is not alone in feeling that, while many native plant

American garden making is entering an exciting, evolutionary stage as gardeners and designers push past the obvious and the borrowed to explore less familiar territory. The California garden of Marcia Donahue holds personal and found art as well as uncommon plants, all placed with evident respect and pleasure. Photo: George Waters

warns, for most regions of the States are complex and varied in terms of soil, weather, and other conditions. Plants which occur in natural wetlands may struggle in drier gardens, while drought-tolerant plants may literally drown in a well-watered border. Plants used to leaner conditions may suffer from rots and fungal diseases when faced with a soft life in pampered garden beds. Mixed borders, with their variety of microclimates, can offer a wider range of settings than the average garden, but even there, unless a good match of conditions can be found, it may be better to admire certain natives in the wild than to try to coax them unsuccessfully into the garden. The beautiful, bronzy native peony, *Paeonia*

gardens are well organized, sensitively planted, and beautifully tended, very few of them push the envelope of design limitations. "It would be quite possible to make a formal garden entirely from native plants," Price points out. "We could make wild gardens that felt primeval, even dangerous or almost menacing. We can make sunny, tranquil gardens, or modernistic ones that are all about shape and form, yet rely on plants rather than architecture to make their point." Not only are many native gardens sadly unimaginative, but some are handicapped by their maker's very intentions. "Too many native gardens seem to have been done as penance for the sins of the world," says Price, who finds them "much more interesting when native plants are treated like other border plants, placed and combined for their own strong points rather than for ecological convictions."

This does not mean that ecological concerns are of no importance in garden design. Indeed, they can and should moderate the scope of our gardens. Gardeners will always be willing to lavish endless care and attention on plants essentially unsuited to their climates, and as long as this costs only ourselves, there is nothing wrong with chasing a dream. However, if we insist on having lush lawns in natural deserts, or treat our plants with toxic pesticides and herbicides that kill birds and small mammals and pollute the ground water, our dreams might need redirection. No matter where we live, we can grow a gardenful of something wonderful without harming the environment or wasting resources. It may take some research to learn what will thrive, but what gardener doesn't like experimenting with new plants?

Edith Eddleman, whose display borders at the North Carolina State University Arboretum include a tremendous range of native plants, comments, "We have such hot nights here in the South, and a lot of traditional border plants simply don't handle it well. I am always on the lookout for plants that grow well in southern gardens, and many American natives turn out to be tolerant of the difficulties of our climate." Visitors are often surprised to learn that about half the plants in these borders are natives, she relates. "American gardeners are just waking up to the riches of our floral heritage, which means

some exciting things lie ahead for us all." Though Eddleman is willing to give all kinds of plants a fair trial, varying conditions to see if they can adapt with a bit of help, she feels that it is important to acknowledge the limitations of her climate. "We can't waste time feeling sorry for ourselves if we can't grow this or that," she says firmly. "We just need to keep trying new things, make mistakes, talk to others. That's how we learn what does work for us. That's how we expand the possibilities."

The concept of regional gardening styles is far more meaningful in North America, where climate and landscape may alter dramatically from one side of a state to the other, than in relatively homogeneous England. If we want to develop garden designs and styles that are uniquely American, we must be flexible and inventive. We must be willing to try things others assure us won't work, and willing to learn from our failures. We need to share accumulated experience, building up accessible bodies of regional knowledge. We have to experiment with different kinds of garden enclosure and structure, seeking out regionally appropriate materials. Plant lovers in every part of the country could be working to develop better plants for their own regions. We can all keep our eyes open for fortuitous seedlings or sports that could result in fine new garden forms. After hard winters or blazing summers, we can select especially adaptable strains of borderline hardy or finicky but wonderful plants. People with time and talent can go further, deliberately breeding stronger, more disease-resistant lines of favorite plants and hybridizing with locally successful species.

In difficult climates or garden settings, it is easy to feel hindered by imposed limitations. Expanded regional plant palettes will help reduce these limitations, but we can also be more inventive in our approach. Penelope Hobhouse often points out to those who credit England's marvelous gardens to the extensive English plant palette that almost any garden effect can be replicated quite faithfully without using any of the same plants admired in the original setting. We can also apply John Brookes' trick of analyzing shape and silhouette, then find another plant which creates a similar impression. Thanks to the enormous wealth of the plant kingdom, we can find healthy, hardy, or drought-tolerant counterparts for virtually any plant. By applying all these techniques, mixed borders can illustrate the precepts of both traditional good design and responsible stewardship. Indeed, more than any other garden style, the mixed border readily marries regionality of design with as many ecological goals as we care to embrace.

TRAINING THE EYE

How we shape and fill our gardens will and should depend on our personal perceptions of beauty. However, a good gardener with an untrained eye may easily create the garden equivalent of a Grandma Moses painting. Such visually naive gardens are not without charm, yet may fail to fulfill their creators' hopes. We can train our eye by looking, as Hobhouse suggests, at art of many sorts, by perusing garden picture books, and by visiting gardens. The idea here is not so much to teach ourselves what is acceptable and therefore "right" in order to copy it, but to acquaint ourselves with standards of design that have remained stable over the centuries. Though it can be helpful to analyze attractive compositions—garden and otherwise—in terms of geometry and proportion, we don't really need slide rules to get the most from our training. It is rather, as Hobhouse says, "Getting one's eye in." Exposure to great landscapes trains the eye to accept certain classical relationships and proportions as pleasing. This carries over into other areas, so that in time, we find ourselves recognizing the strengths and weaknesses of a garden design almost without effort or conscious thought. When we return to our gardens, our new skill seems intuitive. Suddenly, we understand that the borders are all too short, the beds too narrow and too empty. We know almost without thinking that the paths are too skinny and that their purposeless curves annoy rather than soothe the eye. We recognize the excellence of sound plant combinations, and see that others are weakened by imbalance. Poor transitions are revealed as ineffectual because they lack clarity; what they need, we realize, is shared elements from the areas they both overlap and unite. Visual sophistication is a tool like any other; it does not give a garden shape or purpose of itself, yet a trained eye can guide a skilled hand to wondrous effect. It teaches us not to mimic classic English and European gardens, but to use the same underlying principles to organize our own.

Penelope Hobhouse refers us to Impressionist painters for inspiration because they explored nature in terms of color and light. Anybody mystified by color theory could benefit from immersion in Impressionism and later modern schools as well. Look at as many examples as possible: Van Gogh for pure, saturated colors and their complements which turn crude contrasts into resonating combinations. De Kooning for mass, shadow, and light. Matisse for shape, Monet for texture, Manet for interplay of form and color. If they are to plant artfully, garden makers must learn to see and analyze in these terms. It is not enough to assemble a marvelous collection of plants, or even to grow them well, or to carefully grade flowers and foliage by tint and tone. We must learn to organize big picture focal points, then surround them with supportive details. We must discover how to play with plants as Impressionists play with paint, working them into patterns of light and color, compositions of mass and shape, playing off textures as well. Fortunately, the results aren't graded by arbiters of Good Taste, nor must we complete our training in a given period of time. There is no final exam for garden makers, just the constant lab of the garden itself. An idea or experiment, once set in motion, may take several seasons or many years to come to fruition. During that time, other parts of the garden will be altering, and our own tastes may even change before our attempts at artful gardening have matured. This is as it should be, for flux is the proper state of a garden, as it is of anything alive. Our ideas and abilities are continually developing as well. Armed with increasingly sophisticated design tools, we can engineer and control our garden effects. As we gain confidence, we can take equal pleasure in happy accidents. When we know enough to adapt the classic design tools to our own ends, our gardens can meet traditional visual criteria, yet be individual, free, and fun.

In North America, the challenge is eagerly taken up. For us, the informal "art garden" style has a strong and natural appeal; it suits our taste, our architecture, our attitudes and life-styles. When suc-

WINTER This small section of my garden is overlooked by my kitchen window, so it needs to be furnished all year long. Dense interplanting allows a constant flow of color as the seasons roll by. In winter, the woody backbone frames bulbs and evergreen perennials hidden during lusher seasons.

Trees: *Pear (Pyrus communis 'Bartlett')*; ***Evergreen shrubs****:* Euonymus fortunei *var.* radicans *'Silver Queen',* Juniperus virginiana *'Manhattan Blue',* Mahonia bealii, Rhododendron *'Hong Kong',* R. yakushimanum; ***Deciduous shrubs:*** *Witch hazel (*Hamamelis × intermedia *'Diane')*; ***Evergreen perennials:*** Bergenia *'Rotblum',* Euphorbia amygdaloides *'Rubra',* Helleborus foetidus *'Wester Flisk',* H. orientalis, Kniphofia caulescens, Polystichum acrostichoides; ***Bulbs:*** Crocus tommasinianus, Eranthis hyemalis; ***Grasses:*** Miscanthus sinensis *'Strictus'*; ***Vines and climbers:*** Euonymus fortunei *var.* radicans *'Emerald Gaity',* Hedera helix *'Buttercup'*; ***Ground covers:*** Sagina subulata *'Aurea'.*

cessful, art gardens are enormously satisfying, exciting to make and to see. Some failures are as exciting as success, for they are clearly leading in new directions. Others demonstrate the baby and the bathwater dictum; Our flamboyant independence is famous, yet the accompanying disrespect for authority may lead us to flout rules without considering what lies behind them. Gardens which aim simply not to be English or classical are fueled by negativity. They are often quite ugly, and even at their best are rarely as strong as gardens which reach toward new, though as yet undefined artistic goals. Where such gardens fall short, Hobhouse offers some observations and suggestions. While there is no set pattern that will automatically yield a gorgeous garden, certain basics hold true in all situations. "The greatest fault seems to lie in dotting plants, either as single specimens or as plant associations, stuck in any-which-way," she notes. Massing plants and placing them in purposeful

SPRING *The pear tree and several of the evergreen shrubs bloom now, joined by spring bulbs, early perennials, and certain deciduous shrubs. The winter palette is now bolstered by:* **Deciduous shrubs:** *Sand cherry (*Prunus × cistena*), lilac (*Syringa vulgaris *'Sensation'*), Weigela alba *'Java Red';* **Perennials:** *Euphorbia sikkimensis, Hosta *'Sum & Substance', *Iris douglasiana *'Terra Cotta', *Ligularia dentata *'Desdemona', *Paeonia *'Coral Charm', *Primula acaulis;* **Annuals/biennials:** *Cordyline australis (in pot) (tender perennial);* **Bulbs:** *Fritillaria meleagris, Muscari latifolium, Narcissus *'Spellbinder' *and* 'Tete-a-Tete'; *Ranunculus ficaria, Tulipa *'Couleur Cardinale' *and* 'Princess Irene'; **Grasses:** *Miscanthus sinensis *'Strictus';* **Ground covers:** *Milium effusum *'Aureum'.*

relationships will strengthen any design, but especially an informal one, as will repetitions of important plants or plant groups. "Gardening is an art," she points out, "and, in natural gardening, the plants must be arranged as if one were painting a picture inside a definite frame," taking into consideration the shades and tones, texture, and form of each component. "It is much more difficult than formal gardening because the arranger needs an artist's eye as well as horticultural skill, so that the plants will actually perform as you imagine."

Imagination, in many ways, is the key element in garden planning. It is dangerously double edged: a powerful ally, yet it can also be a powerful enemy. It is a tool that must be harnessed to be of any use. Where is the value in training the eye, in exposing ourselves to the very best and highest forms of garden making, if we allow the experience to spoil ourselves for anything less? Would-be garden makers must hold fast to their dreams, yet not permit dreams to devalue reality. Americans, ever battered by potent media hype, need encouragement to resist

SUMMER *Shrubs have leafed out, and many early and late bloomers now act as foliage plants. Warm weather brings on the annuals as well as mid-season contributors, including:* **Deciduous shrubs:** *Smokebush (Cotinus coggygria 'Royal Purple'), St. John's wort (Hypercium 'Rowallane Hybrid'), Rosa glauca;* **Perennials:** *Alstroemeria 'Ligtu Hybrids', Euphorbia sikkimensis, Helianthemum 'Henfield Brilliant', Hemerocallis 'Terracotta Baby', Iris pseudacorus 'Variegata';* **Annuals/biennials:** *Digitalis purpurea 'Sutton's Apricot', Gazania 'Talent';* **Vines and climbers:** *Clematis × durandii, C. 'Moonlight', Royal Velours', Rosa souliana, R. 'Climbing Shot Silk';* **Bulbs:** *Lilium 'Molly' and 'Regale';* **Ground covers:** *Alyssum 'Apricot Shades' (annual); Viola 'Antique Shades'.*

the tyranny of perfection. When we study garden books for inspiration, we need to remain aware that the images we are seeing are works of art, not candid snaps. Page after page of fabulous images, each more wonderful than the last, can fire a tremendous enthusiasm which dies a painful death when we step through the garden door. We tend to see our gardens through a filter of unreality, holding them up against impossible perfections. Keep in mind that they really are impossible; if you visit those gardens, you may well find the scene that captured your heart, but it may not be quite so overwhelming when framed by more or less than the photographer chose to include. You may be hard pressed to find your favorite image, until you realize it was taken from a window, or from a ladder, or from flat on the ground. Whole sections of famous gardens may delight you more than those that are much photographed, for not all gardens or borders are equally photogenic. Since viewing a garden is an act of imaginative participation, the eye instinctively groups certain things and ignores others, something a camera cannot do. Comparing our own gardens to picture gardens is comparing apples to oranges.

AUTUMN *Potent color bathes the late season borders in a last gasp of glory. Quiet for much of the year, these now come into their own:* **Shrubs:** Cotinus coggygria *'Royal Purple'*, Rosa glauca *(hips);* **Perennials:** Aconitum *'Kelmscott'*, Helenium autumnale *'Butterpat'*, Helianthemum *'Henfield Brilliant'*, Kniphofia caulescens, Ligularia dentata *'Desdemona'*, Rudbeckia *'Goldsturm'*; **Annuals:** Helianthus annuus *'Autumn Beauty'*, castor bean *(*Ricinus communis*) 'Impala'*; **Vines:** Rosa souliana *(hips)*, Vitis coignetiae; **Bulbs:** Crocosmia *'Lucifer'*, Dahlia *'Bishop of Llandaff'*.

THE CAMERA AND THE EYE

Like imagination and visual training, a properly used camera is an excellent tool for border builders. Even if you never take a single picture, just walking through the garden framing—or attempting to frame—garden pictures and vignettes will underline design strengths and expose any weaknesses. It's quite fun, really, to focus eyes dazzled by lovely pictures through the little frame of the camera eye; when we turn the trick around, what we see may surprise us. Discrete chunks of our own gardens may read as well as anything in the glossy books. Our carefully weighted focal points may indeed carry themselves as poised and distinguished garden pictures. Hazed with late, long angled sun or early morning fog, a camera lens may make our borders look as lush and endless as those on any English estate. Then, too, the camera makes distractions like telephone wires, neighboring houses, and road signs scream for attention, pointing up unsuspected holes in perimeter hedges or barriers. Indefinite border sections are suddenly seen to lack sufficient structure. Plant groups you vaguely like but aren't quite satisfied with prove too complex or insufficiently interesting to frame into a great shot. All the un-

If your borders disappoint you, try looking at them through a camera lens to find flattering angles and identify strong vignettes. The camera is also a fine tool when analyzing design flaws and weak spots. Photo: Mark Lovejoy

Photographs may show us where we have succeeded in making a memorable combination but need to give it a sturdier background. Conversely, a blank bit of border may be revealed as a great piece of framework that lacks a centerpiece. Sometimes it helps to draw on the prints, sketching in a spiky yucca or a graceful, weeping crab apple to see which shape suits the situation. It's rather like putting together a puzzle in which we must design the missing pieces. (If you want to try a number of variables, tape the picture to a piece of cardboard with a cover sheet of clear Mylar. This can be drawn on and sponged off many times, if you use water-based markers.)

John Brookes, the English garden designer, likes to use black-and-white pictures of gardens, because it eliminates the distraction of color. He recommends drawing directly on garden snapshots to determine the silhouette of perimeter planting or border section. "Lots of people begin by planting something, then messing around to see what will go with it," he notes. "It's far easier to decide what shapes and silhouette you want, then find plants that fit the patterns." Even when working remedially, within established borders, Brookes finds this technique valid. "You try different shapes until you find the one that works best, then, again, choose an appropriate plant to fill that spot." Slides are also useful, both because seeing pictures projected and enlarged strengthens their impact and because, if reversed, a slide image becomes mysteriously unfamiliar. It is all too easy to be sentimental about elderly plants or one's own combinations; like good parents, good gardeners eventually learn that loving dispassion is of more lasting value than sentiment. When the scene is stripped of personal attachment by a novel perspective, we can analyze its faults or triumphs purely on design merits.

sightly details which the conscious eye rejects or eliminates are utterly evident to the merciless camera.

Taking pictures in our own gardens and analyzing them in terms of design can be equally helpful. The human eye has a tendency to organize and relate things which the camera records with impartial verity. We see a little clump of white lilies here, a patch of white phlox there, and unconsciously tie them together. The camera shows them as unrelated bits and blobs which weaken the overall composition.

All these techniques sharpen one's eye and ability to recognize essential design elements. However, when you read advice to think of your garden in terms of pictures, it does not mean photographs so much as coherent assemblages, plant groupings that are mutually supportive and enhancing. Whether they photograph well is beside the point, so long as they work in reality.

BASICS

Traditional herbaceous borders are perhaps the most labor-intensive gardens ever devised by humankind, and it is a common assumption that mixed borders are equally demanding. Mixed borders can of course be as wasteful and exacting as any garden, yet with a bit of thought, they can easily be made or adapted to serve the principles of conservation and responsible consumption as well as those of good design. My own borders, filled to the brim with plants of all types, some of which are in active growth all year

Caring for a well filled mixed border can seem a daunting task, yet when the border soil is in good heart and many of its plants are sturdy independents, the tasks prove relatively few and richly rewarding. September, author's garden. Photo: Mark Lovejoy

long, might be expected to present a nightmare of needs. In fact, this is not so. Simple and practical in design, ruthlessly stripped of any plants that need cosseting, fed by healthy soil, and kept more or less free of weeds by mulches, my borders are surprisingly efficient and easy to maintain.

To get this way, my garden has been built as much around limitations as strengths. Before the garden and I could achieve equilibrium, I had to be utterly honest about how much time and money could go into it, as well as how the garden might reasonably be expected to perform given those limitations. Visitors sometimes say, "It's easy for you; you work at home, but I have a regular job, and I could never keep up with all this." As mentioned earlier, the key to successful garden keeping is not so much unlimited time as it is organization. I would love to spend hours every day in the garden, but I can only count on putting in a few hours a week, squeezing in extra time during the garden's rush seasons of spring and fall. The modesty of our budget meant that fancy irrigation systems were out, as were major hardscape elements, which we decided to build ourselves over the years. It also meant that I couldn't hire in help, so my available time simply had to be enough.

On the plus side, I have learned to whip through a border section, taking care of obvious problems in very short order. (My mother did housework this way, saying firmly, "A man on a fast horse would never notice," about any deficits.) One of the benefits of parenthood is that you learn to accept compromises readily in order to survive; this helps in the garden as well, where limited time and energy often mean things don't happen exactly the way we want them to. Perhaps most importantly, I deeply enjoy the work. I can also count on my husband, Mark, to help out with heavy digging and hauling, tree pruning, and compost making. The work is not always easy, for me or for anybody, yet no true gardener grudges the personal cost of garden keeping. Indeed, for many of us, it is both soothing and satisfying. Gentle exercise, the intimate connection with our plants, just being outdoors every day, even if for a few minutes, are all rewards that make garden work one of gardening's pleasures.

I had to be honest rather than hopeful about the garden, too, in order to assess how best to develop it. The presence of mature trees and shrubs makes for more shade than sun, and means the soil is almost everywhere permeated with roots. In its natural state, our soil is lowly dirt, a heavy, rather sterile acid clay that drains slowly and dries like concrete in summer. The northwestern climate is such that our winters are usually mild but always wet, while summers are dry, though not necessarily hot. Plants that rot easily tend to disappear quickly in these circumstances, as do those which resent summer drought. Common sense would suggest that we rely heavily on woodlanders and wildflowers, and we did indeed plant many. However, experimentation has taught me that many sun-loving plants will tolerate certain kinds of shade. There are roses and peonies, lilies and clematis that bloom generously in light or dappled shade, and scores of perennials perform well in the half sun that is often the best the cloudy maritime Northwest can offer anyway. I give preference to plants that naturally thrive in clay, but as our soil quality improves, we find that more plants succeed each year.

When we made the first beds, we dug in as many soil conditioners as we could lay our hands on. Aged stable sweepings, grass clippings, raw compost, and shredded leaves were added in quantity to improve both the texture and nutritional qualities of the raw clay. Where compaction and root intrusion were worst, we added coarse grit to open and aerate the soil and improve drainage. Where borders ran beneath mature trees, we dug a coarse grade of hydrophilic polymer (the largest size of Broadleaf P4—see page 46) into the bottom fourteen inches of improved soil, so that border plants could tap into their own reservoirs despite root competition. We tilled in bone meal, cottonseed meal, and green alfalfa, then let the new soil mellow in place for a month before retilling and planting. All these efforts paid off handsomely as the plants settled in quickly and put on new growth.

We also set up a composting system that would be ongoing and easily sustainable. At first, we relied on a nearby stable for manure and wood shavings, and the neighborhood school for large amounts of grass clippings and leaves. (The local school district decided not to use any pesticides or herbicides on the children's play area, so we knew these were free of possibly damaging chemicals.) As the garden grew, it provided an increasing supply of raw material itself. Now, every few months, we have a truckload of compost with which we can make new beds, tuck in new plants, or replenish older plantings.

Garden maintenance has also been streamlined as much as possible. The shape of each bed is designed as much with edging and mowing in mind as ease of getting at the plants within. Shapes are large and simple, and the line between the lawn and the borders is kept clean with a foot-powered edging tool. Wide beds have tiny access paths or stepping-stones to facilitate weeding and other chores. Mulches suppress weeds and conserve moisture. The plants are arranged in like-minded communities, so the same general care will do for each entire area. Permanent plant supports and climber tripods (made from apple branches) remain in place all year round, simplifying and reducing the need for staking. Forethought, and understanding the needs of your plants can eliminate most problems, but there are always plenty of unexpected ones to keep things interesting. Fortunately, most gardeners are as adaptable as their gardens. A good rule of thumb, when any aspect of the garden proves too difficult or demanding, is to ask a few home questions. When wet lilies or ancient trellises crash in a high wind, when dogs romp through young borders, when moles cavort through your favorite combinations, it helps to step back a bit and think: How important is this, really? Can I live with it? Might there be a simple, short-term way to cope? What might be an acceptable approximation? Compromise and common sense can often put a new face on a seemingly impossible situation.

In practical terms, the basic principles of gardening are pretty much the same for mixed borders as for any other kind of garden. Covered in enormous detail elsewhere, they need not be duplicated here. I include only a few specifics which may influence the way mixed borders in particular are made and maintained. Perhaps the first of these might be

Soil work repays the gardener's efforts many times over with dividends of moisture retention and strong, steady plant growth. Here, a work crew at Wisley has renewed a herbaceous border's soil and marked it out with lime to guide its replanting. In mixed borders, such thorough soil preparation is only done once. Photo: Cynthia Woodyard

considered attitudinal. Though it can be a challenge to live as lightly as possible on this earth, as gardeners we have the opportunity to improve the condition of our own particular bit of it. To me, in my garden, this means building the soil on a continuing basis. It means encouraging variety, preserving antique and endangered plants, and procuring absolutely everything from responsible sources. It means not employing toxic pesticides, herbicides, or chemical fertilizers. It means using water thoughtfully, and improving or not impairing the quality of the water that passes through this piece of land, whether it be rainfall or stream water. All of us who garden have a particular responsibility to be good stewards of our earth, for we owe the very source of our passion to earth's abundance.

SOIL

If mixed borders had a slogan, it would be: "Make Beautiful Dirt." Indeed, in any garden, soil is the crucial element. No single thing contributes so much to the health, progress, and good looks of a garden as does soil in good heart. In mixed border making, the goal is not so much to convert the entire garden to the idealized sandy loam, but rather to improve whatever you have as best you can, then to choose plants that will appreciate the strengths of the natural situation. No matter what its type, a decent garden soil should nourish roots and allow air to get in and water to get out. How you go about improving your soil depends on where you live and what materials are readily available, but those goals are the same everywhere. It is a sad fact that dirt is not a romantic topic, and few gardeners come to their art with a full blown appreciation for their most elemental medium. However, the longer you garden, the more you come to appreciate good soil. You know you have really made it when the idea of tasting soil as farmers do no longer seems weird or repugnant, and when you, too, can tell a good deal about soil by smelling and feeling it.

These, however, are side issues; the essential fact is that soil work pays a major dividend, and quickly. Everything you plant will perform better and longer in response to the dirt work you do. Even native plants will grow better when tight soils are opened, heavy ones made to drain, and sandy ones enriched with organic amendments. Furthermore, healthy soil promotes healthy plants, especially in mixed borders, where the variety of plants with different needs reduces direct competition for the same nutrients and trace elements. I am often asked about pests and diseases, but have very little information or advice to offer. As big and complex as this garden is, the plants are almost invariably healthy, thanks, I am convinced, to our soil improvements.

Dirt work need not be especially arduous. Though some swear by the spiritual benefits of double digging, I am no longer one of them. After double digging all the beds in our small city garden, I realized why the ubiquitous garden boys of Gertrude Jekyll's day had vanished without a trace; her beds were dug fully three feet deep, and it probably killed them all. Soon thereafter, I read that Graham Stuart Thomas no longer digs soil amendments and conditioners in, but simply adds them as feeding mulches each year. I immediately began experimenting with layering amendments and conditioners on the soil surface and found that, in established borders, this is indeed all that is really necessary. What's more, healthy mixed borders that get regular feeding mulches do not need to be taken apart every three to five years as herbaceous borders do. Individual perennials will always need periodic division, but the bulk of mixed border plantings can be considered as more or less permanent, so long as the soil is not neglected. Exhausted soil makes a garden decline quickly, and careless artificial feeding can promote overly lush, excessive growth that is often disease prone. The steady nourishment available from healthy soil promotes the slow but regular growth increase that allows garden plants to remain attractive and in balance with the garden's design for many years.

Where I want new beds, we no longer dig or till, but begin with either ready made soil or compost. We mark off the general shape of the new bed, lay down a thick layer of wet newspapers, burlap sacks, or horticultural barrier cloth, then pile on the good soil (at least a foot thick; eighteen inches is better yet). Rake it, shape it, and mulch it, and it is ready to plant. Obviously, if the site is full of brambles, this doesn't quite do the trick, but for grass or ordinary weeds, it is remarkably effective, and perfect for instant gratification types. Longer term beds are made in much the same way, but instead of using ready made soil, we make on-site compost piles of garden detritus and whatever else is plentiful; usually leaves, grass clippings, wood chips, or sawdust. I rarely add lime to these piles, since the neutral compost buffers the acid clay nicely, but we do toss on the odd pail of wood ashes. Every foot of raw compost gets a thin topping of soil, and when the piles reach three feet, all is tilled under or turned by hand and left to mellow for a few months, or anywhere up to a year. By then, the compost is usually coarse but beginning to degrade nicely. We add bone and soy or cottonseed meal or whatever else we want, till or turn again, and cover the new bed with a deep coat of mulch. A month or so down the road, the worms have turned our mixture into lovely, fluffy soil, and the new bed is ready to edge and plant.

MULCHES

Mulch is an invaluable tool for mixed border makers. A dense mulch, spread thickly, can suppress weeds on newly claimed soil, suppress unwanted seedlings, and encourage composting in new piles. Thinner mulches will do the same things in an established garden, as well as conserve moisture in summer and protect plants from frost heaves and damaging cycles of thaws and freezes in winter. Mulch keeps the mud off the faces of the flowers of spring, and hides fading bulb foliage beneath a concealing blanket. In damp, cool climates like the maritime Northwest, deep mulches (up to eight to ten inches) can almost free the gardener from the need to water plants, but where summers are hot and dry, such a thick mulch can be wasteful, for it may take more water to keep the mulch wet than the plants would need for themselves. In such situations, a thinner mulch will be more effective. Many gardeners use thick winter mulches, then reduce them selectively with the advent of spring. Old mulch can always be reused or added to the compost pile.

There are dozens of good mulch materials, among them shredded leaves and bark, cocoa bean or buckwheat hulls, salt marsh hay or chopped straw, stable sweepings or stall litter. Where choices are broad, one can select materials with a handsome texture and color, but it doesn't matter overmuch; in mixed borders, the mulch will only be on show during the cooler months, for by late spring, you should no longer be able to see much of the soil surface within the beds. Since I live near Seattle,

Mulches come in many guises, since suitable, readily available materials will vary regionally. In Seattle, so much importance is placed on good coffee that an over-roasted batch is considered fit only for foot service. Author's garden; coffee beans courtesy of the Good Coffee Company, Seattle. Photo: Mark Lovejoy

where coffee is a local obsession, my mixed borders are often mulched with coffee chaff. It's quite attractive, a pale sand color, and so light and fluffy that it can be piled on several inches thick without threat of smothering small or young plants. Best of all, it smells wonderfully domestic, like a fresh cup of morning coffee. When local coffee roasters overcook a batch, the oily black whole beans make an elegant mulch for our garden paths. The paths themselves are made of the natural burlap sacks the coffee beans arrive in, which also underlie many of the smaller beds.

Burlap alone makes a good mulch where you want to kill off grass or weeds without chemicals or digging. Simply pile on as many layers of burlap as you can muster, and all but the most pernicious weeds (things like blackberries and horse tails) will be vanquished in a few months. It is simplicity itself to make new beds under established trees or shrubs this way, but the burlap should be placed on top of a layer of horticultural barrier cloth first. Otherwise, when the burlap rots, the tree or shrub roots will wander up into your nice new soil to compete with your perennials and bulbs.

You won't be able to use the tiller on such beds, for the loose bits of unrotted burlap will cling to its tines, but they are easily hand turned after a few months. Here, too, if you make the bed with already finished compost, no digging or turning is needed, and the bed can be planted immediately.

Though we do use a wide variety of mulch materials, one we never employ is peat moss. Though often recommended, it is in fact a wretched garden mulch and horribly expensive. For one thing, peat dries out quickly in a sunny or windy site, and once dry is very resistant to rewetting. Then too, we are learning that peat is not quite the renewable resource we once considered it to be, and may take hundreds of years to replenish. There is really no need for huge tracts of Canadian bog to be denuded just so our garden beds can be uniformly brown; shredded bark does the same thing at a fraction of the cost while utilizing a by-product that would otherwise be wasted.

No matter what sort of mulch is used, in mixed borders one must take particular care not to smother the crowns of woody plants as well as those of perennials when mulches are applied. If a deep mulch is called for, heap it on as thick as you like where no plants are placed, but slope the blanket down to a mere few inches near the trunks of trees and shrubs, and be sure that perennials are not covered over.

FEEDING MULCHES AND FERTILIZERS

Feeding mulches are intended to restore soil nutrients, and may be varied according to need. Here in the maritime Northwest, for instance, the soils tend to be acid, rich in potassium and rather low in phosphorus. Across the mountains in western Washington, where my mother gardens, the soil is alkaline or neutral, and requires somewhat different amendments. Soil tests and local county extension agents can tell you how your particular soil is composed, and what you might want to add to it. Certain things, however, are universal. Virtually all soils benefit from conditioning agents, materials that add humus, and improve texture and tilth. These include manures, humus, and compost, all of which contain a modest nutritional value. Many gardeners use aged, screened compost as a mild feeding mulch in autumn, often fortified with raw bone meal. Unsteamed meals release phosphorus slowly, which is what we want for good root growth during the slow, cold season ahead. Cooked bone meals are better used in spring, when the plants are ready for a quick fix. In my borders, a spring feeding mulch might consist of finished compost blended with rock phosphate, kelp meal, aged manure, and alfalfa pellets (the kind used to feed farm animals). Aged manure and alfalfa are a synergistic combination that releases the nutrients locked in each ingredient in forms especially accessible to plants.

If you begin a garden on soil that is basically sound and good, a regular diet of such mulches may provide all the nutrition your plants ever need. However, where soils are depleted or poor in quality to begin with, it can take time to improve them to that point. In these cases, artificial or chemical fertilizers are welcome additions to the pantry. However, it is worth noting that many pelletized fertilizers, and those with time-release coatings, won't release nutrients consistently until soil temperatures reach about 70 degrees Fahrenheit. In many areas, this means that pellets set out in spring won't be feeding your plants until summer arrives. Where springs are cool, supplement with foliar feedings of fish emulsion or a good all-purpose liquid fertilizer. Many pelletized fertilizers also work best when placed a few inches down in the soil, rather than on the soil surface. If the package directions indicate that this is so, scatter or place the fertilizer pellets before spreading your compost mulch, and both soil and plants will be well fed that season. Foliar feedings are also a fine flower booster if administered in early summer when the mid- and late-summer bloomers are just showing bud. Daylilies especially benefit from foliar feeding when in first bud, and any with a tendency to rebloom will do so with goodwill if fed with Peters' 20-20-20 or something similar early in the summer. Once the garden soil is properly enriched and balanced, similar effects can be gained, and summer weary plants rejuvenated, with a dose of manure tea, made by soaking a sack of chicken manure for a few days in a barrel of water.

DRAINAGE

Though few American garden books address this subject, quite as unromantic as dirt, it is a vital one. Many garden fatalities attributed to pests and diseases are in fact victims of poorly drained soil. A garden doesn't have to be a standing bog to need better drainage; plants can smother from lack of oxygen at the roots, or drown from excess moisture held too fiercely by a retentive soil. Even those who garden on lighter soils may need to improve drainage, for certain sand-based soils also contain tiny clay particles which can lock up when wet, causing puzzling puddling to occur. The gardener may rightfully be mystified by sand that does not retain water very well, yet drains poorly. In these cases, adding some coarse grit or very fine gravel along with masses of humus will help enormously, turning tight soil into the well-drained sponge that so many plants prefer. Heavy, stiff clay also improves with this combination, though here the proportions of grit to humus can often be reversed.

Where wet, mild winters leave excessive losses in their wake, the true culprit is probably rot rather than frost. Here it helps to make gravel pockets for plants with stout storage roots. Rot prone bulbs like crown imperials and certain lilies do well when manure is kept away from the bulb by a layer of gravel. Dig the holes a bit deeper than usual, filling the bottom with a rich mixture of manure and compost. Cover that with a layer of gravel, set the bulbs in place, then cover them with a blend of gravel and compost. The bulbs themselves may be set on their sides to keep water from accumulating in the stem scar (the stems will still emerge straight, despite the bulb's tilt). Blend more grit into the fill soil, and top the area off with a mulch of gravel, as growers of alpines often do. If you like, you can cover the gravel lightly with compost and bark or leaf mulch to blend in with the rest of the garden. Feeding mulches will percolate down to the bulb's roots with each rain, and excess water will drain freely away.

Where large sections of garden drain badly, tile drainage systems may be laid out beneath the beds and lawns. These are, however, expensive to install and clog readily, and it may prove more practical to improve drainage selectively, putting the most effort into important spots. The rest of the area can be planted with tolerant plants, perhaps natives that like tight soils, or bog dwellers of various sorts, or riverside plants accustomed to both drought and sog. Raised beds also assist drainage, even when made with heavy soils, for simple gravity flow can be remarkably effective.

In any situation, but especially where hardpan soils underlie garden areas, giving each new bed or border a base of several inches of fine gravel will promote better drainage. (The gravel sold as "⅝ths with smalls" is a useful size which packs nicely to a hard surface.) The gravel may be covered with a foot or more of topsoil and compost, which is then shaped to give the bed's edges a gradual, natural slope. The soil is held in place with mulch, aided by fast-knitting ground covers along the border's front and sides. (To soften the transition from bed to lawn, and minimize grass infiltration at the border edges, you can set concrete, tile, or stone pavers at the bed edges, with mat-forming or creeping herbs running through them.)

On steep slopes or banks, you can get the difficult combination of runoff and poor drainage. Here, gentle terracing will help, as will covering the slope with natural jute netting, which will degrade reasonably quickly. This can be covered in turn with a rough textured mulch like shredded bark, held in place by the netting. The largest possible divisions of ground-cover plants can be set in gravel-lightened and mulched holes, each with a wide rim; this way, water is caught as it rushes by, yet the excess will drain away freely.

Berms of earth, the ultimate raised beds, have been popular with designers in recent years, since they help block unwanted views and reduce street noise. The soil in them is often very heavy fill dirt, totally unimproved, while their sides are sloped in an abrupt and highly artificial manner which encourages rain to sheet off rather than soak into the ground. If the berm is gently terraced and deeply mulched, the water rush can be moderated and the soil slowly improved. If well planted, with a shrubby backbone placed along the top and various mixed border elements wending down the sides, such a berm can make a splendid mixed border. A few shrubby islands here and there will further reduce runoff, while making for greater winter interest as well, and the complex planting will mask the unnatural outline of the berm, which so often looks as though a subway station runs through the yard.

WATER

Water conservation is already an important issue for everybody, gardener or no, and it isn't going to get less so. Mixed borders can of course be as water guzzling as the next garden, but they may also be designed to be both water efficient and largely drought tolerant. Improving soils to take fullest advantage of what water they receive, mulching appropriately, and choosing drought-tolerant plants for naturally dry sites all make for more responsible gardening. Since they also promote plant health and simplify garden care, such measures should really be viewed as assisting rather than restricting the garden maker. Good soil in particular makes water management a much simpler proposition. Thanks to generous amendment, our stiff, rather sterile clay now actively supports plants of many kinds, while our winter losses from rot have been greatly reduced. Filled with humus, it holds water nicely even during droughts, yet now the plants get plenty of air as well. Our deeply mulched borders remain full and attractive all summer, though they are watered only once each month between May and October, a time when we seldom enjoy measurable rainfall. (The persistent myth that the Pacific Northwest is one big rain forest dies hard, but, in fact, our summers are typically dry.)

In mixed borders full of thirsty trees and shrubs, the perennials and bulbs around them are apt to dry out quickly, losing to the demanding root systems of the woody plants. Two relatively new horticultural products offer the border maker passive but powerful assistance. Horticultural barrier cloths, generally promoted as weed smothering mulches, are also useful for keeping the root sytems of woody plants away from those of less competitive companions. Woven of chemically inert polypropylene, barrier cloths are available in various qualities and weights, but all allow air, water, and nutrients to pass through, while stopping (or at least discouraging) root penetration. The heaviest grades are highly durable, and can be considered more or less permanent root barriers (they deter moles as well, a nice side effect). This permanence makes their proper placement important; beds built on barrier cloth can never be tilled, and must be dug with the same care as beds containing buried drip irrigation lines. It is easiest to spread the barrier cloth directly on the ground where mixed borders are to be made, with raised beds piled on top of them. If working around established trees and shrubs, be sure to leave a circle several feet across around each trunk. The new soil must be sloped down to the old level and held in place with jute netting or open textured ground covers, otherwise the mature plants may smother before they can adjust to the altered conditions.

Barrier cloth alone can greatly reduce a water bill, but the use of hydrophilic polymer gels will help even more. These are long-chain polymers that can absorb and hold tremendous volumes of water for their weight. In dry form, they resemble coarse grains of rock salt, but when hydrated they look like quivering chunks of clear gelatin. When I first saw the stuff, it was oozing out from under a potted border chrysanthemum, looking for all the world like escaped ice nine. I soon learned that these polymer gels belong well below the soil surface, where they act as tiny reservoirs for plant roots, releasing extra water on demand. Derived from corn and other natural starches or from synthetic polymer acrylics, the gels may last anywhere from a few months to between three and eight or ten years in a garden setting, depending on such conditions as soil type, exposure to sun, and composition of the gel. (Starch derivatives break down faster than acrylics.) Those which persist for a few years buy plants the time they need to establish competitive root systems. If necessary, gel applications can be renewed by digging up the plant, refreshing the soil and adding gel, then replanting. With larger established plants, one can poke deep holes all around and through a plant's root zone and add hydrated polymers as needed, though this is seldom necessary once a plant is well settled in. No matter what their initial composition, when they disintegrate, the gels break down into natural compounds, mostly water with small amounts of ammonia and carbon dioxide.

There are many kinds of hydrophilic gel on the market, of varying qualities and size grades, with names like Water Grabber, Supersorb, and Broadleaf P4. Though little known in America, they are widely used in England, predominantly in large container plantings and nursery greenhouse pots, as well as in borders. They are also available as a fine slurry used to keep cuttings and seedlings from drying out. For border use, the gels should be thoroughly hydrated (which takes several hours) before they are blended into the soil. In new beds, they can be worked into the entire area, which is then covered with an additional inch or two of soil and a good layer of mulch. In established beds, gel can be mixed into soil and hole whenever a drought-sensitive plant is moved, divided, or added to the border.

Hydrophilic polymers not only help plants get through drought periods, but give them a good start in spring as well. When this bed of Primula florindae *was planted three years ago, the large plant on the left had its planting soil amended with Broadleaf P4. It is consistently the first plant to bloom and the last to flag. Author's garden. Photo: Mark Lovejoy*

It is important that the gel be evenly mixed into the soil, because big clumps of unmixed gel can lead to anaerobic conditions which promote rots and molds. It is very difficult to tell whether unhydrated gel granules are evenly distributed, so prehydration is a must. In very heavy soils, gel should be mixed with coarse grit or fine gravel to ensure adequate drainage. In light, porous soils, humus and soil conditioners are added along with hydrated gel.

In my garden, there is an area beneath a large birch where the ground is always dry and rooty. Most of the plants grouped there are vigorous contenders for food and water, but a big *Rodgersia podophylla* was miserable. That was not too surprising considering its predilection for deep, moist soil, but its bold leaves added strength and balance to the group it dominated, and I wanted to keep it there. I dug out the plant, fortified its large root zone with gel, and reset it, and it never looked back. After four years, the rodgersia shows no sign of water stress, even during our August heat waves. Polymer gels also provide some measure of frost protection, for when they freeze, they hold the roots in their grip at 32 degrees Fahrenheit. Even if the surrounding soil gets colder than that, plants with lots of polymer gel around them tend to come through with minimal damage because of its insulating properties.

No matter how many water saving practices you employ, you are almost certainly going to have to supplement natural rainfall at some point. If you want a single watering to last for weeks, make sure the ground is soaked to a depth of at least eight inches. How you achieve this is relatively unimportant, and only experimentation will show you what is optimal for your garden. Where plantings remain relatively static, drip systems are practical and unobtrusive. Gardens with walls may boast wall-mounted soaker hoses or sprinkling devices, and some gardeners enjoy great success with systems of permanent sprinkler heads hidden in the borders, fed by hidden hoses. After losing canvas soaker hoses to rot, plastic ones to sun, and buried rubber ones to shovels, I learned how to use overhead sprinklers properly. Our whole garden is divided into slightly overlapping areas, each of which can be covered by an oscillating sprinkler. Each section of border has a permanent sprinkler station in its interior, usually marked by a flat stone to give the sprinkler firm footing. (It also reminds me not to plant anything just there.) Hoses are threaded along access paths, taking care not to crush or overlie nearby plants. The water is adjusted for total coverage, then left running for as many hours as it takes to penetrate thoroughly. The process is slow, but doesn't require active attention once set up. Since our heavy soil takes up water slowly, I often only change the hoses once or twice a day, watering from the early hours until midafternoon, when foliage needs a chance to dry out before nightfall. It takes about a week to water the entire garden, but since it only happens once a month, it doesn't seem burdensome.

As long as the foliage is allowed to dry out before nightfall, mildews are not a problem in the borders, which, although well filled, are planted to allow large plants plenty of air space.

When we regarded water as free and unlimited, few of us thought much about moderating our water use. Now, when we can't always take a steady supply of clean water for granted, it is a serious consideration. Even where water is plentiful, we should use water intelligently, taking only what we need, and minimizing those needs as much as possible. On the other hand, just having a garden is a service, for flushing rain or hose water through well planted ground can clean it of a number of pollutants. (Of course, if we are using toxic garden sprays, we only

make it worse, rather than better.) Even so, when planning gardens of any kind, it is worth thinking about the water supply, both present and probable future, and planting accordingly. There are a number of ways in which plant use can reduce water use; ground covers can conserve moisture as well as mulches. Many are drought tolerant themselves, or have fine, noncompetitive root systems that share space and water with larger plants. The dry areas of our own country provide us with a host of drought-tolerant plants, many of them already in the border builder's lexicon. Look for natives of the world's great deserts, of steppes and plains and prairies. Quite a few meadow dwellers and woodland plants tolerate summer drought if they get plenty of water in late winter and spring, when they put on most of their growth.

SUN OR SHADE

Most herbaceous borders are arranged to receive full or nearly full sun. Mixed borders, which hold plants of all sizes and kinds, present the gardener with a variety of settings, many of them shaded to some extent. Though the majority of ornamental border plants appreciate full sun, many will perform very well in partial or light shade, especially if their other cultural preferences are acknowledged. Indeed, anybody who has gardened in the maritime Northwest can tell you that the majority of sun lovers from temperate parts of the world can be well grown in less than full sun (our cloudy climate precludes "full sun" as the rest of the country understands it). Shade, often considered a liability, allows the gardener to employ a greater range of plants than a relentlessly sunny site. Bloom may be slightly lighter, yet will often be prolonged days or weeks beyond that in the open. Shade often deepens and protects flower color, and the shelter of the shade-casting plants affords frail flowers protection from wind and rain.

To use shade well, one must be aware of its kind, duration, and intensity. High shade from tall trees which have been limbed up to thirty or forty feet is usually light and dappled, and many plants will grow nicely in it. When low-growing branches are robbing a garden of light and air, removal of a few lower limbs can create a far more hospitable setting for smaller plants. Deciduous trees and shrubs with small leaves create dappled summer shade, lighter in spring and fall and open to light all winter. Most woodlanders and meadow plants will thrive in these conditions, as will early- and late-blooming bulbs and a tremendous range of border perennials. Deep shade cast by walls or large evergreens is a more difficult proposition, one more readily resolved with tough, drought-resistant ground covers than with flowering plants. No matter what kind of shade you have, plants will do better if the shaded soil is in good heart. Barrier cloth, polymer gels, and deep litter mulches will go far to improving the dry, rooty conditions which often plague shaded sites. Margery Fish's handbook, *Gardening in the Shade,* is an excellent resource, but nothing beats ongoing experimentation to find out what will do well in your particular situation.

MAINTENANCE

One of the strengths of the well designed mixed border is that it is relatively easy to keep in good looks. The frameworks and islands of evergreens and woody plants that make up a considerable proportion of the plantings need little more than an annual checkup. Bark mulches keep weeds to a minimum and, if deep enough, may need renewal only every other year. An annual feeding mulch such as compost will take care of most nutritional needs, and even plants on special diets can usually be set straight by a yearly dose of chelated iron or whatever the need may be. Because plants are placed where their natural shapes are an asset, only occasional light pruning should be required, and that mainly for aesthetic reasons. As small trees mature, you may want to trim off the lowest limbs, or reshape the canopy while it is still within easy reach. Unless damaged by storms or disease, little further treatment should be necessary. Shrubs are simpler still, for if relieved

Borders that are groomed regularly may hold their looks very late in the season. If allowed to run together, the natural shapes of the plants become blurred and indistinct, rather than clean and definite as they remain here. September, Withey/ Price garden, Seattle, Washington. Photo: Peter Ray

of misshapen or elderly central canes each year, their pruning takes only minutes. Woody vines may need to be restrained or redirected now and then, but most are relatively easygoing.

Since mixed border plants are positioned according to their physical needs, as well as for aesthetic concerns, they are apt to be healthy and resistant to diseases. Grouping by need further simplifies maintenance because each border section tends to have similar care requirements. Often, two or three tidying sessions each year will suffice to keep entire areas healthy and attractive. In mixed borders, high-need ephemerals are sandwiched between groups of woody plants and low-care perennials which remain attractive for months at a time without fuss. Ferns and grasses, evergreen perennials and ground covers may only need attention once a year, when they are weeded, fed, and thoroughly groomed. Such independent plants may thrive on this modest regimen for five or even ten years before flagging. At that point, a restorative overhaul of the soil and the division of overcrowded plants will renew their performance and good nature.

Experimentation will show how best to space more demanding plants and combinations in order that the borders be well filled yet not so crowded as to invite disease or mask the shapes of the plants themselves. Thoughtful plant placement streamlines border grooming sessions, since groups are designed both to peak and to decline together. This not only avoids the lonely look of a valiant long bloomer shining out amongst fading companions, but allows the gardener to plan color sequences in whole blocks. While the areas devoted to framework and ground covers may themselves have a period of captivating beauty, their main contribution is to provide a consistent setting for ephemerals. Each group of these will provide several high points, the lulls timed to coincide with the glory days of neighboring areas. Each time, one good grooming session will remove traces of dissolution and prepare it for its supportive role as the plants next door prepare to shine. When they flag in turn, the first group is renewed and ready to perform again. This sort of cycling keeps color and interest moving throughout the garden in every season.

In deep mixed borders, plants that need daily grooming should be placed close to the border front or near an access path. Allow them plenty of room and surround them with largely foliar companions, for delicate neighbors can suffer from the frequent disturbance occasioned by their unsightly remains. A choice few flowers are self-cleaning, their petals falling neatly away when they fade. Many others, such as large-flowered daylilies, lilies, and big campanulas are showy offenders whose leftovers can significantly mar a garden picture. Where access is limited, it pays to group long-lasting performers that

need little or no attention for most of the summer. Combinations like the cheerful mallow, *Lavatera thuringiaca* 'Barnsley', creamy pink with a rosy eye, and the tall, airy pink *Polygonatum campanulatum* work together for months without assistance, as do giant catmint, *Nepeta* 'Six Hills Giant', and feathery squirrel tail grass (*Hordeum jubatum*), or the flat plates of chalky yellow *Achillea taygetea* with the pencil thin stalks of intense purple *Verbena bonariensis*. Mixed borders can be tailored to suit the gardener; those with time and inclination can devote a larger proportion of their beds to high-voltage but demanding performers, while those whose time or skill is limited can rely more heavily on stalwarts. Perhaps this is trading spectacle for stability, but it almost guarantees an attractive and tidy garden. As the situation allows, the balance can be shifted to offer more change and greater interest.

Though orchestration of sequencing and seasonal color effects improves with time and practice, regular grooming will do more for the overall appearance of the garden than the most astounding of floral displays. Thanks to innumerable variables, there is no way to plan or chart a border grooming schedule, but during the height of the summer it is safe to assume that the garden will need a good going over at least once a week. A few well-spent minutes each day is optimal, though not strictly necessary; this sort of garden is very forgiving, and rewards even irregular care with generosity. Still, small, frequent groomings keep the garden fresh, and may be equally restorative for the gardener. In any case, it is better to really enjoy the garden than to focus too closely on its state of perfection. The garden is meant to bring us joy, not make us suffer, and relentless perfectionism is a losing game.

To make the best use of limited time, it is important to understand the needs of one's plants. Even for needy creatures, timely intervention will save a good deal of bother and greatly simplify the garden chores. A garden journal can help enormously, for though nothing teaches better than time and experience, we don't all have perfect memories. When my August entries mention tumbling lilies several years in a row, I now write ahead into next year's April space to remind myself to stake those stalks

Grooming the borders is an ongoing job, but one which keeps the relationship between garden and gardener intimate. Weekly tidy sessions are the best tonic for tired gardens, since any pests or problems will be quickly addressed. Photo: Mark Lovejoy

at the proper time. When something looks off balance in July, I note the fact both there and ahead in October, when I can safely remove the offender without harm to plant or garden. Journal notes remind me to feed the daylilies when their buds first show color in order to stimulate reliable rebloom. They jog me to trim hellebore and epimedium leaves in early winter, so the fresh leaves and blossoms can be appreciated unmarred by last year's tattered remains. They persuade me to fill summer gaps in border pictures in autumn or early spring, to sow annuals at the right moment, and to cut back the giant catmint before it smothers its neighbors.

Through disasters and failures, we learn to master sequencing and complex color runs. However, without the help of journal notes, those hard-earned lessons are often forgotten, only to be relearned with

bitter hearts next season. The records need not be lengthy or complicated, just enough to prompt the right action at the right time. The point is to preserve information, building a specific body of knowledge about your own garden with all its individual quirks. We can learn a great deal from books, but the best of them can only hope to be a general guide; in the end, it is our own plants and our own gardens that matter. The more we know about both, the better we can meet their needs. Good records help us organize plants and time effectively; the better organized our garden keeping, the less likely that crises and needless catastrophes will arise. Garden keeping is also far more satisfying when our work is both effective and efficient, and garden records help again on every score.

KEEPING IT ALL TOGETHER

In the mixed border, the round of garden chores differs from the usual garden maintenance schedule in several respects. Here, the immediate aim of all work sessions is to set the stage for the next garden event. The long-term goal is that every area should be at least presentable, while some part of the garden should be in beauty at any given time. Even in a large, complex garden like mine, maintenance is a relatively light though ongoing chore. Large areas of garden are devoted to plants that need very little care—woody plants, ground covers, vines, bulbs, and evergreen perennials—so one or two annual work sessions suffice to keep the bulk of the garden in good trim. Pruning is reduced by proper siting to an aesthetic rather than controlling chore; when plants are given the right conditions and adequate space, their natural growth patterns fulfill rather than spoil the gardener's intentions. The need for watering is similarly reduced by suiting plants to the various settings offered by your garden, by creating shade with trees and shrubs, by improving the soil, and by mulching. Feeding is accomplished through feeding mulches, an annual dose of special supplements for the chosen few, and an occasional midsummer feast of foliar or broadcast fertilizer for hungry annuals and perennials. Since weeds are largely suppressed by mulches, those which make it past that barrier can be removed as soon as noticed, a very light if ongoing job. This leaves grooming, a chore seldom recognized in standard garden books, yet the backbone of mixed border care.

GARDEN GROOMING

Like its human counterpart, garden grooming may be simple and straightforward or an art in itself. How and how rigorously grooming is carried out depends on our natural proclivities; some of us prefer clean, simply brushed hair to carefully coiffed curls. Some will match handbag and earrings to an outfit, while others are content if their socks match. So, too, in the garden, where grooming may mean a quick but efficient weekly tidying of dead or drooping flowers, or a daily manicure for lawn and borders alike. Grooming begins with the lawn, for just as making the bed instantly improves the appearance of a messy bedroom, mowing and edging the lawn makes the garden look crisp and well defined. From late spring well into autumn, most garden grooming is directed at perennials and other ephemerals. As seasonal color sequencing moves visual interest around the borders, the gardener follows, nipping withered blossoms here, heading back lanky stems there, always working with an eye to keeping the overall picture in balance. Long-blooming perennials like *Coreopsis verticillata* 'Moonbeam' or *Aster* × *frikartii* may be gone over many times during the summer, for whenever the fading blossoms are removed, fresh ones appear to take their place. With reblooming iris and daylilies, removing old stems to the ground stimulates the production of new ones. Catmints may be sheared several times during the summer to encourage tighter growth and more flowers. Cutting floppers like oriental poppies back hard results in tidy mounds of fresh foliage. Copper fennel looks handsome when it flowers, but if the seed heads are allowed to ripen, your border will become a fennel farm. Grooming means taking care of these and similar details in good time, and in such a way that the plants are not left disfigured.

When severe treatment is demanded, as for oriental poppies, arrange for screening plants like baby's breath (*Gypsophila*) to cover up until the cut back plant recovers its good looks.

It is crucial not to let sentiment cloud your judgment when grooming a spent area; it seems a shame to cut off that last, lingering rose or this lovely little sheaf of late crocosmia. However, by the time you take away everything that is definitely past its prime, the leftovers tend to look forlorn rather than brave. Do the tidying thoroughly, and the garden will look far better for your mental toughness. Since I can't stand to throw living flowers on the compost heap, I carry a small bucket of water in my garden cart when grooming. All the excised plant material goes on the heap, but any still-fresh bits of foliage and flower and bud go in the bucket. Later I make up bouquets for the house with the garden gleanings, where they bring far more enjoyment than when left as relics of spent beauty in the garden.

Unromantic by nature, maintenance is seldom a favorite part of garden making, yet it is a vital one. Chores like deadheading and trimming away browning foliage improve the look of the border, promote rebloom, and make for healthier plants. Photo: Cynthia Woodyard

The best grooming tool around is the secateur, often called a hand pruner. The Swiss-made Felco bypass pruners are ideal grooming tools, strong, well balanced, and replaceable in every part. The blades sharpen up nicely and hold an edge well, and replacing them takes only a few minutes, even for me. The #8 model is the standard for border work (#9 is the same, but made for left handers), but the rather delicate looking #6 is often favored by those with smaller hands. Bypass pruners are expensive, but worth every penny, because they are so well designed and made. Moreover, they are perfectly suited for this specific task, unlike heavy anvil pruners, which crush and tear rather than cut cleanly. Good border pruners are not just for cutting twigs and branches; they are used to trim out spent flowering stalks of reblooming perennials, nipping them cleanly at the base without damaging their emerging replacements. They can shear shaggy grasses in spring, restrain overly exuberant catmints in summer, whisk away fading foliage in autumn, reshape a straggling holly in winter. With sharp bladed pruners, one can nip the fading roses from a spray while leaving neighboring buds untouched, or remove thick canes cleanly at the base. Used with skill, pruners are capable of both delicacy and strength.

To keep pruners handy at your side, hitch a pruner holster to your belt. My holster rides on the webbing straps of a small fanny pack or waist purse, the zippered compartments of which hold sundries like labels and marking pens, garden twist ties and string, chapstick and tissues. My weeding knife, a heavy, cast-iron affair traditionally used by Japanese farmers, comes in its own sheath, which also slips over the belt webbing. The weeding knife is just the ticket for digging out tap-rooted weeds like dock, which is too slippery to pull properly. Its serrated edge is not very sharp, but serves for severing thick roots (when that is one's goal) or chunking up overgrown hostas and Siberian iris clumps. In spring and fall, a hand trowel should also accompany you on the daily rounds. With this, seedlings and small plants are shifted about, wandering side shoots are restrained, and offsets are removed to pot up for friends or to colonize elsewhere. Much of the fine tuning of the border is done with the hand trowel.

SEASONAL CHORES

While the actual schedule must be indicated by the needs of each specific mixed border, maintenance chores come in waves, corresponding to the five or six seasons of the garden. Though these too differ, both regionally and garden to garden, they may be roughly expressed as spring, early summer, high summer, autumn, and, where winters are mild, early and late winter. Each has its chores, its rhythms, its plants, and its pleasures.

SPRING

In early spring, the borders must be tidied up to prepare for the flowers of spring. Feeding mulches will be spread, heavy winter mulches lightened, weed-preventing mulches renewed. Any seed stalks or rustling grasses left for winter enjoyment are now removed to make room for new growth. The whole garden should be looked over, weeded, and tidied up as necessary. Perimeter plantings, hedges, and evergreen islands can be tidied, fed, and trimmed as needed. Lawns and border edges are retrimmed, and paths are remulched or otherwise put in good repair. Keep track of color sequences, any gaps and ideas for filling them, successes, and places that need work in your garden journal.

In late spring, when late frosts are unlikely, winter losses can be made good, new plants set out, and autumn bloomers divided or reset. Summer-blooming combinations may be altered or fine tuned, and annuals can be set in place. The earliest bloomers, especially bulbs, may now be drooping and in need of grooming. Stakes, hoops, twiggy sticks, and other plant supports should be set in place, and young vine shoots guided in the proper directions. Heavy vines and other climbers can be trained over tripods or tepees of stout poles (fruit-wood suckers of anything over an inch in diameter serve very well) bound together with wire or a rope made of supple willow wands. Long strands of weeping willow can also be used to disguise the wire edges of tomato cages or other metal frames; weave several long strands together to encircle each level. Willow

Tripods or tepees of stout stakes bring climbing plants to prominence and create powerful vertical accents along the border. In more formal gardens, trellis cages or handsome metal frames are more suitable than the rustic sticks which serve so well in casual settings. Photo: Mark Lovejoy

strands can also be woven around and through wooden tripods and tepees to restrain and guide young vine shoots. When it dries, willow is surprisingly strong, and will last several seasons if two or three pieces are worked together. Long, twiggy pieces of weeping birch can also be loosely braided, then woven around wooden or metal supports in the same way to pleasant effect.

EARLY SUMMER

The remains of spring bloomers must be cleared away with care, so that summer plants can bloom unmarred by browning foliage. Where bulb leaves are intrusive, push them gently down to ground level to hide behind emerging neighbors. Bulb leaves can also be covered with a light layer of mulch and still ripen nicely. Mulches should have disappeared by now beneath the fast spreading border plants, but where weeds persist, increase suppressing mulches as needed. Begin weekly journal entries, noting the timing of plant emergence or bloom, good garden pictures, and any gaps or failures. Mark plants that need moving in your garden journal, entering the information in autumn when you will be carrying out the plans you make now. Note, too, average monthly temperatures and weather patterns (if heat waves, drought, heavy wind, or rains are typical, you can prepare for them well ahead of time).

Give annuals, new plants, daylilies, and late or rebloomers a light suplemental feeding (I use Peters' 20-20-20 and a hose siphon). Water deeply and well, but as seldom as possible. Spot watering of young or new plants should be done as needed, rather than by schedule. Garden grooming begins in earnest; a weekly once-over may be supplemented with five-minute daily sessions to keep major offenders like large daylilies and roses clean.

HIGH SUMMER

Grooming and watering are the only regular chores during the warmest months. Keep journal entries current, recording changes you want to make in autumn, things in bloom, patterns of performance, how plants are responding to any special care or situation, and similar matters. Supplemental feeding should stop, lest it promote excessive young growth—prone to disease and winter kill—too late in the year. Refresh tired plants with grooming and manure tea (soak a bag of dried manure in water for two or three days, then feed the resulting liquid to the needy). Water deeply when needed, checking the soil weekly in hot weather. If overgrown or lanky, Mediterranean subshrubs like lavender and santolina should be cut back before August to allow new growth to ripen before winter. By midsummer, grooming is geared toward promoting autumn display. Clear away late stragglers that look wispy and insignificant and replenish annuals.

AUTUMN

Keep grooming light and reduce or stop watering to discourage new or continued growth. Let everything slow down and lapse gently into winter. Leave hips and leaves on roses well into autumn (at least until the first hard frosts) to harden off the canes before winter. Large, established perennials may be allowed to set seed if you want to collect it, or to attract birds. Lift perennials ready for division, and replenish the soil, adding amendments. Plants may be divided and moved as long as mild weather holds;

late plantings should be especially well mulched to insulate unsettled roots (six to eight inches is not too much). Spruce up areas of winter interest with particular care. Grooming is geared toward setting the stage for winter, but let hard frosts be the signal for major cleanup. Where late bloomers still hold sway, avoid severe treatment of neighboring areas until all glory is gone. If this proves awkward, consider planting options that would better support the autumn groups. Flanking groups of low, evergreen shrubs and hardy perennials mixed with spring bulbs are an effective choice.

In a dry year, wait for softening rain before planting bulbs, or spot water deeply where they are to be placed. Set bulbs relatively deep, both for insulation and to reduce damage when sandwich planting (layering shallow-rooted plants above bulbs). Most bulbs will bloom undeterred when planted this way, and those which prefer shallower conditions will soon make their way closer to the soil surface whatever you do. As the borders are cleaned up, renew deep protective mulches and have any winter wraps for tender or half-hardy plants ready to put on as needed. Go over your journal notes, assessing the season past as well as present, and recording future plans as well as tending to earlier ones as noted.

WINTER

Climate shapes the character of the winter season, for where snow falls early, the garden must be ready by late autumn, and winter gardening activities are restricted to the passive ones of admiration and appraisal. Even in the harshest climate, the mixed border can be a haven in winter. Now the perimeter plantings that shape the garden offer shelter and verdant promise of greener times to come. Mid-border islands of evergreens retain their relationships even in the snow. A sheltered seat offers a setting for snow picnics; the winter garden in a snowfall or by moonlight is alive with magic. Deciduous trees and shrubs, spare and graceful, are showcased by the quiet backdrop of green and white. Winter's pause gives us time to study our journal notes, reorganizing our ideas and impressions, and making lists and plans to implement in spring.

Where mild, winter has two distinct parts. Early winter brings the first of the winter-blooming perennials into strength; certain crocus, hellebores, forms of *Iris unguicularis*, and winter jasmine (*Jasminum nudiflorum*) may all begin to flower as early as November. Sheltered spots may be warm enough to lure the gardener out to take coffee in the sun. Though much of the garden is quiet, the hedges are alive with birds, the border's islands alive with winter color.

After the midwinter lull, late winter brings a gentle handful of early bloomers, precursors of true spring. In my garden, the first species crocus, snowdrops, and early perennials may appear in late January. In late winter, where weather is mild, gardeners may begin light pruning of spring-flowering things for shape and control, bringing in branches to force for the house. Mulches may be adjusted around the earliest performers, and a final grooming of winter-battered plants will ready the garden for the approach of spring.

If the garden is not enticing in winter, make notes about what could help. Gaps in boundary and perimeter plantings might be temporarily closed with trellis panels, fencing, or large plywood cutouts of mountains or trees. Make maps in your journal to mark places that need further planting or screening. If there is no place to be comfortable in the winter garden, consider adding a seat in a sunny, wind-sheltered spot. Choose a generously oversized one that can be piled with blankets or waterproof cushions when you use it. Look at books on winter gardens (see Books for Further Reading) for suitable plants that would offer beauties of branch and bark, leaf and berry.

THE JOY OF CHORES

Talk of chores is always daunting, and great lists of seasonal musts can be intimidating, yet the experience of garden keeping is one of the gardener's greatest pleasures. Indeed, for many people, the process of caring for the garden is more rewarding than

Edging the border at Great Dixter, demonstrating that even lowly chores may be performed with style. Photo: Cynthia Woodyard

admiring it. Both bring enjoyment, but weeding is interactive, while admiration is both passive and solitary. Serious grunt work like breaking or stripping sod, moving trees, or double digging a long border isn't everybody's cup of tea (though an excellent way to dissipate anger or tension), but grooming and other seasonal chores put us closely in touch with our plants, and keep us aware of conditions within our borders. Planting new beds, fine tuning older ones, even routine weeding can be as deeply fulfilling as many a more obviously creative act. The personal investment of time and physical attention strengthens the bond between people and plants. Ongoing garden care is what weds the gardener to the garden.

PESTS AND DISEASES

I have relatively little to say about pests and diseases, since my gardens have so rarely been seriously troubled by either one. This is due in part to an unswerving philosophy of tough love in the garden; plants that are prone to problems are given several chances to shape up, but if they don't respond to therapy or change, they get shovel pruned. On the other hand, I am tolerant of occasional or mild damage that might trigger action in others. Because mixed border communities are varied and complex, they seldom attract the insistent pests that plague monocultures. Since problems are minimized by healthful garden practices, the mixed border gardener spends more time on making and keeping the garden attractive than in practicing direct disease intervention. When problems do arise, they tend to be minor and easily remedied. Many are safely ignored, for healthy plants in good soil often succeed in outgrowing trouble. If an attack is light, the gardener may hose off a few aphids or burn a few caterpillar tents and leave it at that, trusting the garden to balance itself. If the garden is already in balance, with the right plants growing well in satisfactory situations, a few pests are nothing to worry about. If anything, they attract more birds to the garden.

Now and then, however, the best arranged garden may suffer more serious depredation. If plants are endangered, or the garden disfigured, action may be called for. However, it generally pays to react with caution, and to intervene in as benign a manner as possible. Wide spectrum sprays may seem to promise tidy dispatch, but very often they do considerable environmental harm without resolving the initial problem. Roger Swain (of Victory Garden fame) has frequently written about the terrible side effects of misused garden chemicals. "The problems are not caused by industrial or agricultural use," he notes. "These substances are expensive, and the profit margin is so slim in agriculture, nobody can afford to be careless or inaccurate with either pesticides or fertilizers, another significant source of pollution." Moreover, he feels, "Although pesticides and herbicides are very dangerous substances, few homeowners bother to learn how to use, store, or dispose of them safely. Worse still, very few people bother to correctly identify their problem, let alone match it to the appropriate treatment, so much of the time, the treatment is worthless. Then, too, few people read the label directions with care. The greatest risk to the user comes when mixing sprays; that is the point at which one is exposed to full concentrations of these substances. Though you may

be using small amounts, if you spill that teaspoon per gallon, you've got a health problem right now." Indeed, Swain points out, the trend in industrial application is to package pesticides and herbicides in such a way that the user never comes into contact with the concentrates. "The homeowner doesn't worry much about these things. If the label says 'use a teaspoon,' they fetch the kitchen measuring spoon, then run it through the dishwasher and figure themselves safe. If it says 'wear gloves,' they might use regular garden gloves, or even dish washing gloves. Even if they discard the gloves after use, were they pesticide proof? How many people use respirators when they spray, or change the filters after pesticide use? How many people are familiar with the laboratory technique the use of dangerous substances merits?"

Swain is well aware that not even the so called "organics" are harmless. "Many people cheerfully spray dormant oils and insecticidal soaps with no protection at all, assuming that these are environmentally benign. However, their effect on the human lung is far from gentle; dormant oils can cause lipid pneumonias, and the fatty acids in soaps do much the same thing. These, too, must be used with respect." In his own garden, Swain controls problems with sound cultural practices. "Most of what people complain about aren't even significant problems," he states firmly. "Insects and diseases are nothing compared to invertebrates. Nobody wants to hand pick rabbits. Deer, woodchucks, moles . . . Let me tell you about beavers. Let's talk about moose." Nonetheless, "Grow everything as well as you can, and put up with a few problems," he concludes. "The real answer to pest and disease problems is tolerance."

If chemicals offer a quick all-purpose fix, they also keep us at arm's length from whatever is ravaging our garden. Some people prefer it this way, yet there are certain satisfactions in resolving problems directly. If enough harm is done, good, clean gardener's rage ought to find relief in squishing slugs or assigning caterpillars to the bonfire. As a child, I was paid a penny a piece to pick Japanese beetles off my mother's roses, drowning them in a little can of kerosene. They seemed beautiful to me, metallic and lustrous, yet I so hated finding them lurking in the heart of a half-eaten rose that their collection caused me no pangs of conscience or distaste. Later, when I lived in Ohio, experienced gardeners taught me that crushing fat hornworms underfoot or pinching earwigs in half was wonderfully effective if done daily. Here in the Pacific Northwest, our worst consistent pests are slugs and tent caterpillars. With both, I have found that a mixture of watchfulness and timely intervention reduces the amount and intensity of whatever preventive measures we decide to follow.

The caterpillars wax and wane over a cycle of several years, but slugs are forever. Here in the Northwest, slugs are something of a local specialty. They may be black or gray or buff or tan, mottled like leopards or striped like tigers. An especially huge, creamy yellow variety called the banana slug is not the thing to step on barefoot in the morning when you let the dogs out or fetch in the mail. Some are enormous, big enough to break lily buds under their weight. Others are tiny but voracious, and find their unerring way into the core of every hosta. Snails, their hard-backed relatives, have joined the throng in increasing numbers, imports from California. Our property is surrounded on three sides by woods and meadows, from which slugs slither on thick, slimed trails by the thousands. What they can do to an innocent garden in a single, undefended night is disgusting. Actually, some plants, like delphiniums and monkshoods, can defend themselves after a fashion. When their first tender shoots are stripped to the ground, they respond by producing a nasty tasting toxin in the next set of leaves, which nearly always make it to maturity unscathed. Hostas, daylilies, and hellebores seem to be endlessly tasty, and must be protected if they are to fulfill their garden destiny in my terms, rather than the slugs'.

The first line of defense is a good offense. Every day before breakfast, I make a tour of the garden and stomp a hundred slugs underfoot, a chore which takes perhaps three minutes on a bad day, or up to twenty on a good one. If we have a cold winter, slug hunting begins in mid- to late January and continues unabated into August. Summer heat (if there is any) and drought slow the suckers down, but they

are present and hungry right up to the first killing frost (if we have one). In a mild year, they never stop. In a garden like ours, full of children and pets, visited by thousands of birds, with a bog and small stream running through, most of the chemical slug remedies are out of the question. One of our dogs once got into some slug bait the neighbors had set out. Our excellent vet sat with us through three hours of epileptic seizures, and though Bosco recovered, he has never been the same. We are not eager to see what the effects might be on a child, and have no wish to poison birds or groundwater either. Still, the garden needs constant defense, so we make choices. In a nostalgic moment, I offered the kids a penny a piece to stomp slugs. They tried to bargain me up to a dime, claiming that the process was icky. Indeed, those with small feet can even find it dangerous, since ex-slugs are still very slippery. We compromised at last, and now I fill up squirt guns filled with a mixture of one-third nonsudsing household ammonia and two-thirds water. A good shot of this will reduce a slug to gray foam in seconds without harming the host plant. (A few plants will show a bit of leaf burn; if this happens, we knock slugs off those plants with sticks before blasting them.) I patrol the garden with spray bottles of the mixture, and whoever hits a hundred slugs first, wins. On a good day, we all make our quota in no time, which, at a penny apiece, is definitely worth two dollars a day. In midspring when slug eggs hatch daily and the hordes are hungriest, and when we are not home to do the daily patrol, I supplement with commercial baits. As mentioned, some are too toxic to contemplate, but a few can safely be used, so long as the proper precautions are observed. Aluminum sulfate, sometimes recommended as a soil amendment to alter pH (it acidifies soil, making hydrangeas bluer), also kills slugs on contact. It can be sprinkled through the border, but since it dissolves in water, it must be replenished after rain or when the borders are watered. Corry's slug bait is a blend of bran with an alcohol analog, metaldehyde. Despite all that dietary fiber, it puts slugs on a fatal bender for, like alcohol, metaldehyde is a potent dehydrator. Such products are toxic to cats and birds and should always be kept away from water, but they can be carefully placed beneath hellebore leaves to protect emerging buds or tucked close about the base of vulnerable plants like daffodils, daylilies, and hostas.

A few plants will be totally consumed if not so protected. Each garden is different in this respect, and though it may vary a bit from year to year, fairly consistent patterns soon emerge. In my garden, for instance, slugs obliterate the terra-cotta colored single chrysanthemum 'Mary Stoker', though her sibling 'Clara Curtis' is not bothered. Silvery, cabbagelike *Salvia argentea* will be stripped to the crown in short order while all the other salvias I grow are untouched. The rounded blue leaves of *Mertensia simplicissima* are irresistible, while those of *M. virginica*, though well chewed, are never destroyed. Red leaved lobelias are favored over green ones, which rarely rate a nibble. Though no relatives are bothered, purple leaved elder needs early protection or it loses all its leaf buds. Pulmonarias and primroses seldom show damage, yet tulip buds and daffodil flowers are always ravaged. For such as these, I begin to set out bait as soon as the first slugs appear. The next day, I may find thirty or forty slugs feasting at each bran pile. The biggest are scooped into a bucket of aluminum sulfate or sprayed with ammonia water, for in spring, when both ground and foliage are saturated, large slugs can rehydrate after metaldehyde poisoning, and will avoid bait in the future (proving amazingly savvy for such a primitive life form).

Tent caterpillars, though occurring less frequently, present more of a threat to the health of the garden than slugs, whose depredations are generally more cosmetic than life threatening. Unchecked, the caterpillars can do a tremendous amount of damage, since they feed on a wide range of plants, sometimes to the point of death. Lilacs and roses, fruit trees and honeysuckles, even daylilies are dinner to these voracious creatures. Here in the Northwest, they appear in varying quantities each year. When infestations are light, we may find only a handful of tents. In a bad year, they strip mature trees to the bone, and walking beneath the canopy of branches, one can hear a steady rustling noise, the crunching of

tattered leaves in a million tiny mouths. Thanks to several natural predators, including swallows and tiny parasitic wasps, a banner year for the caterpillars proves their undoing. As the caterpillars peak, so do their enemies, which nearly always results in a lull of several years without much sign of those sticky gray tents.

However, even knowing that help is on the way, it takes a more organic gardener than I to stand back and do nothing when the garden is under a full-scale attack. For us, vigilance begins in winter, when we prune the fruit trees. We search out and strip the egg cases, which look like bands of Styrofoam, from branch and twig. If there are a lot of egg cases, I make a point of checking other vulnerable trees as well as garden shrubs, and removing all the cases I can find. When the caterpillars hatch, we strip and burn their tents as soon as we discover them, either early in the morning or late in the day, when the caterpillars are resting at home. Where the parasitic wasps (so small as to be almost undetectable to the eye, and not interested in people) are not native, they can be released when the caterpillars appear. These little insects lay their eggs inside the caterpillars, leaving telltale white spots on the caterpillar's body. When the tents are high overhead, out of stripping range, we spray with Bt (*Bacillus thuringiensis*), a bacterium which paralyzes the digestive tracts of leaf eaters, yet won't harm birds or bees. Because this also works against the caterpillars of harmless butterflies, I consider it a last resort, to be used only when there are many tents out of reach, when the garden is seriously threatened, and when spirited attempts to hose them down with water have failed.

However we choose to respond to problems, we need to balance our parental fury over the assault to our garden child with our responsibilities as stewards of our piece of the earth. I personally wouldn't want to breathe the air in a garden where all bugs had been chemically eliminated, and where conditions were so sterile that no disease could find a foothold. Accepting some degree of imperfection is part of finding our place in the natural world.

In spring the Platt garden's subtle winter beauties of silhouette and shadow, berry and bark are enlivened by sheets of bulbs. Winter blooming hellebores flower from late November through April, sheltered by the arching arms of protective shrubs and small trees. Photo: Cynthia Woodyard

Chapter Three

TREES
IN THE
MIXED BORDER

THE GARDEN OF
JANE PLATT

PORTLAND, OREGON USDA ZONE 7/8

"The garden began because I loved trees so," said the late Jane Platt, creator of one of the most acclaimed private gardens on the West Coast. We were talking in her garden, about a year before her much regretted death in 1990. "Gradually, a great many other things found their way in; the shrubs, the rock garden, the perennials all had their day as the center of my attention. Now I've come full circle, and am planting trees again." Mrs. Platt's garden, now under the able care of her husband, is living witness to her fascination with and appreciation for trees. The garden sits high on a wooded hillside west of Portland, protected by the shoulder of the hill from the worst of the fierce winds that sweep the nearby Columbia River Gorge. The property slopes steeply enough that the forty to sixty inches of annual rainfall drain quickly away, despite a heavy clay soil. The garden is a haven for a multiplicity of plants, but it is shaped by its trees.

Trees dominate this tightly planted garden, yet they are so artfully used that they seem to expand, rather than crowd the two-and-a-half-acre lot. Clever placement of larger trees leads the eye outward to the meadows and rolling hills beyond the garden's borders. The expansive view and open lawn preserve a sense of spaciousness often lacking in complex, mature gardens. The majestic treeline, bold and varied, immediately captures the attention, yet very soon the hundreds, perhaps thousands of smaller garden plants claim their own share. Small trees, shrubs, and perennials are arranged in pleasing juxtapositions which give body and depth to this parklike garden. Indeed, in any season, the grand tour should be made twice; once to exclaim over the rarities, and again to savor their placement.

If many of the trees here—*Franklinia alatamaha*, *Eucryphia glutinosa*, *Prunus maackii*—are uncommon, rarer still are the levels of artistry and plantsmanship combined in this garden. Every plant is well grown, and each is sited to advantage. Only experienced gardeners can appreciate the knowledge and ruthlessness required to maintain such standards over time. Few of us are keen enough of eye and stern enough of heart to see, let alone remove, beloved shrubs past their prime, or trees that have outgrown their position. Mrs. Platt was as capable of sentiment as any gardener, but unlike most of us, she never allowed it to cloud her vision. She was well aware that unless the interior balance of a garden is rigorously maintained, the garden as a whole loses character and definition. This one, now over forty years old, has both in spades.

"I wasn't always so careful," she admitted. "Everybody who loves plants uses too many of them, and I overplanted dreadfully in the early years." She always preferred to begin with young trees and shrubs, feeling that they transplant more successfully, but as her first plantings began to grow up, "The garden looked like a jungle," she chuckled. "One day, one of our sons returned after several years in Peru, and told me the garden reminded him forcibly of the headwaters of the Amazon. That's when I began to garden with more discipline and foresight." Though she continued to plant closely, preferring the furnished look of full borders and beds, she began a rigorous thinning program which continues to this day.

Though always interested in the uncommon, Mrs. Platt was no plant snob. Prized among her connoisseur's trees was a small flock of old apples,

relics of a homesteader's orchard that once filled the hillside. Carefully preserved and pruned, each named by the family, these elderly trees became much loved mascots for the growing garden. She also grew many native plants well before that was fashionable, including a towering fir collected as a seedling from the ill-fated slopes of nearby Mount Saint Helens many years ago. A magnificent tanbark oak, *Lithocarpus densiflorus* var. *echinoides*, in an especially silvery form, was selected for her by renowned Oregon nurseryman Marcel LePiniac. He also gave Mrs. Platt the first of what are now thousands of dogtooth violets. "Our pink native, *Erythronium revolutum*, is a terrific self-sower," Mrs. Platt explained, adding that, "Another favorite, *E.* 'White Beauty', is shy to set seed, so I help out by gathering what there is and growing the seedlings on in pots until they're ready for the garden." Now,

Open, rolling lawns and a fascinating tree line characterize Jane Platt's garden. Dense perimeter plantings of small trees and ornamental shrubs create the effect of an informal tapestry hedge, against which borders full of perennials and bulbs display to advantage. Photo: Cynthia Woodyard

the offspring of the original plants carpet the garden in spring, spreading in pale pools beneath blooming trees and shrubs.

Much of the garden is designed as a series of woodland walks. Mrs. Platt loved the Hamamelidaceae, the witch hazel family, and one spectacular area holds ribbons of corylopsis and witch hazels, fothergillas and the little known evergreen shrub, *Loropetalum chinense*, with tufts of the familial flossy flowers in white rather than yellow. Maples were another passion, and the collection of dwarf Japanese maples which filled her rock garden could equally fill a respectable catalog. These are excellent mixed border trees, slow growing and shapely, with leaves as gorgeous in early spring, when many are pink as shrimps, as in autumn, when frost wakens them to flame and ember. Other garden areas are devoted to *Prunus* and *Cornus* species, especially those with lovely bark. In winter, the garden is full of soft, reflected light that brings out rich shades of port and mahogany, lacquered bronze, and glossy black in stem and branch and trunk alike.

Mrs. Platt wove her trees into woodsy thickets, grew them free-standing, and combined them with lower growing shrubs. She surrounded them with masses of bulbs, underplanted them with perennials, and threaded them with vines. She used flowering trees as centerpieces for perennial borders and as vertical accents for shrub borders. Tiny trees make a miniature landscape of her extensive rock gardens. Enormous ones shelter the garden, frame lovely sightlines, and obliterate unwanted views. She used trees with great sensitivity, studying each to determine the role for which it was best fitted by nature. As they aged, she watched their progress closely, removing whatever threatened the overall harmony of the garden. She abhorred tree topping or massive pruning, which she regarded as mutilation rather than control. "If a tree, or any plant, no longer belongs, no longer contributes, then take it right out," she would say firmly. Pruning, she felt strongly, was a minor but constant operation, to be performed on an ongoing basis by the gardener. Indeed, she was rarely to be found without her trusty hand pruners, with which she kept her large and complex garden under control.

TREES IN THE MIXED BORDER

When planning mixed borders, begin by siting any trees you plan to use. More than any other element, trees focus the garden and give it a sense of permanence. These largest plants will shape the flow and placement of the beds, both by their appearance and by their physical needs, present and future. Though the backbone planting, consisting largely of evergreen shrubs, provides more structure and definition, the trees in a mixed border are nearly always the dominant features. Even deciduous trees have a powerful presence all year round, particularly when they have been selected for winter features like skeletal grace and handsome bark. In larger borders, evergreen trees—narrow Irish junipers, glossy hollies, arboreal rhododendrons—can be generously incorporated into the perimeter plantings which give the garden its form. Smaller borders require scaled down plants, little upright junipers like the narrow 'Skyrocket', or myrtle-leaved Portuguese laurel (*Prunus lusitanicus* 'Myrtifolia') in the hedges, or a dainty redbud, perhaps *Cercis canadensis* 'Forest Pansy', with wine-colored foliage and warm pink flowers, as a border centerpiece. Even tiny urban gardens benefit from a tree or two to link the small world of the garden to the greater communities of neighborhood and region. In such situations, large shrubs like evergreen *Kalmia latifolia* or the gray-barked deciduous dogwood, *Cornus florida* 'White Cloud', will act as trees in hedge or border. Since there are hundreds of wonderful small trees to choose among, try not to get seduced at the nursery by a temporarily lovely commoner that can be found in every other yard. Take time to search out choicier beauties that are garden worthy in every season. Make sure as well that your choice is regionally appropriate, and that, in character and size, it will prove of lasting value in the mixed border setting.

In older gardens, where mixed borders are being made amongst mature trees, the selection process should be equally thoughtful and prolonged. When we first came to our present garden, it was amaz-

Trees give a garden character and privacy and provide shelter for the smaller plants tucked under their wings. Woodyard garden, Portland, Oregon. Photo: Cynthia Woodyard

ingly overgrown. Our first impulse—strongly encouraged by a number of professional landscapers—was to clear out the place and start over. Instead, we took several years to assess what we had. Where older trees were jammed together in ridiculous proximity, we studied their lines in summer and winter, seeing which branches were shielding us from neighbors or the road. We tried to look at each tree separately, to judge which, if any, would be shapely were the others gone. Certain things—the dead and disfigured—were removed quite soon, which opened up large sections of the garden for lawn and garden beds. The best of the old trees were cleaned of deadwood, and many within the garden interior were limbed up to provide high, open shade. As a result, the old trees give this very young garden a strong feeling of history and permanence. The borders benefit as well, gaining an immediate impression of the depth that truly arrives only with maturity.

Because trees play such a strong and vital role in the garden, it is very easy to go wrong with them. A stroll through any neighborhood will illustrate the pitfalls of thoughtless tree placement. On every hand, you will see examples of inappropriate trees in unsatisfactory settings. The most common mistake is to choose trees that will be too large for the site in maturity. The most common solution—inexpert and excessive pruning which often amounts to butchery—is unacceptable in mixed borders, where trees are expected to be beautiful. Often, too, one sees trees with the wrong shape for their setting, as when a wide, spreading oak shades not one but two or three gardens. You will also find compact, columnar trees hacked off at the top by power line crews when the trees threaten to interfere with the wires. Here, good selection is ruined by poor placement. Perhaps the most widespread fault of all is planting trees smack against the house, where they will very soon overshadow windows and gutters alike. Their roots often penetrate water and sewer lines, and may cause structural damage to the foundation as well. The worst of it is that a tree so placed never fulfills its promise; its natural shape is ruined from the start. In mixed borders, where trees are given a good deal of importance, wise choices will save a lot of heartache and hard labor. (Planting trees properly is a big job in the first place, and moving them when they outgrow their place or the gardener changes her mind gets harder every time.)

When we choose our garden trees, our first thoughts tend towards foliage and blossom, fruit and autumn color. As valuable as these attractions are, the question of ultimate size should be foremost. On a large country residence, a mixed border of majestic scale might be graced with a river birch that would fill a city yard with roots and shade. Where space is limited, we can often find smaller cousins of beloved plants that will remain lastingly welcome in mixed borders. *Magnolia* × *soulangiana* 'Rustica Rubra', smaller and quicker to bloom, would be a better choice than a Campbell magnolia, beautiful but of heroic proportions. A modest suburban border could host a graceful California buckeye, *Aesculus californica*, rather than the grander horse chestnut, *A. hippocastanum*, or a compact, green-gold *Robinia pseudoacacia* 'Frisia' rather than the robust species itself. In the smallest of city gardens, a fragrant snowbell (*Styrax obassia*) or a slender fastigiate dogwood might be showcased.

The smallest trees can go anywhere, fitting with ease into schemes of all proportions. The largest trees, however fetching, are only suited to outsized settings where they may develop without constraint. The place to remember this is at the nursery, where a future giant may look deceptively delicate and frail. It may continue this act for several years, appearing to fit nicely into the smallest garden. Once its expansive intentions are made evident, however, the tree will become a source of increasing annoyance and rapidly lessening pleasure. Size is not the only consideration; some trees, like many robinias, are quite brittle, and tend to lose their most attractive and important branches at inconvenient times. Willows, too, may shed branches without notice, especially as they age. Birches drop an incredible quantity of fine, twiggy branches in winter, and lesser amounts all through the year. Madronas, though evergreen and handsome, make an unsightly mess when they drop their fat tawny berries in autumn, and again when they shed their large, leathery older leaves in midspring. Fallen holly leaves make weeding beneath these trees most unpleasant, and they seed superabundantly, making vigilant weeding a necessity. Walnuts and certain other trees produce a toxic substance from their roots which inhibits the growth of many garden plants, making it difficult (though not impossible) to incorporate these trees into large borders. All these trees are worth growing, despite their drawbacks, but knowing exactly what to expect from your trees makes it possible to plan ahead, placing them to minimize their weaknesses and take fuller advantage of their strengths.

Before you begin to shop, do some preliminary browsing in the pages of reference books (see Books for Further Reading for suggestions) to give your thoughts firm direction. Ask the advice of your nursery as well, for the staff should be able to give more precise information than a standard reference book about how the trees they sell react over time in your region. If local nurseries prove limited in their offerings, consult your Barton (*Gardening by Mail* by Barbara Barton, see Books for Further Reading) to find specialty nurseries like Mellinger's which offer an exciting palette of garden trees. The thoughtful gardener can—and should—pick and choose with care, selecting a tree that will suit garden and gardener for many years to come.

Once our trees are chosen, their relative placement demands our full attention. It may seem patronizing to point out that the hopeful occupant of a five-gallon can might increase in bulk a hundred-fold, bringing roots and shade in its train, yet it is astonishingly easy to overlook the obvious. One of the best aids to judicious tree placement is to rig a mock-up of the tree as it will look in ten years' time, if not in maturity. Using materials as disparate as a ladder, an old fan trellis, several lengths of two by four and a large tarpaulin or old shower curtain, one can manufacture a working (if unlovely) facsimile of a young tree which may be lugged around the

*Before planting any tree, always learn how large it is likely to become with age. This lovely dogwood (*Cornus controversa *'Variegata') has plenty of room to spread its wings in Helen Dillon's Dublin garden, but its steady increase in bulk might easily overset the gardener's plans in a more modest setting. Photo: Peter Ray*

garden until the optimal planting site is discovered. Another good trick is to photocopy (expanding the image to the largest size) several pictures of your yard, then sketch in the prospective tree in a variety of locations and at several stages of growth. This last method is simpler to carry out, yet flat surface images can be misleading. Besides, few of us are really all that good at perspective or interpreting scale; it is easy to be significantly off when trying to imagine what a twenty- or fifty-foot tree would actually look like in a snapshot where most of the actual measurements are unknown. A mock-up "tree" which occupies real space is far harder to misjudge or misplace. (Just pick a day when you know your neighbors will be out, and spare yourself some embarrassment.)

A further consideration is that of roots. Tree roots can be both powerful and pervasive, and the home owner who tenderly positions a stripling willow over the sewer line invites hygienic disaster. Even when such horrors are avoided, the encroaching ways of tree roots can cause problems, particularly in small gardens. One excellent solution is to spread horticultural barrier cloth over the future mixed border areas (see page 46 for a more detailed discussion). Dry wells must be sloped to protect the crowns of the larger woody plants which may now grow on undisturbed, no longer posing a threat to the health of their border mates. Young trees and the largest shrubs are planted directly into the underlying soil, which may first be improved as necessary. (The barrier cloth can be cut with scissors or a utility knife to make planting holes.) The smaller plants are then arranged in the new soil, which remains free of tree and shrub roots for years. If you want to add or move the woody plants, new holes may be cut into the underlying barrier cloth at any time.

Where trees and shrubs are meant to mingle cooperatively with perennials, bulbs, and vines, it is well to lay out the borders on as generous a scale, both in width and length, as one's property permits. Trees have more presence than perennials, even when out of leaf, and their implicit strength demands an adequate setting. The vital proportions are those of border depth and length to tree height; this can't be reduced to a formula, but use your eyes, and trust them. If the tree rises giraffelike above a low sea of inconsequent plantings, remedial planting will incorporate it more firmly into the border. Where possible, the borders can be expanded outward, to give the tree breathing room, which will allow for the addition of good-sized shrubby companions to balance the height of the tree with their bulk. Whether or not expansion is possible, background and companion shrubs of ascending sizes will anchor it comfortably to the rest of the border. In very young borders, large divisions of tall, chunky perennials or even outsized annuals like castor beans can temporarily relate such a tree to its surroundings while more permanent shrubby companions grow on to full size. A young tree that looks dwarfed by mature surroundings is less worrisome, for time will soon heal that sort of imbalance. While the youngling is growing, treat it as if it were a shrub, and give it accordingly down-sized neighbors. As the tree matures, so will its supporting cast, which may be moved or removed as necessary. Very young companion shrubs may be mixed with perennials, which can be freely rearranged as the woody plants grow. A few years' growth will bring the entire group up to size, and the border can then be reorganized for relative permanence.

Gardeners with tiny planting spaces mustn't assume that mixed borders, let alone trees, are not for them, since any composition which can be arranged in a container will work in a postage stamp garden as well. Think of trees that thrive in half barrels—genetic dwarf fruit trees, red-leaved sand cherry (*Prunus* × *cistena*), slow-growing threadleaf ma-

ples—any of these would make a fine centerpiece for a miniature mixed border encompassing ten or twelve square feet. (Mound your earth for greater planting area.) Set a few glossy, pinnate Oregon grapes (*Mahonia* species) behind your small tree for winter bloom, with Christmas ferns (*Polystichum acrostichoides*) and *Helleborus orientalis* at their feet. All will tolerate the shade they get in summer, coming into their own with leaf drop, when their healthy, evergreen foliage and fat flower buds satisfy the gardener's winter plant lust. Underplant the tree with moss and snowdrops if it is a weeper, or weave a neat carpet of tiny-leaved 'Jekyll's White' vinca beneath a standard tree. Arrange a few long-blooming perennials midbed; *Achillea* 'Hope' and *Coreopsis* 'Moonbeam', the dwarf ice green *Kniphofia* 'Little Maid' and a mini daylily, 'Bumble Bee', or the tall white *Sedum* 'Meteor' would all be good choices.

Intermediate and smaller shrubs in hedge and border link large garden trees firmly to house and garden, creating visual steps down to the more intimate scale of the garden plants. Ross garden, Bainbridge Island, Washington. Photo: Mark Lovejoy

Six or eight clumps of perennials will fit in easily, supplying many months of bloom. Scented 'Black Dragon' lilies could appear in late summer, along with plum-purple gladiolas. Run a swathe of checkerberry (*Gaultheria procumbens*) laced with primroses, early crocus, species tulips, and daffodils across the bed's sloping front, and you will have made a delightful and durable mixed border composition in a space the size of a coat closet.

In a bigger border (anything from twelve to perhaps thirty feet deep) small, graceful, slow-growing trees can develop into prime midborder specimens. Though most large plants will be arrayed along the border's back, an occasional break in this pattern allows fascinating interior views as changes in height and mass lead the eye in and down. Tucking distinctive plants in the resulting low spots within the border's depths makes for visual surprises. A veil of airy plants to the fore of such a half-hidden pocket creates the sense of mystery that builds a garden's character. Place the copper-and-gold-variegated dogwood, *Cornus florida* 'Cherokee Sunset', midborder, burying its base in golden 'Buttercup' ivy and adding a sheaf of wavy hair grass (*Deschampsia flexuosa*) for height and a wheeling, spoke-leaved clump of *Helleborus foetidus* for textural contrast. Screens of gauzy gauras or a haze of late-blooming *Aster lateriflorus* 'Horizontalis' might rise in front of this small picture, bright in spring, tantalizingly glimpsed in summer. When autumn thins the garden, the dogwood presents a prolonged blaze of sunset tints above its golden bed and the long strands of grass are spangled with gilded seeds. When winter stills the garden, the tree lifts its graceful boughs of lavender-gray over gleaming ivy till both are mantled with snow.

Dozens of small trees might similarly shine through the seasons in a garden setting. Specialty nurseries offer a dazzling array of Japanese maples and dogwoods, witch hazels, and mountain ashes. Local nurseries might carry dwarf fruit trees or garden trees with unusual foliage, like purple weeping birch (*Betula pendula* 'Purpurea') or a golden bean tree, *Catalpa bignonioides* 'Aurea'. At sales sponsored by local plant societies, you might find seed-grown rarities unavailable at any retail outlets. Here is a

Few places on earth consistently enjoy fall foliage displays as impressive as those in New England, but many trees color reliably in less favored climates, including European white birch, Betula pendula. *November, author's garden. Photo: Mark Lovejoy*

brief sampler for consideration, all mannerly enough to merit inclusion in a mixed border, where their perpetual graces may be fully appreciated.

It is worth noting that, for these purposes, "small tree" means any with a mature height of between fifteen and thirty feet. The information below is offered with a caveat; the delicate sorrel tree (*Oxydendrum arboreum*) that slowly matures to twenty feet in Seattle soars to a robust seventy in its native Tennessee. Before you make your final decision and buy a tree, call or visit a regional arboretum or botanical garden to get locally sound, specific advice.

DECIDUOUS TREES

Japanese maples, *Acer japonicum* and *A. palmatum* (both Zone 5, to thirty feet), are a varied bunch with numerous named forms. Many are slow growing but others are relatively quick, so it is important to be clear about which kind you are buying in order to place it properly. As a class, Japanese maples are fine garden trees, graceful in every season. Their new foliage and flowers make them as lovely in spring as when autumn brightens their foliage to flame. Those with lacy, cut foliage provide good summer textures, and many are variegated or hold their red leaf color through the hot months. *Acer griseum* (Zone 6, to thirty-five feet) is another splendid small maple grown as much for its dramatic, peeling bark and good garden form as for its vivid autumn leaf color.

Dogwood, *Cornus florida* (Zone 5, to twenty feet). This May-blooming small dogwood has been much hybridized, and there are many delightful named forms on the market. All tolerate or even prefer some shade, making them valuable where mature trees are already in place. Of the variegated forms, 'Cherokee Daybreak' offers pink flowers amid foliage washed in pink and cream, which deepen to raspberry and ruby with autumn. 'Cherokee Sunset' has bronze-red flowers nestled into leaves splashed with orange and copper, and its fall display is incomparable. *Cornus kousa* (Zone 5, fifteen to twenty feet) is shrubbier, but makes a wonderful small tree where space is restricted. Its cloud of creamy flowers appear in June, rather than May, and are a clean white in the form 'Milky Way'. *Cornus* 'Eddie's White Wonder' (Zone 5, slow growing to thirty-five feet or more, if well suited) is a terrific hybrid between *C. florida* and the West Coast native *C. nuttallii* which offers spectacular flowers, fat red fruit, and gaudy autumn color. *Cornus mas*, the cornelian cherry (Zone 4, to twenty-five feet), makes a charming small tree, decked in spring with fluffy yellow flowers, in late summer with its plump red "cherries," and in fall with ruddy foliage.

Fringe tree, *Chionanthus retusus* (Zone 5, to twenty feet). An ardent bloomer from an early age, the Chinese fringe tree is elegant and shapely even in winter. The trunks, often multiple, curve sinuously with age. Slim, twisting branches are lightly clothed with tapered, opposite leaves which emerge in late spring with the catalpas. By early summer, each twig is festooned with an airy plume of silky white flossy flowers that fade to the ivory-buff of old lace. Autumn brings plump blue berries which gleam among now golden leaves. Our native species, *C. virginicus*, is a bit hardier (to Zone 4) and larger in every part—foliage, flowers, and fringe. It can get rather taller as well, topping out at around thirty feet.

Weeping crab apple, *Malus* 'Red Jade' (Zone 4, to twenty feet). When its arching stems are laden with a froth of white blossoms, you will decide that April is this delicate little crab's finest month. It

Paperbark maple, Acer griseum, *is among the most beautiful of garden trees, with a strong winter silhouette, attractive foliage, and wonderfully peeling bark. Photo: Peter Ray*

holds its own all summer, as the swelling fruits tug the branches down. The fat little apples blush delectably as autumn gilds the surrounding leaves, and that, too, is good. Seeing its curving arms outlined in snow, each twig still bearing a plump, rosy apple, you will realize that this tree has a lot of finest hours.

Silver weeping pear, *Pyrus salicifolia* 'Pendula' (Zone 4, to twenty-five feet). Though the willowleaf pear is hardly ever grown in America, the English have it everywhere, and for good reason. This weeping form is a wonderful thing in every season. Its twiggy stems are covered with white blossoms in spring, nicely set off by the silvery new leaves. By late summer, these are tarnished to a lovely, mysterious pewter-green. They take on tints of copper and yellow in autumn, when the hard little nubbins that pass for pears decorate the drooping branches.

Like most fruit trees, this one gains character with age, its winter profile growing more interesting each year. It does, however, suffer from leaf curl and similar blights, so would not be a wise choice where fruit trees are commonly afflicted with such things.

Mountain ash, *Sorbus hupehensis* (Zone 5, to thirty feet, rarely—and very slowly—to fifty feet). Glaucous, pinnate leaves, sheets of whiskery, white flowers, and berries that may range from white to pink, coral, salmon, or rose make this choice little mountain ash a collector's delight. Among the prettiest of winter trees, its upward flung branches with their ruddy, almost purple skin gleam handsomely when wet. It is a variable species, and I have yet to see a homely one, but in the nicest forms, the leaves are decidedly blue with persistent berries of pale, pearly pink.

The silver weeping leaved pear, Pyrus salicifolia *'Pendula', is a delightful little tree which is worked into many border schemes in England, but is less often seen in America. Photo: Cynthia Woodyard*

Fragrant snowball, *Styrax obassia* (Zone 6, to twenty, sometimes thirty feet). Oversized leaves, rounded and drooping, give this little tree an almost tropical appearance. They are normally a deep, clear green, the undersides downy with faint fur; a pale coloring may indicate water stress, for this is a tree that wants damp feet. The frail looking flowers, white and very sweetly scented, dangle in long, loose clusters which are lost to view when this tree is tucked away at the back of the border. Placed well to the fore and, if possible, above a slope or a wall, one looks up into a cool canopy of filtered light, filled with a delicate perfume. In autumn, the leaves fade slowly to copper and tobacco brown, leaving the elegantly angular trunk and tiered branches bare and gleaming like burnt orange and bronze sari silk till spring clothes them once again.

Redbud, *Cercis canadensis* (Zone 4, to thirty-five feet). This North American native holds its own through every season, offering pinky purple flowers in midspring and clear, golden autumn foliage color. 'Forest Pansy', a smaller, slow-growing form, has fuchsia-pink flowers on ruddy twigs, followed in late spring by dusky purple leaves which hold their color nicely through the summer, then deepen to ember red in autumn.

Serviceberry, *Amelanchier* × *grandiflora* (Zone 4, to twenty-five feet) is a hybrid between two natives, and offers multiseasonal charms. In spring, it carries clouds of soft white flowers, followed in summer by fat red fruit that is quickly snapped up by eager birds. Autumn brings red-gold foliage, and winter sees its shapely skeleton.

Witch hazel, *Hamamelis* × *intermedia* (Zone 4, fifteen to twenty feet). Though classified as a large shrub, witch hazels can be pruned into multi-trunked small trees which remain in proper scale for small gardens. All have good-sized oval leaves which often color well in autumn. Fragrant winter flowers make them especially valuable in mixed borders; those of many forms are shades of yellow or gold, but 'Diana' has deep, cinnamon red blossoms while those of 'Jelena' are bronzed orange. *Hamamelis vernalis*, the Ozark witch hazel, colors especially well in fall, particularly in the form 'Sandra', which also offers purple new growth in spring and paint-box yellow flowers in midwinter.

EVERGREEN TREES

Common boxwood, *Buxus sempervirens* (Zone 5, to twenty feet). Though usually treated as a hedging plant, boxwood makes a nice, plump little tree if permitted. Multi-trunked specimens look best when the bottom three or four feet of the trunks are kept clean of twigs, the tops left loose or sheared only lightly for the most natural appearance. Often overlooked, but a plant of solid value nonetheless.

Magnolia grandiflora 'Little Gem' (Zone 7, to fifteen feet). This compact, rather narrow, and slow-growing selection blooms generously even when young, opening improbably huge, citrus-scented flowers on slender grayish twigs. Its thick, leathery leaves are only half the size of the typical southern magnolias, their backs fuzzed with cinnamon-colored indumentum (felty hairs).

Portuguese laurel, *Prunus lusitanica* (Zone 6, fifteen to thirty or even sixty feet). Easily pruned to a several-trunked tree, it usually remains a modest size, but in good soil and an open, sunny site protected from bitter winds, it may make a tremendous standard tree in time. The small, fragrant flowers are thickly clustered on upright spikes, followed by red and burgundy berries. Dark, lustrous leaves with a pleasing little ripple on the edge catch and toss thin winter light all over the garden, even on a gray day.

Laurustinus, *Viburnum tinus* (Zone 7, to twenty feet). Neat, dark green leaves and tightly clustered Victorian posies of pinky white florets with a sharp, spicy fragrance make laurustinus a mainstay of mixed hedges and borders wherever it is hardy. Glittering blue-black berries linger for months, and their gun metal gleam is highly attractive in winter. The old-fashioned form, 'Eve Price', has small, tidy leaves of a matte dark green and is an especially prolific bloomer, with reddish buds on dark red twigs.

Like a column of blue flame, a young Juniperus scopulorum *'Wichita Blue' rises above blood red shrub roses. In maturity, this slim tree will be a much more imposing element in this border. Withey/Price garden, Seattle, Washington. Photo: Mark Lovejoy*

Mountain laurel, *Kalmia latifolia* (Zone 4, twenty to thirty feet). Slow and graceful, this large native shrub can reach tree status in time and when well suited. It appreciates the same conditions rhododendrons do; moist, humus-rich, and acid or neutral soils and light or high shade. The glossy, pointed leaves make a good textural contrast against large-leaved rhododendrons, and combinations of the two make beautiful evergreen hedges or backbone plantings. The species kalmias have pink, cup-shaped flowers, but in named forms they may be pure red, or freckled with rose, or banded in purple. A few, like the reflexed, white 'Shooting Star', have unusually shaped blossoms.

Rhododendrons (zones variable, but 4 to 6 through 10, depending on species and conditions. Height also variable, taller varieties fifteen to twenty feet in time). Long out of favor, rhododendrons earn a place in mixed borders handily, offering evergreen leaves in a variety of shapes and sizes, and flowers which may rival anything in the garden for sheer glory. Though most are shrubby, a number of rhododendrons grow into trees over time. These aspiring types may be pruned into multiple-trunked border specimens or woven into background hedges. *Rhododendron catawbiense*, the Catawba rhododendron (Zone 4, to fifteen feet), is a good looking southeastern native with pale pink or white flowers in great ice cream scoops over ruffs of large, glossy green leaves backed with toasty brown fur. *Rhododendron decorum*, the sweetshell rhododendron (Zone 5, to twenty feet), carries trusses of shell pink or white flowers over dark green, leathery leaves. *Rhododendron fictolacteum* (Zone 6, to twenty-five feet) makes a shapely tree with shaggy bark and long, broad green leaves backed with tawny orange fuzz. The big, glorious flowers are white or deep pink, freckled and speckled with ruby. The white-flowered form is easiest to work into mixed borders, for plants that echo the pink flowers swear dreadfully with those that bring up the copper and orange of the leaf backs.

The garden at North Hill is encircled by native trees and thick shelter belts of shrubs. Small garden trees like the golden false acacia, Robinia pseudoacacia 'Frisia', and a rich combination of shapely conifers act as visual intermediaries between the magnificent woodland trees and the more intimately scaled garden. Photo: Cynthia Woodyard

Chapter Four

SHRUBS
IN THE
MIXED BORDER

NORTH HILL,

VERMONT USDA ZONE 4

Wayne Winterrowd and Joe Eck are garden designers who love horticultural challenges. Like Lawrence Johnston, both men combine an unbridled passion for plants with an intense appreciation for visual artistry. In their own garden, they aim to present their connoisseur's collection of plants in ways that make the most of each individual member while keeping the garden as a whole harmonious. North Hill is living proof that the concept works as well in Vermont as anywhere in the world. Deep woodlands surround the garden, which encircles in turn their weathered wooden farmhouse. Though only fifteen years old, the building persuasively echoes the local architectural vernacular, just as the garden fits easily into its shell of native woods. A small greenhouse off the stone-flagged kitchen preserves a strong visual connection between house and garden throughout the year. North Hill has no winter garden as such, yet when snow blurs the shapes within the garden, the shape of the garden itself is revealed. Shaggy pines and hemlocks, open-armed maples, delicate black twigged birch, sturdy beech—the strength of the native flora and the con-

tours of the land give this garden its distinguished winter presence.

During the warmer months, one experiences North Hill's mixed borders as a seemingly effortless flow of foliar and color effects. In truth, of course, the garden's changes and transitions are carefully orchestrated, directed as much by forethought and considerable horticultural knowledge as by frequent—not to say constant—grooming and controlling measures. This is a highly structured, deliberate garden, yet nothing in it feels contrived or artificial. The living framework of trees and shrubs defines the garden space as apart from, while marrying it to, the native woods which enfold it. Though the garden holds hundreds of foreign plants, the line and scale of those native trees dictate, to a large degree, the overall design of North Hill. "The garden is surrounded by old maple and beech woods, which had been allowed to grow quite close together, so they bore no branches until quite high up," Winterrowd explains, adding, "We were completely lacking in any sort of understory, and so we used smaller deciduous and evergreen trees to satisfy this need." Winterrowd and Eck recognized early on the vital importance of making convincing transitions between the existing forest and the garden space, for without them the garden would always sit uneasily in its niche. "We are firmly committed to the principle that gardens need a frame or setting," says Winterrowd. Moreover, those intermediate understory plantings would fulfill a second, equally important function, that of providing visual enclosure and privacy from neighbors and the road.

North Hill lies on some twenty acres of land, yet the shape of the terrain and especially the location of a small stream made initial placement choices very clear. "The position of the stream meant we had to build house and garden fairly close to the road. That meant we needed screening, for privacy and to create the sense of haven that we were after," Winterrowd recounts. "Wind, too was an issue, and all that taken together meant that we would need at least a back wall of shrubbery." They began by weaving perimeter shrub belts, using tough, densely thicketing deciduous shrubs. In the first stages, these were common things like lilac and privet or honeysuckles, plants which would strike roots quickly and fend for themselves without much encouragement. In most places, the shrub belts were themselves underplanted with hardy, colonizing bulbs and a few woodland perennials. Unifying carpets of *Vinca minor* turned the transition areas into simple but effective "big picture" plantings which hold together all year long.

As these shrubby barriers took hold, choice specimen shrubs and trees were added throughout the garden. Harsh winters limited their choices of evergreens to conifers and deciduous trees, but fortunately both groups present a wealth of shapes, colors, and sizes. Conical *Thuja occidentalis* 'Holmstrup', a freshet of feathery green in winter, and *Taxus × media* 'Hicksii', its looser form and ink green foliage a dramatic foil for the thuja, flank a slim, spreading *Robinia pseudoacacia* 'Frisia', a ferny confection in lemon and lime possessing a handsome winter skeleton. A beauty bush, *Kolkwitzia amabilis*, floats like a chalky pink cloud above the perennial borders, its twiggy branches decked with rusty red seed heads when the midspring blossom is past. A white willow, *Salix alba sericea*, is pollarded (cut to the base) periodically to keep it moderate in size and to gain the shining silver of its young foliage.

As the protective shrub belts moderated the wind and air temperatures within the garden, Eck and

Winterrowd were able to introduce a few broadleaf evergreens as well. A number of good-sized rhododendrons have established nicely in this northern garden, thriving in favored microclimates. North Hill's collection of hardy boxwoods also survives, though several kinds are given winter overcoats, insulated wooden boxes or various sorts of padding, to protect against drying winds and hard freezes. The generous snow cover usually covers these jacketed plants completely, so they are not obtrusive in the winter landscape. Although the perimeter shrubs are mainly deciduous, they still provide a significant measure of year-round screening and shelter from both weather and the outside world. The largest of them further assist the transition in scale from tall forest trees to the more intimate garden plantings. Winter or summer, these shrub belts filter road dust and traffic noises, and all but obscure the few neighboring houses from view.

"We wanted the garden to blend into its surroundings, with the backs of the borders seeming something like the thickened growth one finds at the edges of old forests," notes Winterrowd. "Then, too, the character of some of the features of our site, particularly the stream, demanded a style of gardening that would seem wild, possessing all the diversity of nature itself, even though the plants were often exotic species, and carefully cultivated." Overt control can give a garden a rigid, highly unnatural appearance which would be utterly out of character for the borders at North Hill. What Winterrowd and Eck were after was the artful, hidden control which comes only with experience, and must be implemented with a mixture of good timing and ceaseless discipline. The result is that more formally contrived areas meld into the naturalistic without pause, each transition as thoughtfully crafted as the theme areas—perennial bed, rhododendron dell, rock garden—themselves.

Among the most striking plantings are those along the sloping banks where the small, singing stream runs through the back garden. When North Hill was still a young garden, this area was considered a problem rather than an asset. The ground stayed boggy nearly all year, and despite many attempts to drain it or to fill it in, its character would not change. Fortunately, the garden won the gar-

As the garden melds into woodland, transition areas are made to appear increasingly natural. This area, above the stream and bog, looks almost wild, yet is highly disciplined in execution and maintenance. Lush grasses, ferns, and mosses make a dappled understory to the shrubby plantings which link the garden to the woods beyond. Photo: Cynthia Woodyard

deners over in time. "Finally we recognized it for the treasure it is," says Eck with rueful amusement. "Now it is one of our favorite areas." A small plank bridge of Shakerly simplicity spans the stream, which is elsewhere crossed by rugged stepping-stones. Some of the garden's most magnificent foliage effects occur here, where the enormous, rounded plates of the California umbrella plant, *Darmera peltata*, are played off by frilly ferns and the slim swords of Siberian and other iris. Broad hostas and bold rodgersias center flurries of tiered Japanese primulas and the soft curves of silken grasses. Though

seasonal color is not lacking, it is the thousand shades of green which best illuminate these contrasts of leaf form and texture.

"It's easy to see why the woodland and stream parts of the garden were mixed borders from the first," reflects Winterrowd, considering the consciously naturalistic mixture of small trees, shrubs, perennials, and woodland ground covers which now fill these areas. Though quantitatively similar mixtures predominate throughout the garden, the character and feeling of the blend changes according to the ambience or intended mood in each area. The fact that the perennial border, rose path, and the beds that surround the back lawn are also mixed is due more to a number of chance factors than to any specific decision. Partly, Winterrowd thinks, they turned out this way because "We are inveterate plant collectors who enjoy plants of all kinds. As we brought things home, whether perennial or shrub or vine, they each had to have a proper home." Many of those choice acquisitions were shrubs, which were continually incorporated into the beds along with the ephemerals. What began as happenstance was soon deliberately repeated. "In so cold a garden as ours, plantings purely of perennials or annuals would have seemed very dreary for much of the year," he points out, "so we added bulbs for early and late interest, evergreens and shrubs to carry us through the late autumn into winter. We learned that even the bare shanks of a lilac can be very beautiful, especially when there is nothing else to admire."

By most standards, North Hill holds much to admire in any season. Early and late, when the lush growth of ephemerals is dormant, the native woods and rock dominate the garden. Local stone is a vital element in Vermont. At North Hill, flat flagstones of slate or granite spread in terraces and steps. The good gray fieldstone is layered in walls and laid into paths that lead directly into the heart of the garden. Main paths usually skirt the beds and borders, but at North Hill, they tend rather to divide them. Walking through the borders themselves, one comes into intimate proximity with the plants, and is able to admire them at close hand. "To penetrate the garden, to be within it and surrounded by it, seems to us one of the greatest of garden pleasures," says

Winterrowd. Accordingly, they have contrived their borders to be experienced as a series of walks, rather than something viewed from a certain distance. Each has its own theme and essence, sometimes formal, often relaxed, but nearly everywhere plantings rise and build on every side. The blend of shrubs and small trees makes for enticing interior views, and as one walks the wandering paths, seasonal vignettes are framed and reframed in a changing succession of viewpoints till at last one is thoroughly immersed in the garden.

In recent years, perhaps the most formative influence at North Hill has been a growing fondness for "gardening in the air." Winterrowd comments, "We pay lots of attention to layering the garden upward from the ground in textures and shapes, and building, within lighter masses, more substantial ones." Many of North Hill's borders were originally planted in traditional size order, with the larger things ranged at the backs and smaller ones surrounding the unifying middle-sized plants. "We are discovering the magic of breaking ranks, pulling a taller element forward, letting the mass of a small tree front the border, or arranging for the gaunt but handsome stems of some woody shrub to emerge from a sea of slighter, lower things," Winterrowd comments, adding, "I am always thrilled by rather formal, upright elements in a planting; the punctuation points of a conical evergreen that marks the end or entrance to a garden, or vines trained on stout posts within the perennial border. We have just begun to train buddleias this way, and to use, where we can, woody vines like *Lonicera* 'Dropmore Scarlet' trained as standards."

After some fifteen years, the maturing trees and shrubs give North Hill the look of a garden long in place. The largest plants, the trees and shrubs of the shelter belts and woodland walks, have grown up here, and, shaped by their site, give the garden a rooted sense of permanence. The beds and borders, however, change frequently, from season to season and year to year, filling and refilling with new plants and different combinations. This constant flux keeps the garden lively, and makes it feel like an ongoing process rather than a finished product. That impression is deliberately fostered by Eck and Winterrowd,

who take pleasure not only in expanding the garden with a new rock garden scree or woodland walk, but in the evolution of established areas. "Lately we have begun to focus on frothy, transitory things, especially on annuals—the most neglected group of plants in the mixed border—and on bulbs and alpines," Winterrowd offers. "They bring a sense of heart to the garden, a spontaneity obtainable no other way." Plants in pots and containers are also finding their way into the garden in increasing quantities, an extension of their current fascination with floral ephemera. Though such things require a good deal of attention, often on a daily basis, Winterrowd is willing to pay the price, feeling that "There is nothing that so clearly strikes the note of care and love in a garden than a few handsome pots stood about, full of flourishing tender shrubs, or annuals, or choice alpines."

Time is not grudged at North Hill, a fact made obvious by the dozens of small details which quietly declare that attention is lavished on this beloved garden. A tapestry of tiny plants tucked in an angle of the path, the embroidery of sedums stitching the terrace to the garden, fringes of annual wildflowers between paving stones, choice alpines arrayed in handsome tufa tubs, all speak their tale plainly to those who have ears to hear and eyes to see. Tropicals and tender plants make a surprisingly significant impact in this northern garden, from the huge, drooping trumpets of a deadly datura, scenting the evening air with its sinister perfume, to the tender grasses which spill in restrained curves from elegantly understated pots. The most tender plants are wintered over in one of the greenhouses, but anything which might possibly prove hardy—or even borderline hardy—in a protected outdoor site will be trialed at North Hill. Though they usually hedge their bets by keeping a few pieces of an experimental plant under winter cover, Eck and Winterrowd enjoy taking calculated risks, for that is how both knowledge and garden palette are expanded and enriched.

Supposedly tender plants are often given several chances to prove themselves in this garden. Pieces will be placed in several different microclimates, given different kinds of soil, tried in both an open spot and given the protection of a shrub. Quite often the results of these tests are pleasantly surprising, and so encouraged, the two are constantly pushing the accepted limits of plant hardiness. Wandering along North Hill's wooded paths, one finds stands of meconopsis, the fabled Himalayan blue poppies, considered by most experts as limited to the mild winter areas of the Pacific Northwest. A maturing hedge of yew raises many an eyebrow, as do the many kinds of boxwood, all plants which conventional wisdom would declare too tender to thrive this far north. In some cases, of course, the experts would be right, except that Winterrowd and Eck are willing to put a tremendous amount of work into their garden. Not just the beloved boxwoods, but many relatively tender plants are boxed or bundled up in place each winter. Evergreens that suffer from windburn and sharp frosts get padded blankets of brush and bracken. Each year, the two put several tons of insulating boughs over the garden. Soils are worked and reworked, drainage amended, and fertility assisted by careful, well-timed feeding. Endless grooming and ceaseless vigilance keep both borders and less formally structured plantings in balance.

The growing season at North Hill is short, and Eck and Winterrowd have long sought to extend it by collecting plants of all kinds which perform at both ends of the garden year. Species crocus bloom in late winter, spring, or fall, when they are joined by many forms of autumn crocus, the colchicums. Hardy cyclamen nestled beneath tree and shrub may bloom from summer into autumn or awaken with the spring. The loose knit clan of shrubs which bloom early and color late, as well as those which offer winter beauties are well represented here. Spring-blooming heaths and heathers mingle with prostrate junipers in a rough-textured tweed blanket flung along the entry drive. Euonymus trees, the European spindles, dangle their gaudy seedpods of pink or orange in fall, when the *Heptacodium miconioides* (formerly *H. jasminoides*) blooms like bewildered lilac, and the sweet autumn clematis hangs in frothy, fragrant curtains from the trees. In winter, the eye is caught by details of bark and bough, by graceful lines, and subtle, lustrous colors. By the

stream, one sees the purple and lavender-gray, old gold and fresh Irish green of dogwood and willow. Elsewhere, the startling skeletal stems of whitewashed brambles stand out against the mottled and peeling barks of *Stewartia koreana* and *Acer griseum*. Several dozen kinds of bamboo rattle in the winter wind, and tall grasses rustle in soft sussuration, their warm gold fading to battered brown as the snow advances. At the turning of the year, North Hill is reduced to its bones, its bare outline both revealed and obscured by a thick blanket of snow. It passes this test, like all the others, with banners flying, for even now, in the silent season, it is indeed a green haven, a place of serenity and power.

SHRUBS IN THE MIXED BORDER

Shrubs are the magical element which unite the mixed border, relating trees to perennials, vines to ground covers and bulbs. Relatively carefree, shrubs are the busy border builder's friends, for they provide months of cooperative good looks in exchange for very little. Shrubs alone can make a respectable border, as their enthusiasts are quick to point out, but for mixed border makers, shrubs are valued as much for their supportive ways with other plants as for the wealth of forms, colors, and textures they themselves can supply. Moreover, the introduction of shrubs into the border means that there will be wonderful niches to be filled with choice perennials and bulbs, splendid showcases for ornamental vines, and effective visual connections established between tall trees and intimate garden plantings. Impressively flexible, many shrubs partner equally well with larger or smaller plants, and can successfully join plants with disparate forms as well as those of various sizes. The largest shrubs will frame the garden as a whole or give substance to individual planting beds, and some can be treated as border trees where space is limited. Middle-sized shrubs ease transitions within the garden, and those between the garden

Shrubs unite the larger woody plants of hedge and perimeter plantings to the more intimate arrangements within the borders. Ceanothus 'Marie Simon' is a hardy hybrid of New Jersey tea, C. americanus, *and though deciduous, its twiggy red stems are attractive all winter. Photo: Peter Ray*

and larger scale architectural elements. Compact border shrubs may anchor midborder groups or strengthen border composition. Dwarf and sub-shrubs edge paths or borders or free-standing beds, and marry midborder shrubs to smaller perennial companions.

Some of the most memorable and long-lasting mixed border effects arise through pleasing juxta-positions of foliage. Shrubs with fascinating foliage can pull their weight for six or eight months at a

stretch, passing through several colorful stages along the way. Bitty or bold, long fingered or finely fringed, shaped like stars and moons, swords and shields, shrub foliage presents a tremendous vocabulary of form. Mingled in startling contrasts and soothing combinations, leaves make up the very fabric of the mixed border. The long, leathery leaves of *Viburnum davidii* are strongly veined in deep parallel grooves that run the length of the leaf. When the shrub is underplanted with snowdrops, the bulb foliage curls in soothing repetitions of form and color made piquant by the great difference of size. Golden holly glitters between the smooth, felt-backed leaves of a species rhododendron and the gigantic, embossed ones of *Buddleia nivea*. Lacy leaves like outsized red fern fronds rise from a stooled stump of *Robinia pseudoacacia* 'Ruby Lace', set off by the smoke red foliage of *Rosa glauca* and cabbagelike, midnight red 'Rubine' Brussels sprouts. The oversized gray velour leaves of *Verbascum* 'Silver Candelabra' glow against a backdrop of purple-leaved hazel, *Corylus maxima* 'Purpurea'. Provocative combinations such as these keep the border visually engaging even when there's not a blossom in sight.

Shrubs with golden or variegated foliage can brighten dull corners or lighten a heavy mass of stodgy perennial foliage. A ruffled, cutleaf golden elder, *Sambucus racemosa* 'Plumosa Aurea', or gold spotted *Aucuba japonica* 'Variegata' will illuminate lusterless laurels or somber abelias. Silver-streaked shrubby dogwoods like *Cornus alba* 'Elegantissima' enliven the dappled shade cast by a streamside weeping willow or a gnarled old fruit tree. Such striking plants need cautious handling, however, for used to excess they may look more frantic than fascinating. In moderate doses, variegated shrubs make fine transition plants. Foliage of soft sage and bright olive will marry purple or red leaves to dark blues or somber greens. Mixtures of cream and grayish greens can smoothly link gray border sections to golden ones. Blues and blue-greens are particularly good blenders, lifting dim reds to brilliance, tempering mustardy yellows, cooling acid greens, and waking coppery highlights in muted, blackish greens.

Contrasts of form and habit count as much as those of color and texture, contributing to a stimulating garden topography. A golden mock orange that looks dumpy in isolation may stabilize a pencil thin juniper. Formally shaped boxwood can make a lax, open *Daphne genkwa* look blowsy, but partnered with a windswept Portuguese broom, the same daphne looks delicate and graceful. Thoughtfully placed shrubs will unite hedge and border plants, draw the eye to minor vignettes tucked deep into the beds, and relieve the monotony of pillowy, billowing perennials. When each is placed so that its strengths are emphasized, the community of the mixed border is strengthened as well.

Despite their catalog of virtues, shrubs are often undervalued and sadly misunderstood by ornamental gardeners. Many people assume that shrubs belong in ghettos with others of their own kind, like the ubiquitous azalea borders of the South, the heath and heather or rhododendron gardens of the Pacific Northwest, or rose gardens almost anywhere. Some people see them as strictly fit for house foundation plantings, while in many gardens shrubs never make it out of the hedgerow. The idea that shrubs can rank among the stars of the border may come as a surprise to those who have never considered them as border candidates at all. Often, placement and company has everything to do with the way we view a shrub. Once we begin to evaluate their real merits, shrubs emerge as extremely valuable border plants. Many offer flowers and fruits in profusion, and the class as a whole boasts a remarkable variety of foliage shapes, textures, and colors. Deciduous shrubs, the mainstay of many a summery English mixed border, are delightfully changeable creatures, altering their tints all through the seasons. In spring, their young leaves may be as pink as shrimp or a murky, midnight purple, glittering copper or dandelion yellow. As summer matures, their foliage may turn any of a hundred unnamed tints of green or blue or silver. Autumn calls forth clear gold, deep bronze, and singing reds. When winter draws near, flower gives way to swelling bud, while leaf fall reveals unsuspected beauties of berry and cone, stem and bark.

Supportive rather than stellar, evergreen shrubs possess solid qualities of mass and permanence which balance softer ephemerals. They are invaluable framers, giving privacy to the gardener, protecting the garden from unwanted views, and muffling street noise. In an urban setting, a small evergreen hedge becomes the equivalent of a nature sanctuary, housing and often feeding a surprising number of birds. Structural stalwarts like hollies and rhododendrons, camellias and columnar conifers dazzle only briefly, if at all, yet they shelter their less robust companions and delineate the mixed border all through the year. Dwarf or diminutive broadleaf evergreens like daphnes, cotoneasters, and euonymous may be clustered in green islands which float midborder above the slumbering soil come winter. Whether or not they bloom visibly themselves, evergreen shrubs of all sizes will set off the fleeting flowers of spring, frame the shifting floral effects of summer, and play dark night to the fireworks of fall.

Traditional hedging plants, whether evergreen or deciduous, are rarely eye-catching; their job is to be accepted and passed over almost unnoticed, much like the walls of a room. In mixed borders, the hedge plants may be as distinctive as anything within the beds. In a formal mixed garden, the perimeter hedge might be woven like the tapestry hedges at Hidcote, where evergreen hollies are intermingled with plain and copper beech. All are clipped into seeming uniformity, yet the warm months bring out the beauties of leaf forms and colors, while in winter, the strong skeletal beeches contrast with the solid, glossy hollies. In less formal settings, mixed border hedges might be a blend of fruit trees and naturally shaped flowering shrubs, dense barriers of twiggy hawthorn and shrub roses, or lightly pruned walls of Irish junipers and rhododendrons. In my own garden, the unsheared tapestry hedges are extremely mixed. Indeed, they vary in composition in each area, reflecting the style and color or seasonal themes of each, but all are completely informal, a revelry of shrubby beauties rather than mere backdrops for something else. Evergreen viburnums blend with lilac and weigelas, while bubbling brooms and arching roses are interspersed with fastigiate junipers and glossy, free-form Portuguese laurels. However arrayed, hedge shrubs still serve several functions, defining the borders they enclose and making visual

Mount Etna broom, Genista aetnensis, *becomes the centerpiece of Tintinhull's Cedar Court when in bloom. At its feet, stiff sprays of prostrate cotoneaster make an effective and handsome ground cover. Photo: Cynthia Woodyard*

steps between mature trees and smaller scale plants. It only makes sense to choose plants which are persuasively attractive in their own right, especially where garden space is limited. Far too many schools of garden design treat shrubs purely as architectural materials, formally grouped and often given shapes other than their own. Geometric strips of lavender or extruded bands of boxwood outline paths, while beds filled with amorphous billows of perennials are backed by sheared slabs of yew or laurel. In stirring contrast, the mixed border generally celebrates the natural shapes and habits of its inhabitants. There may well be a few formally shaped shrubs, placed where such conventions are appropriate, yet by and large, the shrubs, like everything else in the mixed border, will be used for what they are, rather than what we can force them to become.

The larger mixed border shrubs may well do backbone or hedge duty, yet the very hedges can melt into the borders, with certain of the backdrop shrubs becoming integral, active parts of the composition. The bays formed between large border-back shrubs provide sheltered microclimates for choice perennials and bulbs that require protection. Whether they bloom early, late, or not at all, big shrubs can be given climbing companions to brighten a quiet phase or enhance their moment of glory. Trained as standards or multiple-trunked specimens, their tops allowed to achieve their natural shape, large shrubs can play the role of trees in small gardens, or receive midborder placement in larger ones. Indeed, it is always worth examining existing mature shrubs with care before yanking them out, for even unprepossessing specimens may possess hidden graces. In my garden, an elderly golden privet, *Ligustrum ovalifolium* 'Aureum' (sometimes sold as *L.* 'Vicary'), had been pruned into a small tree by a hungry goat. The results were not immediately promising, yet by removing all the misshapen or broken branches, a lovely framework of smooth, gray-brown trunks was exposed. A few years' remedial shaping produced a very pretty little tree, and now its lime-yellow leaves enliven a shady corner beneath a wide spreading apple. It is echoed by the similar yellow of *Robinia pseudoacacia* 'Frisia'

which peeks over the top of a nearby *Forsythia suspensa*, an enormous creature which must be forty years old. Over the years, it had tangled with an overgrown English boxwood, *Buxus sempervirens*, fifteen feet high. Though the older shrubs needed quite a bit of tidying to be presentable, box, forsythia, and robinia now complement each other in form, color, and texture, and make a pleasing, large

An informal tapestry hedge can both screen the garden from the outer world and connect it with larger trees in the neighborhood. Its multiple textures provide a pleasing varied backdrop for perennials and bulbs. Nishi garden, Bainbridge Island, Washington. Photo: Mark Lovejoy

scale composition which holds up well across a distance. Seen from closer at hand, the three blend into backdrop for a curving bed of foliage plants and flowering perennials. These flimsier plants are firmly tied into the big picture with a trio of dwarf Alaska blue willows, *Salix purpurea* 'Nana' and a delicate southeastern shrub, *Fothergilla gardenii* 'Blue Mist'.

Used with ingenuity and vision, shrubs can focus unstructured borders, anchor flyaway companions, and shelter exposed ones. Any open suburban garden could be transformed into a mixed border by framing it with a blend of larger shrubs, then bridging down in scale with smaller ones. Evergreen andromedas (*Pieris* species), mountain laurels (*Kalmia latifolia*), and laurustinus (*Viburnum tinus*) might al-

ternate with lilacs and species dogwoods at the border's perimeter, while graceful witch hazels, perhaps *Hamamelis mollis* 'Pallida', could curve in to round off each end of the hedge. A cutleaf Japanese maple or frilly golden elder would focus the newly enclosed borders, while an infusion of small border shrubs like diminutive hydrangeas, dwarf spireas, and barberries would lend them strength and depth.

Not all large shrubs need be hidden away at the border back; certain of them merit a forward position where they will break up smooth border topography with stimulating effect. A white Spanish broom, *Cytisus multiflorus*, will weave a gauzy net some eight or ten feet high, its thready twigs contrasting handsomely with tall border grasses and sta-

Shrubby spines give this narrow border in Hidcote's Wild Garden depth and strength. Their pleasantly informal shapes create pockets at the border's back to fill with seasonal bulbs and perennials. Photo: Cynthia Woodyard

tuesque perennials. Its whippy branches might be strung with a clematis, or support a small semi-climbing rose like creamy 'Windrush' or the burnt sugar blossoms of 'Climbing Butterscotch'. California lilacs such as *Ceanothus impressus* 'Puget Blue' or the powder blue hybrid, 'Cascade', will spill over the border edge like foamy blue fountains in spring, while remaining decently clothed in glossy green, narrow little leaves the rest of the year. If a large shrub is given front line space, those with irregular, rather sculptural shapes work better than blobby ones, which just look like mistakes.

Intermediate shrubs are peace makers, uniting plants of disparate sizes and physical types. There is little enough sympathy between most trees and most perennials, and the two may coexist uneasily in the border unless brought together with firm, shrubby bonds. Species rhododendrons with lovely leaves, like *Rhododendron oreotrephes*, its rounded foliage powdered blue, and the bronzed green hearts of *R. williamsianum*, will link a pear or quince to spears of Siberian iris and wide hoops of hostas. An airy lacer, *Kerria japonica* 'Variegata', with dappled silvery foliage, relates the heavy bulk of a holly to the tall, fluttering columns of white meadow rue, *Thalictrum delavayi* 'Album'. Lanky species hydrangeas, like *Hydrangea aspera* or the grayish *H. villosa*, have stunning, oversized foliage which strikes a balance between the drooping limbs of a silvery blue spruce and ranks of Jerusalem sage, *Phlomis russeliana*. A trio of rosy-belled, evergreen *Enkianthus campanulatus* 'Red Bells', their tidy, tiered foliage a pleasant contrast to the long, pinnate leaves of *Mahonia bealei*, step our eye down from the height of a pink-berried mountain ash to the froth of rues and columbines, toad lilies, and hostas which deck the shady border floor below. A delicate buttercup shrub, *Corylopsis willmottiae* 'Spring Purple', bridges the gap between a stiff-needled screw pine, *Sciadopitys verticillata*, and the rough, rugose leaves of *Rodgersia aesculifolia*. In autumn, the crimson hearts and supple branches of a witch hazel relative, *Disanthus cercidifolius*, carry the stems of a spectacular species grape, *Vitis coignetiae*, a blaze of scarlet and gold, into the waiting arms of a towering Douglas fir. The metallic blue beans nestled amid the long, pinnate fronds of *De-*

caisnea fargesii link the soft blue, feathery foliage of the fatly columnar false cypress *Chamaecyparis pisifera* 'Boulevard' with the silvery blue, sawtoothed leaves of the tender South African honeybush, *Melianthus major*, most often grown as a perennial in this country.

Midsized shrubs may be used anywhere in the border, whether freestanding, in combinations with perennials and vines or bulbs, or grouped more or less midborder. Singleton shrubs will rise like sculpted rocks amid a sea of flowers, their strong shapes and exotic foliage focusing an amorphous mass of smaller plants. The felt-backed leaves of *Buddleia* 'Lochinch' lap like silvery fish scales along its curving, eight-foot stems. Strands of the dusky red *Clematis viticella* 'Royal Velours' dangle amid the buddleia's conical clusters of lake blue florets. Further down the border, the buddleia's colors are echoed by a blue and silvery gray haze of Russian sage, *Perovskia atriplicifolia* (or what is sold as such, though it is probably really *P. abrotanoides*), above which soar the stately trunks of *Hydrangea villosa*. This is a statuesque shrub, with hairy, matte green leaves interrupted by wide lacecap flower heads of lavender-blue. It tends to be leggy, making it a good choice for midborder placement, with peonies and tall daylilies in front and really big perennials like *Angelica archangelica* or its red-flowered relative, *A. gigas*, behind. It could easily serve as a tree in a small border, as could a southeastern native, *Fothergilla major*. This genuinely splendid shrub produces its creamy candles very early in spring, and follows a quiet summer with some of the most sensational autumn color in the garden.

Groups of shrubs, usually smaller in scale than any of the preceding examples, can be placed at or near the middle of the border, where they play altering but always valuable roles all through the year. In winter, they appear as pools of greenery amid the quiet borders, repeating the colors and textures of the hedges and background plantings in scaled down versions. Where broadleaved evergreens will thrive, one can achieve delightful foliage mixtures which play off leaf form, texture, and color, but even where the winter palette is restricted to conifers and deciduous dwarves, shrubby island groups can pro-

In the Platt garden, a midborder cluster of dwarf conifers unites succulent sedums and bulbs with ornamental shrubs and trees. Early blooming bulbs are sandwiched between the island shrubs and the perennials. Photo: Cynthia Woodyard

vide considerable visual interest using needled foliage and cones, bark and berry. These shrubby islands create a strong backdrop for late winter snowdrops and early crocus, and support the more flamboyant narcissus and tulips of spring as well. By early summer, rising perennials have screened off the fading bulb foliage, and though the island groups recede from center stage, they continue their supportive role, propping up flopsy campanulas and shrubby clematis, elevating sweet peas or the cup-and-saucer vine, *Cobaea scandens*, off the border floor, and making firm counterpoint to lightweight perennials. Autumn thins the perennial ranks, and often opens up gaps in the border. If late bloomers are grouped near shrubby islands, such gaps will

merely open vistas through which we can admire autumn's glories. These will be ably seconded by midborder evergreen shrubs, while the deciduous ones frequently offer exciting seasonal color of their own.

In my garden, the midborder shrub islands are expanded with evergreen or winter-blooming perennials, as well as pockets of early and late bulbs. In the narrow, shady border beneath an umbrella-pruned pear tree, a shapely little rhododendron anchors the winter group. A Yakushimanum hybrid, it is graced with the stirring name 'Brandt Red × Yak #2', but its long, elegantly powdered leaves and ruby red flowers make up for any deficiency of imagination in its appellation. At maturity, this rhododendron may exceed two feet in height, and will spread rather wider, but at present, it is about half that size, so its companions have all been arranged to give the yak plenty of growing room. It is flanked by a glossy little sweetbox, *Sarcococca hookeriana humilis*, a compact, slowly spreading evergreen with tiny, intensely honey-vanilla scented flowers in January and February. In a colder place, either its partner here, *Daphne retusa*, or the tougher little *D. cneorum*, could replace the sweetbox. Ruddy clumps of *Euphorbia amygdaloides* 'Rubra' sit behind the shrubs, their upright young shoots, nicely clothed with narrow red leaves, counterbalanced by their sinuous flowering stems which curve under the weight of their showy red and green-gold bracts. These begin to open in January, and remain in good looks for months, fading most unobtrusively in late summer or autumn. At the foot of the pear tree, a stately giant chain fern, *Woodwardia fimbriata*, unfurls evergreen fronds which can be as much as five feet long in favored sites. This is, alas, a very tender species, and when it leaves me for plant heaven, it will be replaced with a smaller Japanese holly fern, *Cyrtomium fortunei*. Between all these plants run small waves of *Crocus tommasinianus*, their lilac-blue brightening late winter, and the nodding onion, *Allium cernuum*, a summer bloomer which produces its drooping clusters of pink or purple lilylike flowers in shade as well as sun. The very pale, creamy yellow *Clematis* 'Moonlight' flowers well in shade, and mine clambers through the yak and up into the pear tree by means of a japonesque dead pear branch, gray with lichen, its twisted fruit spurs curving like arthritic fingers to guide the vine securely to its goal. Low mats of the slightly weedy lungwort, *Pulmonaria rubra*, liable to produce its salmon-red flowers anytime between late November and March, run behind the shrubs, their shabby summer foliage hidden by rising thickets of rosy toad lilies, *Tricyrtis formosana*. Red-stemmed *Helleborus foetidus* 'Wester Flisk' has seeded itself into a modest colony nearby, and its seedlings now link this shrub group with a neighboring island beneath the gnarled old apple tree down the border.

The apple tree shrub island holds a dwarf form of the East Coast native mountain laurel, *Kalmia latifolia* 'Shooting Star'. Compact and slow growing, it is well furnished with glossy evergreen foliage, almost hidden in spring beneath hundreds of reflexed white flowers. Their unusual shape is echoed by a colony of hardy *Cyclamen coum* with richly marbled foliage that sets off their own delicate white flowers with panache. Winter jasmine, *Jasminum nudiflorum*, is bare in winter, yet its slim, arching stems are as vivid a green as many a leaf. Each stem is thickly studded with reddish buds that burst into golden yellow trumpets during every warm spell between November and March. Its neighbor, *Mahonia nervosa*, is a hardy, low-growing Oregon grape with leathery, pinnate leaves that remain reliably evergreen well into Zone 4. The shrubs are threaded with sassy wintergreen rosettes of *Scrophularia aquatica* 'Variegata', the basal leaves heavily brushed with cream. Shiny clumps of *Bergenia ciliata* edge the island group, their faintly hairy foliage catching dew and frost most attractively. Groups of white-variegated 'Cheerleader' tulips and a soft reverse bicolor narcissus, 'Pipit', are tucked into the gaps between the shrubs, as are dozens of checkered lilies, *Fritillaria meleagris*. Their browning foliage is hidden in late spring by feathery meadow rues and the broad-fingered foliage of masterwort, *Astrantia* 'Rose Symphony'.

Across the garden, a weeping birch brushes the ground with its thready black twigs in winter. Here, the shrub island is a large one, for the birch's underskirts are filled with wide ruffles of a layered, evergreen honeysuckle, *Lonicera pileata*. In colder gardens, the drooping *Leucothoe fontanesiana*, planted here in its dwarf form, 'Nana', could replace the honeysuckle, for this lovely native is thoroughly hardy to Zone 4, though it becomes semi-evergreen in really cold situations. Curving arms carry slender, alternate leaves that are a dark, glossy green all summer, then turn rich copper-red during the autumn. Leucothoes often hold their lovely color well into spring, when they echo the subtle ruddy tints in 'Apricot Beauty' tulips and the midnight red foliage of sweet Williams. (Sweet Williams which bloom in dark, velvety reds nearly always have blackish red foliage as well.) Beyond the leucothoe are tidy hummocks of a hardy Japanese wintergreen, *Gaultheria*

Like many of its kin, the evergreen coast leucothoe, Leucothoe axillaris, *colors wonderfully from autumn till spring. November, author's garden. Photo: Mark Lovejoy*

A large and varied group of dwarf and compact shrubs have been developed for border use. The best of them combine the usual offerings of flower and berry with exceptional foliage that extends their contribution over many months. Many, like *Gaultheria miqueliana*, are shapely enough to merit a place in the front lines, where their neat foliage sets off silken small grasses and sprawling sedums. Smooth, regular mounds of *Spiraea japonica* 'Little Princess' provide calming textural relief for busily variegated plants like the showy zonal geranium *Pelargonium* 'Persian Queen'. The bluebeards, frizzy-flowered *Caryopteris* species and hybrids, will temper forceful perennials like the tall, black-eyed magenta *Geranium psilostemon* and the outsized, fuchsia pink *Salvia involucrata* 'Bethelii'. The marbled foliage of a small barberry, *Berberis thunbergii* 'Rose Glow' contains a complex mixture of reds and creamy pinks which can unite quarrelsome neighbors like copper-red poppies and warm pink weigela. Big, blowsy hydrangeas have been bred into demure border shrubs, with some, like the basketball-sized *Hydrangea macrophylla* 'Pia', tiny enough for rock garden placement. *Hydrangea macrophylla* 'Preziosa', in muted rose and purple, and the blue-and-white 'Seafoam' may reach three or four feet in height and girth, making them very much at home in a narrow urban garden.

Spiraea × *bumalda* 'Goldflame' has caught the fancy of many a colorist, for whom its changeable foliage is an irresistible lure. They open in early spring in rich, saturated bronze tinged with red, then soften to coppers and oranges that are delightfully emphasized by 'Princess Irene' or 'Prince of Orange' tulips and the early copper-and-rust-colored intermediate *Iris* 'Tantara'. By summer, the leaves are soft old gold, a lovely color with which the intense pink of their flowers is not at all in sympathy. Those who cannot abide pink and yellow should pinch off the flower buds before they can open, provoking a flush of bright new foliage much complemented by peach and salmon colored Peruvian lilies, *Alstroemeria* 'Salter's Hybrids', and deep blue *Lobelia vedraiensis*. Autumn reawakens the foliar warmth, making this small shrub a surefire companion for rust and copper chrysanthemums and smoky blue

miqueliana, which also remains evergreen into Zone 4. In spring, they are covered with tiny white bells like blueberry blossoms, and their neat little leaves frame a colony of green and gold bracted *Hacquetia epipactis* interlaced with sunny winter aconites, *Eranthis hyemalis*, and feathery clumps of glistening golden *Adonis vernalis*. Behind these small treasures spreads a large colony of *Helleborus foetidus*, their slim-fingered foliage spread in wide fans of dark, lusterless green. Beginning in December or January, these are obscured beneath sagging sheaves of ice green flowers, which continue in beauty through midspring.

The dwarf border shrub, Spiraea × bumalda *'Goldflame' is a colorist's delight, taking on various shades of bronze, copper, gold, and yellow from earliest spring until hard frost. Author's garden. Photo: Mark Lovejoy*

asters. *Spiraea* 'Lemon Lime' is smaller than 'Goldflame', remaining at two feet in height, and its cheerful clear yellow foliage sets off the clean yellow and orange of Welsh poppies, *Meconopsis cambrica*, and the everblooming dwarf daylily, 'Stella d'Oro'. Blue balloon flowers, *Platycodon grandiflorus* 'Mariesii', rise quite late, and are liable to damage from the errant trowel when tucked into the border, but they find a safe home ranged about the skirts of this modest shrub.

When the cats began to take over the front of the border, attracted by the masses of catmints growing there, judiciously placed dwarf barberries, *Berberis thunbergii* 'Crimson Pygmy', convinced them to redirect their attentions. Even without bad cats, these tidy little hummocks, blood red in spring, ruby red in summer, are worthy of a prominent spot. Where two or three are grown together, the delicate red bells of *Clematis viticella* 'Kermesina' or *C. texensis* may be threaded through them, bringing the flowers closer to hand where they may be fully admired. The slightly larger golden yellow barberry, *Berberis thunbergii* 'Aurea' will similarly cradle slate blue *Amsonia orientalis* or sky blue *Viola* 'Maggie Mott', their tones echoed by sheaves of *Penstemon* 'Zurich Blue' tucked behind. A spritely green version, *Berberis thunbergii* 'Kobold', looks like a smooth green stone amid small perennials, and is a useful front line stabilizer where brighter colors might prove distracting.

Bushy little bluebeards, the *Caryopteris* clan, are dainty, small shrubs which are often massed to increase the effect of their airy blue flowers, but they are all capable of standing alone as well. *Caryopteris × cladonensis* 'Blue Mist' blooms in the muted shade its name suggests, a subtle color which lifts the inky red foliage of *Lobelia* 'Happy Returns' or 'Queen Victoria' to prominence or softens brassy daylilies like 'Copper Canyon' or the pumpkin-red of 'Suddenly It's Autumn'. *Caryopteris* 'Dark Knight' produces its bright navy blossoms over a long season, and its supple arms make a stunning home for lax shoots tipped with the firecracker red-and-orange flowers of the shrublike Mexican *Lobelia laxiflora*. A recent introduction, *Caryopteris* 'Worcester Gold', combines sky blue flowers with warm yellow foliage, a knockout when underplanted with low mats of the similarly colored *Veronica teucrium* 'Trehane'.

Butterfly bushes have long been favorites for country gardens, but the sloppy figures and weedy habits of the older shrubs have been modified in a handsome bunch of hybrids. *Buddleia davidii* 'Pygmy Purple' is an arching three footer with slim, gray-green leaves and long flower clusters of a dark, saturated purple which holds its own below bobbing, six-foot wands of angels' fishing rods, *Dierama pulcherrimum*, tipped with rosy pink bells. *Buddleia da-*

vidii 'Nanho Blue' is much the same in size and habit, but with rich cobalt blue flowers that play sky to a stand of yellow *Heleopsis scabra* 'Morning Star' or the warmer gold of *H.s.* 'Summer Sun'. *Buddleia davidii* 'Harlequin' holds maroon-red flowers above long, sage gray leaves lightly brushed with a buttery yellow that fades to cream by midsummer. Coral-bells with red foliage, including several forms of *Heuchera villosa* and *H.* 'Palace Purple', make a very pretty underplanting, interspersed with the oxblood red flowers of chocolate-scented *Cosmos atrosanguineus*, the whole backed by big clumps of purple fountain grass, *Pennisetum setaceum* 'Burgundy Giant'.

There are so many good shrubs for border work, it is impossible to discuss them all here, but it is equally impossible not to mention some of the outstanding candidates. The following passages are not meant to be taken as exhaustive, but only as indications of the possibilities. Since every region has its own outstanding natives, its own favored traditional plants, and its own garden styles, your shrub choices will very likely be different from mine (and so they should be). My hope is that this brief overview will stimulate fresh thinking about the role shrubs could be playing in our gardens. Please note that the hardiness ratings indicated are approximate, and usually conservative. A rating of Zone 3 means it is hardy at least that far north. Multiple numbers, as in "Zones 3 to 5," mean that there are several species or forms, some hardy to Zone 3, others to Zone 4 or Zone 5.

DECIDUOUS FOLIAGE SHRUBS

Corylus maxima 'Purpurea' (Zone 5), the purple hazel shrub, can be kept to moderate height (eight to ten feet) by thoughtful pruning, or allowed to grow into a small, perhaps twenty-foot tree with one or more trunks. Either way, it offers a handsome winter silhouette, each dark twig crowded with fat buds that burst into pleated fans come spring. The new leaves are black, turning wine-purple as they expand. By summer they are a dusky, bronzed green, but au-

tumn sets them alight once again with ruddy purple flames. Pair this with a purple grape vine or the variegated *Ampelopsis brevipedunculata* 'Elegans' for a tremendous fall display, or drape it with an early clematis like *Clematis macropetala* 'Bluebird' or 'Rosy O'Grady'.

Another warmly colored shrub, *Cotinus coggygria*, or smokebush (Zone 5), has whispery, round leaves that quake like aspens, showing their silvery backsides in any wind. They dislike damp, but thrive in full sun and poor, dryish soil, and are excellent mixers at the back of a border, where their midsummer flowers rise like cloudy puffs of purple smoke above the frothy perennials. In fall, the soft green leaves deepen to hot reds, flaming oranges, and smoldering purples, rivaling even the fothergillas for impact. Grown as a specimen, a smokebush may reach fifteen feet or more, but it is easily held to lower height with occasional removal of older branches. There are a number of named forms that color especially well in autumn, like 'Flame', or in spring, 'Royal Purple' and 'Velvet Cloak', both having velvety purple young foliage, and 'Notcutt's Variety', with maroon-red leaves and pinky purple smoke. An American species, *C. obovatus* (Zone 5), gets twice as large in time, and is usually grown as a small tree. In cooler climates, the American smokebush grows fairly slowly, and seldom achieves the size it will in its native Southeast. The leaves are plain, soft green, and its smoke is a muted, thundercloud purple, but its autumn color is outstanding, and where rooms allows, this big shrub can be matched with one of the colorful grape relatives for an unforgettable fall display.

The American elders, *Sambucus* species, are handsome creatures, but most are large and encroaching in habit, hardly suitable for the average backyard border. However, both native and European elders offer a number of excellent garden forms, all too seldom seen, which will make strong textural contributions to the mixed border. An ultrahardy elderberry, *S. canadensis* (Zone 3) has a pretty garden form, 'Aurea', with large, lacy leaves of greeny gold, brightest in full sun, and an exotic looking fernleaf form, 'Laciniata', with very finely divided foliage. Both make medium-sized shrubs,

Both the dusky purple hazel, Corylus maxima 'Purpurea', and the frilly golden elder, Sambucus racemosa 'Plumosa Aurea', are splendid border shrubs which lend themselves to numerous color combinations. Author's garden. Photo: Mark Lovejoy

perhaps six to eight feet, and produce flat clusters of whiskery white flowers in spring, followed by dark burgundy-black fruits. (This is the plant elderberry wine is made from, and there are more named clones sold as fruiting shrubs than ornamental.) A European elder, *S. nigra* (Zone 5), with scented, creamy flowers and black berries, comes in several fine forms, among them 'Marginata', in which the pinnate, oval leaves are edged in cream, and 'Aureo-marginata', in which the edging is pale, golden yellow. An especially handsome form, 'Purpurea', can work into almost any color combination, for it has dark purple young leaves that fade to greenish plum, while its flowers are tinted pale pink. (This makes a wonderful showcase for pink clematis.) The European red elder, *S. racemosa* (Zone 6), also comes in many enticing garden forms. The golden cutleaf, 'Plumosa Aurea', boasts leaves like frilly golden

feathers along slender, curving stems, tipped in spring with loose clusters of small, pale yellow flowers. The red berries which follow are usually snapped up by birds quite quickly, but are lovely while they last. A very slow growing form, 'Tenuifolius', is so divided as to look needled, and makes a strong contrast to wide, strappy grasses and bold verbascums.

Butterfly bushes, the buddleias, are a varied race, including both diminutive border shrubs like *Buddleia davidii* 'Pygmy Purple' and towering *B. nivea*, which can reach fifteen feet or more. Many have unusual foliage, long and tapered, their fronts embossed with deep veining, the backs lined with pewter. They may be arching shrubs or small trees, vase shaped or weeping, though most need time to develop their characteristic form. Their common faults (especially among the large-flowered hybrids) are

This small barberry, Berberis thunbergii *'Atropurpurea Nana', fits comfortably into mixed border schemes, and makes an excellent edging plant in larger gardens. Garden of Helen Dillon, Dublin. Photo: Peter Ray*

shapelessness and ill proportions, both of which may be corrected by hard annual pruning. Among the best border candidates are *B. japonica* (hardy to at least 6° F), a thicketing species with supple, five-foot wands tipped with long, sea blue flower panicles. This rather lax creature is an excellent mixer with border hydrangeas and bold-leaved peonies, and can appear well to the fore of a large border. Silver buddleia, *B. alternifolia* 'Argentea' (Zone 7), is a graceful weeper, most dramatic when trained as a small (eight to ten feet) standard and allowed to cascade its silvery leaves and soft purple flowers at the border back.

Hydrangeas exhibit a wide range of forms and sizes, from the tiny mounds of *Hydrangea macrophylla* 'Pia' (Zone 6), seldom over a foot in height and girth, to the stately heights of *H. aspera* (Zone 7), twelve to fifteen feet or more when well pleased. This last is but one of a group of large, treelike hydrangeas, most of which have big, rather hairy leaves, often in muted or grayish greens, and wide, lacecap flower heads in lavenders and quiet purples. They are often confused in the nursery trade and gardens alike, but whether sold as *H. sargentiana*, *H. villosa*, *H. aspera* 'Villosa', or anything else, they are well worth growing (all probably Zone 6 or 7). The oakleaf hydrangea, *H. quercifolia* (Zone 5) is native to the American Southeast, a valuable foliage plant that flourishes in shady borders. 'Snowflake' is an especially good form, with large, long-lasting flowers and terrific autumn foliage color of purple and red and bronze. *Hydrangea macrophylla* (Zone 6), the typical border hydrangea, is divided into two camps, the hortensia hydrangeas, or mop heads, with shaggy heads like outsized lilacs, and the lacecaps, with a few, big sterile florets outside a broad circle of starry little fertile ones. There are an enormous number of named forms in varying sizes and colors, such as 'Snowcap', a big, bushy mop head with globular flower heads of flat white; 'Blue Wave', a middle-sized lacecap with clear blue sterile florets; and diminutive 'Generale Vicomtesse de Vibraye', a tidy little shrub with big mop heads in bright rose and purple. In general, hydrangeas offer bold foliage that colors well in autumn and long-lasting flowers that retain much of their beauty even

in death. Their large foliage is rather tropical in effect, and helps balance fidgety border compositions. They are shallow rooters that do not tolerate drought, and will strongly appreciate the addition of hydrophilic polmer to their root zones.

The color of any hydrangea is affected by the pH of the garden soil, so if you are surprised or unhappy with what you get, you can influence the flower color by amending the soil. Alkaline soils make blue hdrangeas pink or red, but adding an acidifier can bring back the blues or clarify muddy whites. Harsh pinks and reds can be tempered with a tad of lime.

EVERGREEN SHRUBS

Where broadleaved evergreens flourish, the mixed border maker may draw upon a tremendous palette, but elsewhere, serene simplicity will be the keynote in winter. There will still be shrubs in plenty, but the garden's chief delights will be subtle ones of bark and berry, silhouette and shadow. A corylopsis holds up its curving arms with a dancer's grace, each twig bearing trembling drops of rain. The smooth, burnt orange bark of *Styrax obassia* has the sheen of sari silk when wet. Deciduous azaleas hold the snow like mounds of frozen blossom. Tree dogwoods are tightly clothed in lavender-gray, while shrubby ones spread bare, burnished twigs in gleaming thickets of old gold or blood red. Pyracanthas may be covered with berries of terra-cotta or warm yellow as well as crimson. The slim-fingered beautyberries (*Callicarpa* species) are studded with tiny fruits of periwinkle or purple. Bare, bushy *Symphoricarpos* 'Mother of Pearl' carries fat little berries, opalescent as a dove's breast. Ivy berries are bitter blue-black and much admired by hungry birds, which are themselves a decorative addition to the winter garden.

Gardeners in zones five and points south have an extraordinary selection of evergreen shrubs from which to choose. Further north, however, the list is dauntingly short. Rather than give up, ardent gardeners all over the country are continually experimenting to push the limits of hardiness. Many have

The doublefile viburnum, Viburnum plicatum *'Mariesii', looks rather like a lacecap hydrangea, and is more reliable in northern gardens (to Zone 4). Photo: Mark Lovejoy*

managed to coax broadleaved evergreens to grow for them far beyond their normal climate boundaries. Windbreaks, fences, and barriers of deciduous shrubs and mixed conifers all help to moderate a harsh climate, and creating excellent soil conditions may also be of value. To discover which broadleaf evergreens will thrive in your area, visit public gardens, parks, and nurseries in deep winter. Some plants will look great, others adequate, and a few may be obviously suffering. At worst, you can build a working list of serviceable evergreens that may not stir your heart, but do survive in your region. Sometimes you will find that supposedly tender plants can thrive in protected pockets with a favorable microclimate. In truly harsh regions, the choice may come down to whether you prefer to look at bundles of burlap or plastic or a deciduous garden framework. A judicious leaven of conifers, and a handful of reliable broadleaf shrubs (usually small ones are the hardiest) can provide winter effects as

delightful in their quiet way as the lusher look created by bolder foliage.

In colder climes, it is tempting to pack the border with conifers in order to gain winter presence, but this is seldom wise. Conifers create dry, rooty shade, have inhospitable underskirts which can defeat all but the most determined climbers, and are too stiff to be good mixers. In judicious amounts, however, they are indispensable mixed border members. Slender junipers like *Juniperus virginiana* 'Skyrocket' find a ready home here, for they are relatively inoffensive in terms of roots and shade. Prostrate or fountain-like, midsized junipers come in lovely shades of green, blue, gray, or gold. Their sterling qualities are lost in mass landscaping, but singletons placed in mixed borders display remarkable textures and quirkiness of form. Feathery *J. virginiana* 'Grey Owl' or the curiously angular *J. squamata* 'Meyeri' can make a distinctive contribution to the mixed border. Narrow, silvery arrows of *J. scopulorum* 'Gray

Gleam', the delicate, frothy *J. s.* 'Lavender Chip', and the prostrate, startlingly blue *J. horizontalis* 'Turquoise Spreader' are all gardenworthy, and any would set off a spuming fountain of maiden grass (*Miscanthus sinensis*), or a colony of fuzzy pasque flowers (*Pulsatilla vulgaris*) to a nicety.

Rockroses (*Cistus* species) are midsized Mediterranean shrubs with tough, often leathery leaves designed to conserve moisture. The foliage is often attractively crinkled and furred, and the flowers are like single roses, usually pink or rose, sometimes white, centered with golden tufts of stamens. Though usually rated hardy to 15° F, half a dozen common varieties (sold as named cultivars of *C.* × *hybridus*) are reliably root hardy to 0° F, and often come through such cold periods unscathed if they

Several Mediterranean culinary herbs can double as evergreen border shrubs, including Lavandula *'Fred Boutin', a particularly hardy form with extra long flower stems. The lamb's ears at its feet is* Stachys byzantina *'Countess von Zeppelin'. Author's garden. Photo: Mark Lovejoy*

have snow cover. *Cistus creticus*, a species rockrose from Crete, is particularly suited for mixed border work in sunny, exposed sites. This compact, well-clothed shrub achieves an overall spread of four or five feet, and if old branches are trimmed out every year or two, the plants stay handsome for years. The small, gray-green leaves are rippled at the edges so the silvery undersides show up nicely, and the chalk pink flowers bloom all summer. Like all cistus, *C. creticus* mixes wonderfully with Meriterranean herbs such as bay laurels, upswept rosemaries, and sprawling lavenders. It partners well with blue-flowered shrubs like California lilac (*Ceanothus* species), *Caryopteris* 'Dark Knight' and 'Heavenly Blue', or Russian sage, *Pervoskia atriplicifolia*.

Where Scotch broom (*Cytisus scoparius*, Zone 6) is hardy, it may naturalize all too well, giving the whole family a bad name. These underrated workhorses are invaluable border plants with a tousled, windswept look, handsome for eleven months of the year. For a glorious month or so, they are either big with promise or making good on it, smothered in bubbling blossoms that seem to tumble off the leafless twigs. They do have a few faults; for a week after their bloom is spent, they are a sorry sight, but fidgety gardeners can speed recovery by gently shaking off the browning flowers. (Those who wasted their money on fancy rubber rakes will find them excellent broom groomers.) Brooms are short lived, having roughly a ten-year life expectancy, but they bulk up quickly, making them a great choice for impatient gardeners who want fast results. *Cytisus scoparius* blooms in a harsh, chrome yellow that mixes uneasily with anything but green, but its various forms and hybrids extend the color range through palest clean yellows to soft pink, lilac, or peach, or intensify into vivid coral, garnet, or bright burgundy. Portuguese broom (*C. albus*, Zone 5), makes a sprawl of white flowers on glossy green twigs. Angular and dramatic, white Spanish broom (*C. mulitiflorus*, Zone 6) can rise to ten feet in a few years, and its open, airy character makes it an unusual accent for the middle of a large mixed border. All brooms have a lovely, wiry texture that will lighten a heavy border, and all make a fine place to hang a summer-blooming clematis.

There are lots of small daphnes which fit comfortably into mixed borders. The lowest growers make fine edging plants, while the compact, mid-sized ones can smooth transitions between larger shrubs and perennials. Evergreens for winter islands include the garland daphne (*Daphne cneorum*, Zone 4), a low sprawler covered with tight clusters of rosy blossoms, well graced with the family perfume, in late spring. This prostrate creeper likes a sheltered position where summers are hot, otherwise accepting full sun. (Put stones on the spreading branches to encourage rooting at the nodes.) Winter daphne (*D. odora*, Zone 7) smells even better, perhaps because the flowers have few challengers when they bloom in late winter. The variegated 'Marginata' has leaves bordered in butter yellow, which make a pleasant splash in winter, but purists prefer the plain form, feeling that the rose-pink flowers are not seen to advantage against the yellow leaves. Both are good border mixers, requiring little or no attention but resenting pruning. It is seldom necessary, for the plants grow slowly and neatly to their ultimate height of five or six feet. Though *D. odora* tends to be informal in habit and style, *D. retusa* (Zone 6) is a tidy little creature with chalk pink flowers in April. It has a rather formal habit, and looks at home among fine-textured companions and in intimate settings.

Quiet and unassuming, the Japanese bell-flowered *Enkianthus* species are the kind of plants which are increasingly appreciated, for their charms are subtle but many, and given the humus-rich, acid soils they crave, they never misbehave. Redvein, *E. campanulatus* (Zone 4), can reach the height of a tree in time, and may be treated as such in small gardens, trimmed of lower branches and trained into a multi-trunked specimen. Small, rather waxy bell flowers appear in late spring, their soft white stained with pale red. This makes a lovely, fine-textured hedge plant or border back shrub, as will the rather similar *E. cernuus* (Zone 5), which is a more compact plant, and offers reddish bells in late spring. The dainty *E. perulatus* (Zone 5) is a midborder shrub which slowly reaches six or seven feet, covered in spring with pinkish ivory bells.

Glossy, pinnate, hollylike foliage, fragrant winter or spring blossoms, colorful new growth, and bronze or red winter color combine to make mahonias, the leatherleafs, excellent mixed border candidates. They are good mixers, particularly valuable in shaded borders, where their long leaves contrast well with small woodland perennials and bolder foliage plants. As a class, few tolerate direct summer sun, and all prefer an open, humus-rich soil, acid to neutral. The exotic forms are all fairly tender, but quite a few of the native Americans are hardy and make useful border members. These include Oregon grape, *Mohonia aquifolium* (Zone 5), six to eight feet tall, with sprays of warm yellow flowers in midspring. Its bright red or bronze new growth begins to glow in late winter, and it carries its berries, black with a pewtery bloom, over the winter. Long-leaf mahonia, *M. nervosa* (Zone 5), looks something like a leathery fern, rising perhaps two feet tall. It makes a fine ground cover to blend with ferns and trilliums, and blooms in late spring, with blue berries to follow. One exotic mahonia well worth seeking out is the Chinese leatherleaf, *M. bealei* (Zone 6). At ten to twelve feet, this architectural, upright plant belongs toward the back of the border. Its long, large leaves are carried on elongated stalks, making this leatherleaf quite showy in a restrained sort of way. Late winter brings its large flowers of clean yellow, soft but bright, and very fragrant on the cold air, followed by faded, powdery blue berries. It requires shade and some shelter from harsh winds to keep its good looks. Prune this and all straggly mahonias by cutting flowers for the house, taking the stems off above where you feel a thickened node. The result is briefly awful, but the plants will soon fatten up nicely.

Andromedas, the *Pieris* species, are gracious shrubs, neatly furnished and bandbox trim. A bank of quiet greenery all summer, andromedas become delightful in winter, when the incipient flowers dangle in strings like little pink peas. Early spring turns them to open sprays of waxen bells, and often wakens lovely color changes in the young foliage as well. *P. floribunda*, the mountain andromeda native to southeastern America (Zone 4), may exceed its usual

Lovely textural effects may be achieved when evergreens are sympathetically combined, here Chamaecyparis pisifera 'Filifera' *and* Pieris japonica. *Nishi garden, Bainbridge Island, Washington. Photo: Mark Lovejoy*

six to eight feet in favored sites which offer rich, acid to neutral soils and filtered or light, dappled shade. In drier situations, a handful of hydrated hydrophilic polymer mixed into the shrub's root zone can spark a dramatic improvement in looks and performance. The flowers of this native are held in upright, rather than dangling clusters, most conspicuous in the form 'Grandiflora'. *Pieris japonica* (Zone 5) is even more attractive, with larger, glossier foliage that emerges coppery red, deepening to lustrous green by midsummer. The species gets fairly tall, as much as ten to twelve feet over time, and grows especially well in shady sites and retentive but open soils that are free of lime. There are many named forms, most of them rather smaller than the

species, among them the brilliant 'Valley Valentine', with big, blood red blossoms and pinky red new growth, and the diminutive 'Purity', an excellent candidate for midborder island groups, producing its masses of clean white flowers in late spring even in extreme youth. A splendid hybrid between *P. japonica* and an unknown oriental species (very likely *P. forrestii* or *P. formosa*) may be sold as either 'Forest Flame' or 'Flame of the Forest' (Zone 6 or 7, and well worth trying in a sheltered spot further north). Compact and densely clothed, it boasts large, dangling clusters of ivory flowers amid stunning new growth, which passes through four or five distinct color changes on its way to summer green. In early spring, the small new leaves are cherry red, softening over the next month to a clear, warm valentine pink. This gives way in turn to soft ivory, which by late April or May takes on tints of yellow and chartreuse which become deep green by June. It is tremendous fun to play off these changes by matching them with other flowers. In my garden, the red stage is reflected by a very early red-and-white-striped Kaufmanniana tulip, 'The First'. To match the pink phase, a little Greigii tulip, 'Corsage', comes into play, followed by a reverse bicolor narcissus, 'Pipit', greenish yellow and ivory, and a soft yellow rhododendron, 'Hotei', finishes off the progression.

Rhododendrons, beloved furnishers of Victorian gardens, have long been out of fashion, but their potential should not be overlooked, particularly since a few rugged species are hardy to Zone 3. (However, it must be admitted that they won't look very nice there unless they are well grown and sheltered from drying winds.) These shallow rooters appreciate open but retentive soils that are rich in humus. In light or dry soils, hydrophilic polymers will be among the useful effective amendments, even reducing the unsightly leaf curl that is the shrub's natural water conserving mechanism. The key to using rhododendrons well is to consider their overall appearance, selecting for distinguished form and handsome leaf color, with flower color weighing in almost as an afterthought. We don't buy the first couch we see just because it's the right shade of blue—this is a furnishing plant, so give preference to those that are well crafted. Species rhododendrons show a fascinating variety of foliage and form, ranging from minute to majestic. They are a natural choice for shade border backups, but many slip easily into place in the mixed border. As a general rule, the smaller the leaf, the more sun a rhododendron can tolerate, and quite a few species with very small leaves can take full sun if their soil is suitable.

The curving, glossy leaves of *Rhododendron bureavii* (Zone 6) have darkly felted undersides that give them the look of artifacts. The shrub itself appears to be bundled in a cozy arctic anorak lined with warm cinnamon-colored fur. It is a compact plant, slow to increase and slow to produce its flowers, usually rose, but sometimes pink or white, but anywhere it thrives, this plant would rate a prominent position even if it never bloomed at all. A variable species, *R. oreotrephes* (Zone 7) is among the most beautiful in its best forms, in which its rounded foliage is glazed with grayish blue, their undersides even bluer. The flowers, too, are varied, but prettiest when bell shaped and softly colored with pearly highlights (though the many rosy pink shades are also pleasing). This species is quite tolerant of sun and moderate drought, in form a spreading shrub that can grow tree tall in time, and can be pruned into a very shapely specimen. A good midborder species, *R. williamsianum*, spreads its intricate branches very slowly into four- to five-foot mounds smothered with heart-shaped little leaves. The rather bronzy new growth sets off its big bells of warm, reddish pink in late spring, making it an excellent companion for ruddy peonies and red sand cherries (*Prunus* × *cistena*). This rhododendron insists on getting plenty of light and air, responding to shade and shelter with leggy, sloppy form and sparse bloom. At the border front, dwarf rhododendrons can be woven together with rock garden birches and dwarf elms in a lovely foliar tapestry, or placed among low, early-blooming perennials. *Rhododendron* 'Ptarmigan', small and spreading, is clothed with tiny, gray-green leaves and produces little clouds of pure white flowers centered with the blackest of stamens, adding up to an altogether distinctive little shrub for the front of the border.

When placing shrubs in the border, and most especially when planning and constructing midborder shrub groups, it is vital to remember that young shrubs must be given room to develop their natural shape and mature size. Both broadleaved evergreens and dwarf conifers can be disfigured, damaged, or killed outright if smothering perennial foliage is allowed to intrude on their air space. Deciduous shrubs are often more forgiving in terms of health,

Most junipers get no respect in elevated horticultural circles, yet they offer the border builder multiple virtues: lovely textures, a variety of forms, foliage in many shades of green, yellow, or blue, reliable winter color, good health, and good company manners. Used with flair and imagination, they can earn their way into the best of borders. Photo: Mark Lovejoy

yet they are equally susceptible to crowding, and will seldom achieve attractive shapes in excessively close quarters. The open pockets left for seasonal bulbs can provide an adequate buffer zone if all but the lowest, slowest perennials are kept outside these bulb zones. Winter-blooming perennials vary in both hardiness and strength, so look for mild-mannered companions or space them generously, filling in with suitable ground covers. It is always a good idea to choose less aggressive ground covers for use around choice, slow-growing shrubs, especially if you can only find very small specimens, as is so often the case. In sunny, open border areas, the ground may only need the general, good amend-ment appropriate for all border plants. In shady places, however, the ground is likely to be infiltrated with tough roots from trees and larger shrubs. A good handful of hydrated hydrophilic polymer mixed into the planting hole of each shrub (and those of most perennial woodlanders as well) will assist their establishment and reduce their need for sup-plemental summer water for years. The polymer should be kept out of the bulb pockets, however, lest it promote bulb rots. Where the border soil is heavy, a handful of grit mixed into the planting hole will loosen and aerate clay or tight soils, and will be especially helpful for bulbs and plants which re-quire sharp drainage.

The simplicity of lawn and unclipped hedge provide both structural support and a quiet contrast to the complex mixed border plantings. Photo: Mark Lovejoy

Chapter Five

PERENNIALS
IN THE
MIXED BORDER

THE WITHEY/PRICE GARDEN

SEATTLE, WASHINGTON USDA ZONE 8

Pulling in to an undistinguished cul-de-sac in a quiet Seattle suburb, few people would suspect that an extraordinary garden lies hidden at its heart. A tall thuja hedge shelters the last property on the road, cleanly separating a rustic looking craftsman bungalow from the ramblers and split-levels that fill the neighborhood. Here, in the space of about half an acre, Glenn Withey and Charles Price have pulled off one of horticulture's great challenges. In their garden, the myriad treasures of the collectors' trove combine in a flowing whole. Here are not dozens, but hundreds of vignettes, created with plants that command the attention of the most jaded plantsman. At the same time, the visual excitement and serenity of the overall gardenscape draws respectful praise even from the architectually inclined.

The garden encircles the modest house, built in 1956 by Withey's father, in deep and verdant embrace. Hedged about on every side, it is a pool of calm, undisturbed by the clamor of heavy traffic along the strip malls a few blocks away. Enter the low gate set in that anonymous thuja hedge and the

suburbs are obliterated. While the neighboring yards are blandly uniform, in this garden, every microclimate has been developed. The narrow property is divided into some half dozen rooms and walks, each with a distinct theme of color, character, and plants. Transitional plantings relate each new section to the last while preparing the eye for what is yet to come.

A formal herb garden greets the visitor upon entering the garden. From it, a small flight of steps leads to double borders which run vertically along the north side of the house, ending in a second, horizontal pair of borders which wrap around the bottom of the house. Below them an oval lawn divides the upper garden from the gently sloping lower beds. At one side, a spring/fall garden is tucked beneath a spreading plum tree, its great branches brushing the ground to hide the area in summer. Across the lawn, a vine-covered arch signals the entrance to a tidy vegetable plot and a hot border filled with vividly colored foliage and flowers. The south side of the house is sunny and sheltered, its plantings Mediterranean in flavor. A round pool and small patio lie near the upper end of the house, where a branching path directs the visitor to an unsuspected area hidden behind the garage and a screening arborvitae hedge. What was once a driveway that ran the entire back length of the property

Theme plants like Miscanthus sinensis *'Variegata', golden* Hakonechloa macra *'Aureola', and* Geranium riversleaianum *'Mavis Simpson' make powerful, unifying repeats on either side of these double borders. Photo: Mark Lovejoy*

is now a woodland walk, cool and shaded in summer and cheerful with early bloomers in winter and spring.

Framed by tall hedges and mature fruit trees, its beds well furnished, the plantings tightly knit together, the garden appears to be at its peak, perhaps fifteen or twenty years old. It comes as a shock to learn that until May of 1986, there was little here but lawn. The fruit trees were put in by Withey's parents when the house was built, the hedges added as the neighborhood was developed. Apart from some peonies and hydrangeas which Withey's father had ordered from Wayside Gardens in the fifties, "It was pretty much a clean slate," recalls Withey. "We started the garden and our business, Withey/Price Landscaping and Design, that same spring." Though running a young business and creating a large, complex garden at the same time might be considered a tough proposition, it was compounded in their case by the fact that neither partner lived at the garden site. Withey's mother, who owns and occupies the house, agreed to let the pair make the garden, "But I'm not sure any of us knew what we were letting ourselves in for," Withey now admits. "Gardens like this really need almost daily care, and there have been many times when following up a full day's work for clients with hours in our own garden felt like too much. Still, it was our best option, and much better than having no garden at all." Now, Withey's mother is thinking about moving, and the fate of the garden is uncertain.

"A lot of people can't imagine putting so much effort into something that may not last," reflects Price, "but we knew from the start that it might work out that way. It's just another risk we decided to take. For us, this garden has been worth every hour and every dollar that we put into it."

"If we do have to leave, we'll have a huge plant sale and start again somewhere else," adds Withey, viewing the possibility with equanimity. The two have already faced a number of challenges in developing the garden, and come through them all as gainers. When the upper section of an elderly poplar hedge that shelters the woodland walk had to come down in 1990, scores of hostas, species rhododendrons, and other shade-loving plants were suddenly exposed to full sun. This became an opportunity to restructure the entire area. Shortly after the poplars came down, a failing basement pump required replacement. This time, the entire upper portion of the garden had to be removed to make way for heavy machinery and a full work crew. The round reflecting pool was installed after this upheaval, and the upper garden replanted yet again. "We weren't exactly looking forward to the changes," admits Withey, "But they did give us a chance to try some things we might not otherwise have done. Gardens always change sooner or later anyway, so gardeners have to be prepared to deal with change." In their own garden, the pair actually welcome change, particularly the constant alteration of color and form that comes from the concentrated use of perennials.

Through a local plant society, The Northwest Perennial Alliance, both Withey and Price act as mentors for advancing gardeners intrigued by perennials. Under their guidance, the NPA is installing huge mixed borders in the nearby Bellevue Botanic Garden, where visitors will be able to see and learn how to use perennials well in garden situations. "People readily accept the idea of periodically changing the decor of their houses, their wardrobes, even their cars," Withey reflects, "but for some reason, the idea of changing their gardens seems more difficult. Perhaps it's because plants are alive, and people feel more attachment to living things, but the result can be stagnation. Gardens have to change, they can't just be made and maintained indefinitely."

"We see garden making as a continuous evolution," echoes Price. "We have learned not to get complacent, but always to look at the garden with a critical eye. We have also learned to be ruthless with plants that don't perform adequately in a given situation. With the flood of new perennials entering the market, gardeners can afford to be more demanding all the time. Perennials especially must earn their keep; they should have wonderful flowers over a long period, interesting if not exceptional foliage, and acceptable garden behavior. There are just too many good plants to waste garden space on second rate ones."

The beds and borders in their own garden change not only with the seasons, but from year to year, for Withey and Price are constantly trying out new plants, new combinations, new ideas. "This garden is not like anything we would design for a client," cautions Price, "It's far too labor intensive. For us, though, it's both a proving ground and a source of active personal pleasure. This is where we experiment with plants and ideas. Here, we can try things that probably won't prove practical, just because we think they might be wonderful. We take risks that we wouldn't expect clients to take, because through trial and error, and by risking failure, we expand our limits, broaden our understanding, and gain spe-

cific information. Besides, to us, trying something new or unlikely is just fun."

Most of the deliberate changes the two employ occur in areas designed primarily for summer interest, where perennials play major roles. In the long double border below the herb garden, the central theme plants have been more or less stable for several years now, but the breathtaking vignettes for which Withey and Price are best known alter nearly every year. These borders seem to be bubbling over with blossoms, their tumbles of flowers and foliage arching in romantic excess. However, to anyone looking

In the purple border, a dark leaved elder, Sambucus nigra *'Purpurea', sets off the tiered yellow pompoms of Jerusalem sage,* Phlomis longifolia, *and silvery spires of biennial Scotch thistle,* Onopordum acanthium. *Photo: Mark Lovejoy*

down the gravelly path which divides them, it is obvious that these borders are shaped by more than mere abundance. In profile, traditional herbaceous borders curve like a rolltop desk, the plants massed in shapeless billows of color. Here, the structure of each plant is as important to the total picture as the color of its flower or the shape of its leaf. A number of theme plants are used throughout these borders, making rhythmic repeats, though at irregular intervals. Tall, architectural daylilies, glittering arcs of silver striped *Miscanthus sinensis* 'Variegatus', shaggy spills of golden *Hakonechloa macra* 'Aureola', and the metallic blue domes of 'Jackman's Blue' rue (*Ruta graveolens*) are grouped and regrouped in shifting combinations. The velvety, nonflowering lamb's ears, *Stachys byzantina* 'Silver Carpet', and great mounds of shell pink *Geranium riversleaianum* 'Mavis Simpson' soften the border edges, spreading well into the gravel of the broad central path.

In between clusters of these theme plants run perennials of many kinds, themselves grouped in telling combinations. The gilded blades of the hakonechloa blend with clumps of *Hemerocallis* 'Happy Returns', a gently colored sister of 'Stella d'Oro' with similar habit and performance. Starry sprays of *Agapanthus* 'Bressingham White' open behind them, while chalky yellow cape fuchsias, *Phygelius aequalis* 'Yellow Trumpet', dangle yard-long, curving arms laden with tubular flowers over the shorter plants. Strands of the intense indigo *Clematis* × *durandii* snake through everything, uniting this vignette with lofty clumps of dark blue globe thistles nearby and bringing out the blue highlights in the ground hugging mats of the stachys. The color run is a piquant mixture of the soft and the definitive, and although many of these plants have similar, straplike foliage, they are varied enough in form, size, and color to keep the assemblage attractive even when no flowers are to be found.

Those neighboring globe thistles, *Echinops bannaticus* 'Taplow Blue', anchor another outstanding combination dominated by color and form. The architectural spikes of the thistle make a stiff backdrop for the creamy, variegated leaves of pale pink *Phlox paniculata* 'Nora Leigh'. Above them open huge curling white lilies (*Lilium auratum* 'Imperial Gold'). The

A signature combination of yellow grass, Hakonechloa macra *'Aureola', gray lamb's ears,* Stachys byzantina *'Silver Carpet', and the sprawling* Geranium riversleaianum *'Mavis Simpson'. These same plants are used in various combinations all along the double borders. Photo: Peter Ray*

pale mauve *Clematis* 'Comtesse de Bouchaud' romps through the feathery thuja hedge above, its flowers reinforcing the rather washy pink of the phlox, the gold of its stamens repeated in the gold banded lily. "It's a great pity, but we will probably have to replace the globe thistles," Price notes with regret. "They suffer mite damage which gets worse each year, and soon they will be too disfigured to keep." Rather than soak the plants with toxic pesticides, Price will choose something less susceptible but equally bold in form to use in their place.

Opposite this group, on the shadier side of the

border, is a fetching combination in which plant shapes and foliar textures play a strong role. More golden hakonechloa, blue rue, stachys, and 'Mavis Simpson' geraniums are centered by a majestic specimen of the same variegated miscanthus repeated elsewhere in the border. Alongside it are clusters of *Astilbe* × *arendsii* 'Brautschlier' (generally sold in this country as 'Bridal Veil'). "We really like this particular astilbe," Price comments with approval. "The blossoms are quite open in form, it holds its color a long time, and it fades to an attractive, rather creamy shade of beige." By the end of the summer, the geraniums have spilled out in all directions, flowing around the astilbes and lapping over groups of hostas, 'Gold Edger' and 'Bright Glow', both good yellows which can take a fair amount of sun without scorching. The great, fan-shaped miscanthus makes a powerful focal point for the flurries of smaller foliage around it. Here, as in similar combinations in these borders, the big grass catches the eye, then draws attention to the subtle interweavings of its companions.

The double borders end in a pair of island beds which jut out from the hedges on either side in matching, convex bell curves. Transitional plantings of deeper blues and golds have prepared us for the sunset splendors of these beds, the key colors of which are rich and regal purples. That on the north side runs from purples to midnight blues and crimson, while the southern bed holds purples lightened with gold and cream, silver and lavender. The north bed holds a host of roses, many of them English roses, hybrids of old and new roses bred by David Austin. Though the maritime northwest has a modified Mediterranean climate, with wet winters and dry, usually rainless summers, average temperatures are relatively low, and summer days are often overcast. Heavily doubled roses often ball under these conditions, molding in the bud before they can open. The English roses, single or double, perform better and longer than many of the older roses from which they were bred, and Withey and Price have used them extensively both in clients' gardens and in their own. This bed holds over a dozen, ranging in tone from the doubled crimson 'Prospero' and dusky purple 'Othello' to the rosy 'Immortal Juno'

and lavender-pink 'Heritage'. The roses are joined by generous quantities of plants of all persuasions which provide serial pleasures from early spring through autumn. Four hundred drumstick alliums, (*Allium sphaerocephalum*) are scattered throughout the bed, their egg-shaped heads a deep color somewhere between maroon and magenta. A purple birch, *Betula pendula* 'Purpura', at the back of the bed is highlighted by deep-toned asters, among them *Aster novi-belgii* 'Coombe Violet', lilac-blue *lateriflorus* 'Coombe Fishacre' which has purple tinged leaves, and periwinkle blue *A. cordifolius* 'Little Carlow'. Small-flowered *Clematis viticella* hybrids, including the red-black 'Royal Velours' and purple-red 'Etoile Violette', run happily over shrubs and between perennials, linking each combination to the next.

Across the path, the south border holds a similar array of woody and ephemeral plants. Here, the spectrum violets and purples of rose and lily are brightened by tints of apricot, peach, and salmon, and cooled by blues, silvers, and grays. A bushy purple-leaved elder with soft pink flowers (*Sambucus nigra* 'Purpurea') centers the bed. This vigorous shrub is cut back hard each year, both to keep it in scale with the other plantings, and to promote the especially rich leaf coloring associated with its new growth. 'Lagerfeld', a tall hybrid tea rose with enormous, fragrant blossoms of silvery lavender, rises nearby, underplanted with seersucker hummocks of *Hosta seiboldii* 'Elegans' and a restrained blue Lyme grass, *Elymus pubiformis*. A silver-variegated kerria with single, cream-yellow flowers (*Kerria japonica* 'Variegata') makes delicate lacework above the broad hostas. This dimunitive kerria is low growing and open in habit, and mannerly enough for the smallest of borders. Peach-and-apricot 'Lady Anne' lilies and shrubby blue *Salvia uliginosa* are paired several times, their color notes replaced in autumn by the late-blooming *Chrysanthemum* × *rubellum* 'Mary Stoker', a pale terra-cotta sibling of the strident 'Clara Curtis', and mounds of *Aster* 'Royal Opal', making swirls of soft blue, lavender, and purple.

The silvery kerria and blue hostas unite the purple borders to the blue and gold plantings along the south side of the house. Windows overlooking this

Blood red 'Othello', an English rose bred by David Austin, blooms at the bottom of the double borders beside Papaver orientale *'Beauty of Livermere'. Photo: Mark Lovejoy*

part of the garden made it desirable to create areas of winter interest here, so the ebullient ephemerals of summer are supported by pockets of evergreens, both shrubby and perennial. Evergreen ground covers and perennials, early blooming hellebores, and tall sedums which dry attractively are arranged with dwarf shrubs like *Ilex crenata* 'Golden Gem', its gilded leaves mottled with green in summer. Species rhododendrons offer beautifully textured leaves, some felted with rust or faun, others spreading in glossy whorls. Here, too, are pleated fans of evergreen *Iris foetidissima* 'Variegata' and the spiky flower heads of winter blooming euphorbias. All winter, subtle ripples of shifting color blow through these beds as bulbs bloom and new growth brightens the evergreens. True winter bloomers include helle-

bores, *Iris unguicularis* in several forms, winter pansies, *Pulmonaria rubra*, and a number of primulas. *Jasminum nudiflorum* opens golden trumpets during every warm spell, and tiny-leaved *Azara microphylla* scents the February chinook, the warm wind that heralds spring, with vanilla and honey.

In summer, this part of the garden is sunny and dry, thanks to the reflected light from the house and garage. Mediterranean subshrubs and heat-loving perennials surround a patio of Arizona sandstone, further embellished with gaudy tropical annuals such as *Pelargonium* 'Persian Queen'. The round pool has its regular edge obscured by wandering traceries of gray, green, and gold *Helichrysum petiolare* 'Variegata'. Color runs here are warm rather than hot; clear yellows deepen to gold, salmon, and orange, with cool ocean blues for contrast. A sweeping clump of *Cortaderia* 'Sunstripe' near the pool echoes *Caryopteris* 'Worcester Gold', a hybrid with narrow yellow leaves and whiskery, sky blue flowers. Their colors are repeated by yellow and blue pansies. Rosemaries and lavenders, sages and thymes flourish in the shelter of the patio area, as do sedums, of which Withey and Price are fond. Here, tall clumps of *Sedum maximum* 'Atropurpuraeum', with nearly black leaves, stand above lax tumbles of pinky purple 'Vera Jameson', rose-red 'Ruby Glow', and their slate-and-smoke colored sibling, 'Sunset Cloud'.

The house wall is hung with shrubs and vines which frame the windows with flowers. A Moroccan broom relative, *Cytisus battandieri*, has silky, hand-sized, silver-fingered foliage, and conical clusters of bright yellow flowers that smell distinctly of fresh pineapple. At its feet are coppery grasses in several sizes, interplanted with blue agapanthus and a Japanese bluebell (*Mertensia asiatica*), its blue, spoon-shaped foliage waking metallic highlights in the dim grasses. Salmony 'Abraham Darby' English roses blend the lemon yellow foliage of *Choisya ternata* 'Sundance', a Mexican mock orange, with the bronzed red flowers of *Phygelius* 'African Queen' trained on the wall. Similar combinations are repeated down the length of this border, which is anchored at its nether end by a blue lacecap hydrangea as old as the house, its jagged leaves softened by a trailing, dark blue clematis, 'The President'.

East of the house lies a pool of lawn, bordered to the north by mature fruit trees. The largest of these, an old prune plum, shelters the spring/fall garden. Furnished with branches to the ground, the plum forms an umbrella of foliage which hides the plants within during their unsightly summer resting stage. Mosses have been encouraged to spread here, making a verdant carpet for spring crocus. "We plant at least a thousand at a time, and add more each year," says Price, who favors *Crocus tommasinianus* hybrids for their propensity to self-sow. Numerous hellebores are grouped here, among them a rosy strain of *Helleborus orientalis*, scented and red-stemmed forms of *H. foetidus*, and the pewtery, purple-belled *H. torquatus*. Several dozen of the hybrid seedlings were raised by the late Kevin Nicolay,

botanical artist and plantsman extraordinaire. One of his life goals was to breed a pure black hellebore, and though Nicolay did not live to see his project through, Withey and Price are carrying on his work, hand pollinating the best of the seedlings each year, and evaluating their offspring. "It would be wonderful to get a really coal black one we could name for Kevin," says Price quietly.

After circumnavigating this large and tightly planted garden, it is a fascinating exercise to retrace one's steps in the opposite direction. This time, one discovers hundreds of plants which were inexplicably missed before. "The plantings are quite complex," Withey comments with dry understatement. Indeed, one can visit here every month of the year and find a different garden each time. Withey and Price are blessed with the true gardener's eye and instinct for placement, gifts that can only be developed but never taught. Though their garden is still quite young, its plantings display the depth and complexity of a garden many years established. This owes something to the mature framework planted by Withey's parents long ago, against which the more recent borders are firmly framed. For the most part, it reflects the time and unstinting effort which the pair have invested, not to mention their out-of-pocket expense. Gardens like this do not come cheap; indeed, they can scarcely be bought, except with the hearts' blood of their makers.

Withey agrees, saying, "You really can't pay people to garden like this. I make gardens for a living, but working here serves as therapy for me. Gardening is the most soothing thing I can do in a frantic and often painful world. I know it is just a small counterpoint to all the environmental damage that is ravaging the natural world, but to try and heal my immediate environment makes me feel better personally."

Price, who is mulching the deep double borders with a thick layer of washed cow manure from a local dairy, pauses to add a further thought: "Too many people are in a hurry to get their gardens made, but are much less interested in caring for them. They are actually missing a lot, because garden work is very restorative." He interrupts his mulch spreading and looks down the long borders.

"Garden making is a slow and lengthy process. Impatient people always want the biggest possible plants, for an immediate effect, but that is often dead wrong," he says decisively. "Large plants should be used sparingly." He points out that big trees and shrubs tend to outgrow a site too quickly, throwing both the garden's design and the growth of surrounding plants off balance. "It's much better to use small, choice plants that will grow up on site; that way the garden remains in scale and retains its pleasing proportions for many years," he explains. "Plant for the future, but allow plenty of rewards for the present. That way, after five or ten lovely years, the garden will be approaching a new peak of perfection, not hideously overgrown." As he returns to the job at hand, he adds with a smile, "Nothing lasts forever, of course; even the best gardens need periodic adjustment to keep them fresh."

PERENNIALS IN THE MIXED BORDER

Perennials are the life blood of the border, for their very essence is of change. Chosen with an eye to continuity and sequencing, perennials will pour through mixed borders in waves and washes of color from the first moment of spring until winter's killing frosts. A handful of ultra-hardy perennials will challenge winter itself, blooming through snow to prove that nature never really sleeps, and the garden year never need end.

The mixed border offers numerous pockets into which perennials may be tucked. They can run in rivers or rivulets between shrubs great and small, pour through the bays between background trees and shrubs, and lap in wavelets behind the border's firm edge. The clustered, shrubby midborder islands, so prominent in winter, sink in summer beneath rolling floral breakers to take up secondary positions, providing solid counterpoint to foamy masses of blossom and lending physical support to flopsy plants.

Perennials can offer far more than flowers and when attention is given to contrasts of foliage form, color, and texture, combinations remain attractive with or without flowers. Author's garden. Photo: Mark Lovejoy

Perennials waken the quiescent garden framework; their artful combinations and complex groupings give those strong, silent background plants purpose, transforming them from empty box to vital walls and encircling arms. Hedges and trees and shrubs can shape a garden, and may even call it into being, but in themselves, they are ever only staging. Say "garden," to yourself, and the mind's eye conjures up images not of yews or privet, but of a vague greenness full of sun and birds, and everywhere flowers, humming with bees. Perennials bring mixed borders to life, full to the brim and fairly bubbling over with bloom. Such potent flow of life and color cannot come without cost, but the cost need not be improbably high. In the garden, as elsewhere, we get exactly what we pay for, yet it is very possible to pay relatively little and get a tremendous lot. Bargains exist in everything; the trick is to recognize the true values and avoid the illusory sort. When selecting perennials, we must thoughtfully define our wants and needs before making final choices, for only when we know exactly what we want can we bargain wisely.

There are a great many tough, hardy perennials that deliver unstintingly over a long period—enough to build a garden that blooms for many months almost anywhere in the country. Despite their reputation for neediness, many perennials belong in that benovolent class requiring only a modicum of well-timed care in return for their kindness. Many of these are so obliging that we are tempted to overuse them, working them into all our schemes. When we further explore the wealth of color and form offered by perennials, our faithful standbys are apt to be left behind. Such progress is often praised (in Seattle, advancing gardeners tease each other by saying, "Are you still growing that old thing?" about any common plants) yet it has its dangers, for snobbery is as senseless in the plant world as in the human one. Before dismissing those first loves, it is worth looking at them with careful attention, for they didn't achieve classic status by accident. Gardeners whose supply of perennials is limited can still make full and fine use of what they have. Indeed, a sympathetic garden maker can work wonders with the most pedestrian plants, placing them with such understanding that we see them as their first discoverer did, with delighted eyes. Good company can be equally uplifting, and a supportive mixed border setting brings out the forgotten strengths in many a weary workhorse. Enchanting gardens are often made with whatever plants come readily to hand, and there is less value in seeking out wondrous rarities for our mixed borders than in learning to use ordinary perennials extraordinarily well.

The happy corollary is that a complex mixed garden full of choice perennials may also be arranged to deliver without excess charges, a process made comparatively easy in mixed borders. Here, the combination of woody and perennial plants proves synergistic, for perennials give the garden framework of woody plants life and purpose, and in return it boosts the impact of their performance manyfold. Whatever kind of garden we make, choosing perennials that will perform in it without fuss is a matter of experience as well as taste. The more we get to know our site, the better we can guess which perennials will enjoy it. The more we learn about perennials, the easier it becomes to look beyond their pretty faces. Perennials must earn their way into our mixed borders with a combination of long-lasting, overall good looks, appropriate habits, and durable company manners. Selecting them for what they look like blooming away on the pages of a catalog or in a pampered nursery pot is akin to choosing Miss America by her swimsuit. We need to see this girl washing dishes, hiking up a mountain, and raging mad before pronouncing her The Most anything. With perennials, as with people, the whole picture counts. Happily, the perennial palette now available to us is so wide that we can afford to be very choosy, settling only for those with beauty and easygoing, cooperative behavior.

The role of perennials in the mixed border is significantly different from that in the traditional herbaceous border. Images of those billowing, immaculate English borders often subconsciously set our mental standards, yet such gardens are too exacting to be practical in contemporary terms. Indeed, even in England, such borders are museum pieces, relics of the days when the upper classes could readily command an ample, inexpensive, and skilled labor force. However unmanageable, those traditional perennial borders are dream makers, and many a smitten traveler has returned home determined to recreate their wonders in the backyard. In much of North America, success is unlikely, thanks to various realities of climate, and even where the dream is realized, its real-life drawbacks are legion. Six or more months of barren ground, and hundreds of hours of labor can seem a poor exchange for three months of glory, especially where one modest yard must serve the year-round needs of a whole family. For most of us, the enormous, ceaseless struggle for

Images of perfect English borders can frustrate North American gardeners struggling with difficulties of climate and site. Tintinhull's borders, with their masterful arrays of form and texture, their color runs rich and subtle, their sequences seemingly endless, are well worth emulating in style, if not in content. Even where the plant palette is limited by regional realities, the principles which underlie these borders may be followed with sure success. Photo: Cynthia Woodyard

fleeting (and never guaranteed) perfection is simply too high a price to pay for not enough garden. Perhaps even more important is that few traditional European gardens welcome use the way that North American home gardens usually do. Though magnificent, those grand gardens are really walk-through showplaces which invite our admiration but do not make us comfortable or at ease. They are hands off gardens, not interactive, rather made for passive pleasures. A working garden, one in which people live and play and relax, should feel more like a living room than a museum exhibit. Fortunately, there is no reason a comfortable garden can't be both

stylish and beautiful. Mixed borders, always furnished, offer all sorts of opportunities to use perennials for excitement and drama without sacrificing garden or gardener to their needs.

In the kind of year-round mixed borders proposed in these pages, perennials are used to not to achieve a blow out extravanganza of summer color but to extend their color as far as possible through every season. This does not preclude a colorful summer garden—indeed, the generous use of perennials will almost guarantee that much—but it does mean that color will flow through various parts of the garden at differing rates and schedules. The thoughtful interweaving of perennials with other kinds of plants can further guarantee that no part of the garden need be utterly empty or dull even during its off seasons. In year-round mixed borders, perennials never stand alone, but are placed along with a host of bulbs, vines, shrubs, and so forth, all of which share seasonal strengths. One bed may shine in winter and spring, while another will be furnished yet quiet at those times, then burst into floral flames in high summer and fall. Within each group, the plants will be arranged in microcosm just as they are more generally in the garden as a whole. Mutually supportive plants are given compatible companions, and placed so their strong points are emphasized, their weaknesses hidden or tempered. Such treatment increases the visual value of every member of each group, but it is especially rewarding with perennials, both simplifying their care and amplifying their impact. Rather than struggling to maintain a borderful of temperamental beauties, the gardener is assisted by a stalwart staff of plants which frame and support the perennials. When one section's hour of glory is over, its perennials are tidied up all at once and given a light feeding mulch to renew their energies. Thanks to woody and other companions, and to well-arranged foliage combinations, the area is left not bereft but perfectly presentable, well able to support in turn neighboring areas where the torch of pure color has passed.

However, such mutually supportive interactions rarely happen by accident. To put perennials to best use in mixed borders, we need to know how they behave in mixed company, whether they tolerate shade, or root competition, or drought, or constantly damp soil, and how they grow over time in our part of the world. We must be able to see them as whole plants, concentrating not on their flowers, or even foliage, but on the shapes and sizes they will achieve in maturity. Perennials are as variable as any other plant group, yet they, too, fall into the common shape categories of spike and pyramid, smooth mound and arching sheaf, sprawling wedge or tufted tussock. Those who find perennials difficult to place satisfactorily might follow the example of John Brookes, planning out perennial groups in

terms of shape and size before thinking about specific plants to fulfill those roles. If limited experience with perennials makes spot assignment difficult, find a good nursery with a knowledgeable staff. Armed with your diagram and site requirements, you will be able to ask the right questions, and elicit appropriate suggestions. Instead of saying vaguely, "I can't find anything to plant under this little maple tree I have," you can say, "I am looking for a pyramidal plant, between five and seven feet tall, that blooms in mid- or late summer, preferably in either white or soft yellow. It needs to grow well in light shade and tolerate heavy, acid soil." Of course, the specifics change every time, but the more of them you can provide, the better the chances of coming up with a lastingly satisfactory answer. Books like *Right Plant, Right Place* by Nicola Ferguson or Graham Rice's *Plants for Problem Places* are also very helpful (see Books for Further Reading).

Local or at least regional knowledge is especially useful. Most general garden books have a regional bias toward the northeastern states, and what works in Boston may or may not apply to a garden in Michigan or Montana. Check the library for regional garden books and local plant society bulletins and newsletters. If you haven't been gardening for long, or have recently moved to an unfamiliar region, it is well worth seeking out mentors, whether from garden clubs and plant societies or through a good nursery. Familiar perennials may behave quite differently in new surroundings, and there are probably a host of regionally appropriate unknowns waiting to be discovered. For many of us, plant hunting is as fun as garden making itself, but finding out about the plants is at least as important as finding them.

Wherever you live, it is always worth giving unfamiliar perennials a season of quarantine in a nursery bed, especially if they come from a family with take-over tendencies. Indeed, any perennial spoken of as "easy" or "quickly spreading" should be viewed with some suspicion. It may be just what you need to fill a difficult spot, but it might also make you pay for years for a monentary indiscretion. Mystery campanulas, which often turn out to be the dreaded *Campanula rapunculoides*, can become the scourge of a garden. Certain artemisias, perfectly well behaved in sand, become rampant thugs in clay, while the statuesque plume poppy, *Macleaya cordata*, which travels fairly slowly in heavy, acid clay, races through sandy borders at lightning speed. It is a significant advantage to know such things before you plant, and will greatly assist you in controlling the ongoing balance of garden groups and relationships.

The sociability or independence of perennials must also be taken into account when planning border placement. Some plants, like *Rodgersia tabularis* and bear's breeches, *Acanthus mollis* var. *latifolius*, need a good deal of elbow room to grow well, let alone develop their proper shape. They also have large leaves that go on expanding throughout their growing season, and can easily smother lesser companions that are placed too closely at hand. Such plants are best paired with very early crocus or minor bulbs, their underskirts filled with a durable, undemanding ground cover like *Ajuga reptans* 'Atropurpurea', with any companion perennials ranged at a generous distance from those territorial leaves. Perennials of very different temperaments, like *Euphorbia griffithii* 'Fireglow', with its slim, rambling stalks, and the Chinese *Morina longifolia*, with its elegant, prickly basal rosettes, may put themselves into closer proximity to neighbors than would be suggested by garden book planting rules. If you rush to free them from encroaching companions, they simply move, or languish, depending on their abilities. It is the gardener's task to watch such developments and to determine whether a plant needs rescuing from aggressive neighbors or is demonstrating a preference for company. While we can make general rules about family behaviors, there are always plenty of exceptions to keep us on our toes. Those who have grown the implacable circle flower, *Lysimachia punctata*, or its lovely cousin, *L. ciliata* (which is once again considered *Steironema ciliatum* by those busy botanical taxonomists), would have every reason to consider the family as unfailingly encroaching. Indeed, even the dark-leaved *Lysimachia ciliata* 'Purpurea', often said to be a slow mover, becomes an amiable thug in retentive soils.

A Himalayan mountain dweller, Morina longifolia, *arms itself against browsers with leathery, stiff-spined foliage. It is a short-lived perennial which dies out in exposed positions, but will seed nicely if given a comforting carpet of creeping herbs like thyme or oregano. Author's garden. Photo: Mark Lovejoy*

However, if we applied what we knew about these plants to a demure European loosetrife, *L. ephemerum*, planting it in poor, dry soil with aggressive companions to try to keep it within bounds, we would probably lose it. *Lysimachia ephemerum*, with gray-green leaves and soft, grayish white flowers, is a tall, elegant clump former that not only does not run, but needs deep, moist soil and partial shade to increase at all.

Some plants need the company of their own kind in order to shine, while others look formless until they stand alone. A season or two in the nursery bed will usually resolve this question, one worth asking as well of plants already in the border. We often assume that big plants should be singletons, or planted at most in threes, while smaller ones need to be grouped for impact. Before tossing a perennial that has failed to meet your expectations, look at it with a critical eye and analyze whether it might be visually stronger if free standing, or whether it might look better in a group. If the latter seems likely, ask further whether that group would have a definite shape of its own, or whether it would need balancing with bolder forms. Try several formations and evaluate them as well: if a cluster of three is good, is five better? Grouping plants can be tricky business, for while too few may look skimpy, too many become either amorphous or boring.

We are always being encouraged to plant in drifts so that the impact of our plants will be increased. However, in small spaces, a single good-sized plant can easily read as strongly as a whole wave of the same plant would in a garden fifty times larger. In those large, traditional borders, plants are often massed in order to read well from the house, and so should ours be, but it is as well to remind ourselves that those estate manors are at least the equivalent of several city blocks away from their borders, which might easily take up a couple more blocks themselves. The concept is terrific, but needs to be scaled down to suit the typical North American lot, urban or suburban. Most of our mixed borders are to be lived in and enjoyed at close range, so our plantings need to be visually entertaining from a few feet, rather than a few blocks, away. It is all very well to aim for a generous abundance, but in a small garden, generosity must be balanced against the need for variety. Even in a large garden, the eye reads great sweeps of the same plant in an instant and moves on, seeking further stimulation. In a small garden, oversized drifts and excessive repetition of theme plants may dissolve the borders into shapeless smears of mere color. What's worse, using too many of the same plant greatly limits the flexibility of color sequencing and multiseasonal display in a small space. Plant your perennials in quantities and groups that are appropriate for the size of your own garden, and don't worry about rules designed for estates the size of the whole neighborhood.

Perhaps the most common fault one sees in perennial borders is shapelessness. This, too, can be traced back to the prototypical English border, where plants are disposed in unbroken masses with the profile of a rolltop desk. Such indefinite arrays work fine where there is a great deal of architectural and structural support to balance them, but in small gardens, they tend to look like floral mush. Amorphous arrangements of perennials are best avoided by paying proper attention to the strengths and merits of each plant that goes into every mixture and every group. Their shape and ultimate size should dictate the border placement of perennials every bit as much as the tint of their petals or leaves. The prime directive of the mixed border holds here in spades: every perennial should be put where it can be appreciated as fully as it deserves, and where its natural shape and habit are assets, rather than liabilities. The artful interpretation of this simple design rule is often the magic element that elevates humdrum components into a breathtaking border. Where all the plant material is choice, sensitive placement makes for stunning vignettes at every turn. Without it, the border may be full to bursting, its color flows clever and successful, yet it will fail to capture our lasting attention. Unless our visual interest is piqued and held, a glut of sheer color brings no lasting pleasure.

Border perennials are most rewarding when their various forms are alternated or arranged in visually intriguing ways. Attention to background structure helps as well, for a froth of pinnate foliage or lacy flowers gains definition and importance from a backstage curtain of large, plain leaves. Just as strong verticals within the border are counterbalanced by billow and bun, the multiple shapes of the border ingredients are held together by the solid, calming framework plants. However, when the finest plants are blobbed together into a senseless jumble, their individuality and essential structure are obliterated. No matter how lovely the colors, mere smudges of color do not compensate for sloppy placement. This happens in famous gardens as well as amateur ones, so if you recognize this very common fault in your own beds, don't feel stricken or unduly ignorant. Do, however, move those plants

Potent verticals like foxgloves lead the eye skyward, balancing the bulk of a shrub rose in full bloom. Garden of Daphne Sewart, Bainbridge Island, Washington. Photo: Mark Lovejoy

narrow border, such a plant functions as a full stop, and takes on the structural role of a small tree. In a good-sized mixed border where nothing much is going on, an imposing focal point can give the planting heart and pull the entire display together. For this, we may look to power perennials such as Chilean rhubarb, *Gunnera manicata* (which always sounds like Italian food, rather than an outsized foliage plant). Though most often used as a bog plant, gunnera grows nicely in the border, so long as it is not permitted to dry out. It won't reach its full ten feet in height there, but its rough-textured, jagged umbrella leaves a good yard across will still get attention. Where gunnera is tender (it can survive zero degrees F with a protective mulch), any of the ornamental rhubarbs might fill the bill. *Rheum palmatum* combines the stout red stems of pie rhubarb with outsized, red-backed leaves that are boldly lobed and deeply toothed, and sends up big, creamy plumes of flowers in late summer. 'Atrosanguineum' is redder in stem and leaf, and has pinky red flowers to boot. *Rheum alexandrae* likes wet feet, and if its basal leaves are not especially showy, its tall stems, covered in overlapping greeny yellow bracts like so many scales, are most definitely eye-catching. Hardier still are the culinary rhubarbs, many of which are highly impressive in both leaf and flower. They strike a strongly exotic note in a border setting, where surprisingly few people will recognize them. (My father, on the other hand, once waded halfway into a deep border to cut the stalks of a Himalayan rhubarb, *R. emodi*, which looked like breakfast to him.) Another giant, the European sea kale, *Crambe cordifolia*, is a stunner in early summer, when it sends up thick, head high stalks bearing billows of ivory blossom that float cloudlike above the border. After the florets fade, the netted mass turns biscuit buff, remaining attractive well into autumn. Crambe's big, coarse leaves look exciting in spring, particularly in the golden foliage form, 'Aurea', but by midsummer, they are tatty and starting to brown off, and need a shelter belt of high-rising lilies and spiky globe thistles to hide their sorry feet. In a border burdened with too many rounded and mounded plants, trios and quintets of well-manured delphiniums, in roughly triangular groupings, will function—like church spires—as a visual excelsior, lifting the eye triumphantly skyward.

Uprising plants of all sizes and heights are useful for breaking up undefined masses of border perennials. Even lowly ground covers may provide valuable verticals, as when woolly lamb's ears, *Stachys byzantina* 'Cotton Boll', sends up its fuzzy, two-foot rods spangled with fluffy balls of purple and silver, rising in small thickets at the border's front. Evergreen rosettes of *Veronica gentianoides* lap low and glossy at the border's edge all winter, elongating into long, floral spears of baby blue (or white, in the form 'Alba') in summer. Narrow-leaved Siberian iris or the broad, blue blades of intermediate iris provide valuable textural contrast throughout the mid- and front border, as do the related sisyrinchiums, stiff yuccas, spiky *Cordyline stricta*, and upright border grasses like *Carex buchananii*. If crowded and crushed, their strength of line is lost, but given enough room to develop and display their true form, such plants make dramatic interruptions to formless flower froth. In a sunny border, *Veronicastrum virginicum* 'Album', the clean white form of our native Culver's root, builds into a stately midborder vertical, with cool icicle white flowers tipping neatly whorled stems of tidy, grayish leaves. In shadier spots, the creamy yellow and sage of a variegated figwort, *Scrophularia aquatica* 'Variegata', spreads in broad mounds, its blooming stalks climbing in gentle curves some four or five feet high, and opening sprays of tiny, blood red flowers in late summer.

Certain perennials have a distinct upward thrust, yet are obliging enough to make good mixers, like the rust-and-ruby-stained stems of a running spurge, *Euphorbia sikkimensis*, which spin in airy, whirling columns between chunky border shrubs. The lacy lady fern, *Athyrium filix-femina* 'Multifidum', can cozy in between small shrubs or stand free at the border back, spilling upward in slim-waisted fountains, and lightening heavy foliage with her green feathers. Further back in the border, *Boltonia asteroides* 'Snowbank' stands four or five feet tall, a delicate yet substantial mass that never needs staking, even when its hundreds of branchlets are laden with fizzy white asterlike flowers in late summer. *Boltonia asteroides* 'Pink Beauty' (a chance seed-

Soft, whorling spires of Euphorbia sikkimensis *provide a settling contrast to the mounded* Spiraea × bumalda *'Gold-flame' and a cloud of purple fennel. Author's garden. Photo: Mark Lovejoy*

cils of *Verbena bonariensis* rise in transparent curtains before banks of salmon and copper daylilies and shafts of china blue and white *Aconitum × bicolor*. Sinuous white bottlebrushes of *Cimicifuga ramosa* sway above a small ivory lacecap, *Hydrangea macrophylla* 'White Wave'. Wandering wands of *Guara lindheimeri* screen the pink-and-white hollyhock blossoms of *Lavatera thuringiaca* 'Barnsley' with a thin veil of its own pink-and-ivory flowers, their tints matching in both bud and blossom. Angels' fishing rods, *Dierama pulcherrimum*, make a thick tussock of strappy, irislike basal foliage, above which rise long, supple rods, curving under the weight of the silken bells, rose or purple or pink, that dangle like heavenly bait from their tips. Set at the border back, they will bob above lesser plants, but placed near the front, the bright flowers nod at face height to receive the study they deserve.

An excess of verticals can make a garden look terrified, if not spaceward bound, but these potent shapes are brought speedily back to earth by jagged blobs, plants with a rounded but irregular silhouette. Most of these are bold of leaf, giving them a pleasing solidity that can anchor flimsier plants. In shady spots, the willow gentian, *Gentiana asclepiadea*, makes tumbling mounds like green waterfalls, each leaf node bearing a bright blue trumpet in late summer and fall. Broad hostas are also effective balancers, such as the great, golden 'Sum and Substance', which makes rounded mounds a good yard across when well suited, or blue-gray 'Krossa Regal', with its long corduroy hearts curving off tall, sturdy stalks. Near the front of a sunny border, lady's mantle, *Alchemilla mollis*, unpleats its fan-shaped leaves in solidly earth-bound hemispheres that are made even larger by the lax stems of fluffy green spangles that pass for flowers in this species. Though small, these blossoms dry well, and the curving sprays are always popular with flower arrangers. This is just as well, for only let a few stalks go to seed, and you will see tiny green fans winking up at you, with microscopic dew drops sparkling on every hairy leaflet, all over the entire garden. Large, scallop-leaved coralbells like ruddy *Heuchera villosa* or the popular hybrid 'Palace Purple' are equally steadfast, binding sheaves of tall daylilies or iris firmly to their side.

ling discovered by Edith Eddleman) is equally upright, and carries its thousands of tiny, baby pink stars well into autumn. Many of the true asters make splendid verticals at the border's back, notably *Aster novi-belgii* 'Climax', six to eight feet of deep green foliage covered in fall with periwinkle blue flowers (white in the form 'White Climax'), and the unknown species sold as 'Latest of All', which gets to ten feet in good soil, and brightens the last days of autumn with its cascades of deep purple flowers.

A few very tall perennials merit a forward position, where they will weave a see-through scrim through which the border may be viewed. Airy pen-

Anything similarly bottom heavy and weighty in effect will serve to keep skybound companions grounded. It is interesting to note that these plants succeed best in their role in informal borders, while smoother, more regularly shaped shrublets or mounding grasses do not. Their place is in formal borders, where the plants are not required to meld, but almost to keep their distance from one another. Plants with informal symmetry are sympathetic in form both with their perennial partners and the woody plants around them. Their very irregularity wakens subtle, barely perceptible echos of outline that help bind the various elements of the natural or informal border into unity.

Perhaps the majority of perennials are rounded, smooth-edged plants, many of which read as an unbroken whole, flowers and all. Unrelieved by more interesting shapes, smooth blobs of this sort make for bland looking borders with boring topography. This simple shape is often predominant in herb gardens, and in those roadside strip plantings sometimes scorned as "bun and bump" gardens. However, the fault lies in placement, not in the plants themselves, and it is the garden maker's job to learn how to use this common shape to advantage. Mounding perennial herbs like golden marjoram or oregano will rise like rough stones between cornlike sheaves of an apricot-colored daylily 'Three Bars' and the whorling leaves of peachy *Alstroemeria* 'Ligtu Hybrids'. *Nepeta mussinii*, the border catmint, has a marked tendency to shapelessness, but plants sheared in midspring will form tight, smooth mounds which soften, yet hold their shape, when decked with their deep blue summer flowers. Mounded catmints are not especially interesting on their own, but tucked between dwarf shrubs and edging perennials, they repeat in pleasing rounds down a lengthy stretch of border, and placed deeper in the border, they will marry taller perennials with incompatible hues or temper harsh, modern colors. Catmints also make memorable duets with the stacked, moonlight yellow plates and silver lace foliage of *Achillea taygetea*, or the pink and gilt brushes of squirrel's tail grass, *Hordeum jubatum*.

The rough, wrinkled gray velvet leaves of horehound, *Marrubium vulgare*, look lumpish when crowded between large border plants, but its big, silvery hummocks make a striking counterpoint between lax tumbles of midnight purple *Sedum* 'Vera Jameson' and a salmony native catchfly, *Lychnis cognata*. If smooth mounders are big enough, they become character plants in their own right, but only when given sufficient room and good company. A well grown clump of *Aster* × *frikartii* can be five feet high and an easy eight across. Crammed into a billowy border, it is a mere lump of lovely color. Set off with a purple-leaved *Rosa glauca* behind shaggy headed red 'Rubine' brussels sprouts at the side, the aster is transformed into a great, unbroken curve of blossom sandwiched dramatically between the more complicated shapes of its companions.

Big, crinkled leaves of Heuchera *'Palace Purple' are comfortingly earthbound, stabilizing the uprising shoots of fuzzy gray* Ballota pseudodictamnus. *Author's garden. Photo: Mark Lovejoy*

The most satisfying combinations work on several levels. Achillea taygetea *and an oversized catmint,* Nepeta 'Six Hills Giant', *are complementary in form, texture, and color, and both plants perform over an extended period. Author's garden. Photo: Mark Lovejoy*

Perennial billowers are another common form which needs thoughtful handling to give of its best. These puffy plants quickly become indefinite when massed, but used more sparingly, they can counterbalance bolder shapes and set off angular ones with their softness. Many are excellent succession plants which fill in awkward gaps left by earlier bloomers. The old-fashioned favorite, baby's breath (*Gypsophila paniculata*), forms a frail bubble of blossom three feet across that contrasts well with the spiky foliage of *Kniphofia caulescens* or the ruddy stalks and coarse leaves of ruby kale. Where baby's breath grows well, it is an ideal follow-up for Oriental poppies, which, though enchanting in early summer, become sprawling disasters by July. I used

to think the cats had been fighting in them until I noticed the same effect in gardens without pets. Those frustrated by the poppy's nasty ways will be heartened to hear that, as soon as it begins to topple, poppy foliage can be cut back hard. It will soon be back, forming a modest and tidy mound. In the meantime, gypsophila placed beside or in front of the poppies will obligingly spill its pink or white seafoam into their former airspace. Our native hippo spurge, the white-flowered *Euphorbia corollata*, does much the same thing, and has the advantage of tolerating the acid soils which the gypsophila detests. Giant woodruff, *Galium aristatum*, is another baby's breath lookalike that not only tolerates heavy and acid soils, but offers the further advantage of blooming well in partial or filtered shade. Though not the rampant aggressor its ground cover cousin is, *G. aristatum* spreads fairly quickly, forming a tidy, ruffled carpet that bulks up by midsummer into a yard-high mass of airy stems and tiny, long-lasting white flowers.

Taller billowers play a protective role, drawing a kindly curtain across parts of the border that are in seasonal transition and performing an engaging entr'acte to distract our eyes from the temporary disarray. Meadow rues (*Thalictrum* species) make attractive thunderheads spun of netted, thready stems and tiny flowers. The tallest of them are scrim plants extraordinaire, screening all that lies behind them in a floral haze. *Thalictrum rochebrunianum*, whether the straight species or the fine garden form 'Lavender Mist', can exceed seven feet in deep, humus-rich soils, and will flower equally well in full sun or dappled shade. Quite similar, but more delicately crafted, is the Chinese *T. delavayi*. This lovely thing reaches six feet in a sheltered position, where it will open expansive panicles of warm lavender (or clean white in the form 'Album') above fluttering, blue-green foliage. A warm, lilac-purple form, 'Hewitt's Double', blooms a bit later, arriving in mid-August to accompany *Aster* × *frikartii* 'Monch' and the shrubby, blue-flowered *Clematis heracleifolia*. *Thalictrum flavum glaucum* (also sold as *T. speciosissimum*) makes lacy five-foot columns of steely blue foliage that set off their puffy bursts of chalk yellow flowers to perfection.

Certain perennials have enough presence to qualify as architectural, even sculptural plants which anchor and focus softer mounds and masses. Globe thistles, *Echinops ritro* 'Taplow Blue', with their needle-studded flower balls poised on long stalks like so many vegetable maces, have a strong garden presence. Even when out of bloom, their great, toothed leaves, rich green backed with gray, rise powerfully amid shrubby looking peony foliage and grassy day-lilies. Bear's breeches, *Acanthus mollis*, with its thick mounds of long, jagged leaves, easily dominates a borderful of smaller foliage, even without its head-high stems full of tubular, mauvy flowers. A hardier species, *A. m. latifolius*, boasts broader, glossier foliage that makes up for its unwillingness to bloom.

The chimney bellflower, Campanula pyramidalis, *is an ardent, long blooming perennial which tolerates a wide variety of sites and situations. Behind it spills a cloud of giant woodruff,* Galium aristatum, *a good substitute for baby's breath* (Gyposphila elegans) *in heavy, acid soils. Author's garden. Photo: Mark Lovejoy*

Both of these plants are best reserved for borders where an extra five or six square feet of ground space can readily be spared. Elsewhere, the compact *A. spinosus* will be preferred, despite the extreme prickliness of its narrower foliage. Its cousin *A. s. spinosissimus*, has even more dissected foliage, armed with truly ferocious spines that make weeding around it a memorable experience. This form is much sought after by collectors, but it must be considered a curiosity rather than a great garden plant, for it is the least effective of the family.

Another prickly clan, the sea hollies, make natural garden sculptures, their thistlelike flower heads surrounded by blue-and-silver bracts that suggest Elizabethan ruffs or a jester's ragged points. Picnickers on European beaches take care not to sit near the dune sea holly, *Eryngium maritimum*, broad and many branched, and covered with the widest of gun metal gray bracts above spiny, bluish leaves. The stiff, spiky rosettes of our native rattlesnake master, *E. yuccifolium*, do indeed mimic gray-blue yuccas, though the flowers that open in small sprays above their four-foot stems look more like frosted white thistles than the open, creamy bells of true yuccas. The South American *E. agavifolium* has stout basal leaves like spined daggers, and its odd, knobbly flowers clustered along lanky stems look like punk art constructs amid washes of lush leaves and frothy flowers. Biggest and bluest of the bunch is *E. alpinum* 'Superbum', a magnificent midborder plant with rounded basal leaves and stiffly branching stems, each tipped with a plump blue thimble encircled with lacy metal fretwork of cobalt and silver. There are several other beautiful garden forms, including 'Opal', with shimmering lavender-blue bracts, and 'Blue Star', stained a deep night sky blue. Though smaller than its bold relatives, *E. varifolium* is just as forceful, thanks to splendid branching sprays of starry, glittering blue-and-silver flowers. Any of these swashbuckling sea hollies will shake up a tame planting of border debutantes to lastingly delightful effect.

Big, potently shaped foliage can have as much impact as a mass of flowers, and some perennials would qualify as focal points even if they never bloomed at all. The oversized gray velour leaves of *Verbascum* 'Silver Candelabra' effortlessly wrest pride of place from far showier bloomers, forming fat cabbages some five feet across, each great leaf embossed with deep silver veins. In midsummer, the multibranched, five- or six-foot bloom stalks carry innumerable, upright spikes of soft yellow flowers that light up the garden like so many flaming candles. The South African honeybush, *Melianthus major*, outshines many a brazen bloomer with the sheer magnificence of its glistening silver-blue foliage, huge and sawtoothed. In Zone 9 or 10, it is an evergreen shrub ten or twelve feet high, bloom-ing in late winter or early spring. Where winter lows seldom drop to zero degrees F, the honeybush acts like a perennial, rising late in spring and opening its shaggy oxblood red flower plumes in August. (Honeybush is hardiest in a sunny, sheltered position and in rich but well-drained soils.) Statuesque *Phlomis russeliana*, with its curving angel wing foliage and tall, tiered blossom stalks, can settle a restless bed, as will a shapely behemoth, *Salvia involucrata* 'Bethelii'. A much better plant than the straight species, the long, pointed leaves of this form may be over a foot long, stemmed and veined in magenta. Its sinuous arms are long and lax, and wiggle through and behind neighboring plants, so that their enormous flower spikes of shocking fuchsia pink appear in astonishing juxtapositions, now laced through a slumbering weigela, now scrambling up the ropy stems of a purple grape, aflame at summer's end. In general, distinctive perennials display to best advantage as singletons, or in well spaced groups of three, so their power is not diminished by clutter. These and similarly bold perennials are excellent transition plants, reconciling soft-edged ephemerals with the dominant shapes of evergreen shrubs and trees.

THE ART OF COMBINATIONS

Perennials have many attributes that earn them a solid place in mixed borders, and color is just one of them. Contriving entrancing color combinations is as genuine an art form as painting on canvas, though fraught with even more challenge, and far harder to control. Strong North American sunlight can wash out pastels that sparkle under cooler skies. Quixotic weather might retard bloom in one plant but not in its companion. A warm spring may bring several months' worth of flowers into bloom all at once. Differences of soil pH or trace elements can alter petal coloration (as can many other environmental factors), throwing off the color values in a careful combination. Colorists court failure with every attempt at color sequencing, coaxing numerous different plants to bloom in a (hopefully) unbroken chain of color. Good art is always a risk, however, and it is nobler to fail spectacularly than never to try at all.

To improve the odds, we must undergo a kind of apprenticeship that prepares us to paint well with perennials. Before artists begin to develop their own personal styles, they study the basic materials and techniques with which pictures are made. Free experimentation is a valuable part of the training, for only by testing and trying things without preconceptions can we discover overlooked or unconsidered possibilities. Plants, too, must be studied this way, as raw materials with variable qualities and characteristics, before they can be used to fullest effect. Artists are often encouraged to train eye and hand by copying the work of past masters, not in order to emulate them, but to understand the process by which those great paintings were made.

When we weave our own borders, we certainly don't have to copy the successes of others, but unless we understand how they came about, it may take a long, long time before we enjoy lasting and encompassing successes of our own. As in any art form, intuition counts for a great deal, but education is at least as valuable, providing solid, reliable tools that work where intuition may not. We should, indeed, aim to express our own personal aesthetic, but when the process is at least partially conscious, rather than entirely accidental, things move forward a good deal quicker. When we are equally familiar with our plants and the mechanics of our own taste, we are truly prepared to paint in living color, with perennials for pigment.

Taste is not necessarily the established factor it might seem, for it is subject to change, and in most of us it is but poorly understood in the first place. This is very natural, for in general it is enough for us to know that we like or dislike something. We only need more information when we are trying to create something personally pleasing. At that point, we need to know the ins and outs of our own taste, not just what we like, but what we like about it. Quite often, our tastes are complex; we admire more than one kind of pattern, more than a handful of colors. What we need is not an exhaustive catalog of likes and dislikes, but a deeper understanding of the categories they fit into. I, for instance, dislike mushy, vague compositions, and prefer cleaner-edged ones, in which every plant plays a specific part. On the other hand, I am made uncomfortable by tidy, sterile-looking plantings where each plant stands alone, neither meeting nor melding with the others. Then, too, I prefer a naive, haphazard garden made with love and unflagging interest to the best imitations of gardens that belong to other countries and cultures. These are the building blocks of my garden taste, and would-be border builders need to understand their own such predilections, even before thinking about color.

Our taste in color would seem a simpler matter, yet it, too, has its subtle points. It is not enough to know we like blue and orange—which blue? which orange?—or even to say we prefer cool colors to hot ones. We need to understand the way we like our main colors tempered, whether by secondary hues that are deepened with a touch of black, as when pure red is stepped down to ember and ruddy ash, or softened with white, in a run of ever-lighter pinks. Sometimes we want both effects, looking for grayed pastels to tone down strong, clear colors. Moreover, we are apt to prefer certain effects in sunny spots, and others in shade. Some people dislike seeing hot, heavy colors in shady spots, but love them in sun. They must remember to choose their plants, not only by color but by placement, avoiding red and black lobelia hybrids or coppery orange *Ligularia dentata* 'Othello' even though they admire the plants themselves. Others may like bold, primary colors in a hot spot, but want to see clear pastels in shade. Some of us want crescendos, cool colors building to hot ones, while others like unbroken washes of colors with a consistent value. We may prefer brilliant mardi-gras gardens, or restrained affairs of blue and green and gray. A few people prefer even subtler color effects, weaving complex foliage tapestries in which flowers play a very minor role.

Color themes are a useful tool for the border artist, particularly those whose love of plants gets out of hand. Where indiscriminate plantings do not add up to satisfying pictures, it helps enormously to rearrange them according to simplifying themes. Even in a small garden, separate parts of the border may be designated for hot and cool colors, with transitional shades worked in between. Where space permits, single-color borders are wonderful fun. White gardens have been popular for decades now, and there is no reason why we can't create similar havens for peach or salmon or yellow or blue flowers, if that is our pleasure. Some collectors get a tremendous kick out of rainbow beds, often circular in shape, with flowers and foliage carefully graded by spectral hue and integrated with shade and tint. Sunset borders may hold hot, heavy colors, while twilight gardens can feature the lavenders, blues, and creamy yellows that are so effective at dusk. A frilly pink and white border would suit a Victorian house trimmed with lacy white gingerbread, while a sleek modern condo could stand up to a sassy red and purple and black one.

The obvious way to begin planning a color theme border is by choosing pairs and trios of plants that bloom in colors you like together. However, it is important to keep both eyes and minds open, for very often the obvious is not enough. Basic combinations like blue, white, and yellow can look disconcertingly harsh, while a pink and silver one may look pallid rather than interestingly pale. Optimal assistance may come from unsuspected sources, for as any artist knows, the world is full of strange and complex colors. I remember having a trendy hairpiece made as a teenager and discovering with amazement that my strawberry blond hair had as much green and beige in it as red and copper. Similarly, portrait painters find smudgy green shadows and muddy ecru highlights in the loveliest of faces. Color theory considers complementary colors to be those opposite each other on the color wheel—red and green, purple and yellow, orange and blue— pairings that contrast very strongly. When gardeners talk about colors being complementary, we usually mean they bring out attractive qualities in each other. A well known art school challenge proves instructive here; students are directed to mix up the ugliest colors they can muster, then told to find out how to use those colors beautifully. Many off shades, not prepossessing in themselves, may prove a necessary ingredient in a complex composition, balancing a trenchant color, clarifying a murky one, or amplifying a retiring shade you want to lift into

Most people enjoy combinations which offer gentle contrasts of color. Here, the Siberian iris and columbines have equivalent color values, resulting in a quiet harmony. Garden of Daphne Stewart, Bainbridge Island, Washington. Photo: Mark Lovejoy

prominence. Some of the more boring shades of pink and blue are extremely useful in this regard, as are oddball pastels like chalky salmon or violet or lemon, colors that manage to be both vivid and pale.

As we grow more ambitious about border painting, we may begin to welcome colors that we previously ignored or deliberately excluded. Just as there are no bad plants, only poorly placed ones, there are really no bad colors. Part of the education of a garden maker is learning to appreciate the worth of every color. It is also important to look past our own preconceptions about what we enjoy looking at. Those who think they hate pink and yellow, or purple and orange, may well admire precisely those combinations when presented in subtle tints and complex groupings. Pairing magenta pink *Geranium psilostemon* and mustard yellow *Achillea* 'Gold Plate' gives quite a different effect from matching the starry, shell pink pincushions of *Astrantia major* with the chalk yellow pokers of *Kniphofia* 'Little Maid', or the rosy pink of *Sedum* 'Autumn Joy' and the greenish yellow of *Phygelius* 'Yellow Trumpet'. Purple and orange do tend to conjure images of Easter eggs or sixties dresses, yet in a border employing an extended range of hues and well matched color values, this combination can be highly attractive.

Few gardeners appreciate magenta, yet when tempered with ashy, gray-tinted colors, its beauties become obvious. A hybrid form of the common European terrestrial orchid, Dactylorhiza, with Rodgersia pinnata 'Superba' at the Royal Botanic Garden, Edinburgh. Photo: Peter Ray

Purple includes colors from near black to strong lavender, while orange can mean citrus or copper, chalky peach or vivid salmon, warm apricot, or tangerine sherbet. My own purple-and-orange border holds not blobs of grape jelly and orange peel, but dozens of colors, both subtle and bold, and intermingled with foliage in many greens as well as cream and butter, sage and olive, steel blue and muddy red. It doesn't please everybody—and there's no reason why it should—but it often provokes a surprised compliment from visitors who had never thought to admire those particular colors before. Magenta is a much maligned color which strikes fear in timid hearts, yet it can win those same hearts if cleverly partnered. Put snapping magenta 'Sheer Madness' petunias between shocking pink dahlias and flat orange calendulas and watch your visitors cringe in distaste. Back that same petunia with black hollyhocks and cool pink and white *Lavatera thuringiaca* 'Barnsley', front it down with ashy pink masterworts (*Astrantia major* 'Rosea') and slate blue catmint, *Nepeta* 'Blue Beauty', and it will be almost universally admired. (Nothing I know of is truly universally admired.)

The trick to combining colors successfully is to expand our working palette, going beyond the basics to take advantage of all the thousands of intermediary shades. Obvious pairings can be perfectly successful; few people will quibble about a match between rose-pink and silver-gray, or clear blue and citrus yellow. However, the obvious and easy can also become boring over time, especially when repeated in every garden book one sees. Sooner or later, the advancing gardener is apt to outgrow the bland security offered by timid pastels and want to explore new country. No sooner do we venture past those reassuring pastels than we find ourselves up to our necks in possibilities. Happily for us, the world is full of color and form and scent and texure. No matter how elevated a gardener you become, there are always more plants to know and learn to use well. Garden artists are the luckiest folk of all, for their canvas may be endlessly repainted, their palette constantly renewed.

To get that extended palette to work its potential magic in our own borders, we must recognize what

REMEDIAL PASTELS—*Pretty Pastels* *This typical border holds a pastel melange of perennials with a few bulbs and annuals. Though pretty all summer, the border offers little interest in spring and fall and none at all in winter.*

Shrubs: Lavatera thuringiaca *'Barnsley*; **Perennials:** Achillea millefolium *'Lavender Beauty'*, Alchemilla mollis, Artemisia stelleriana *'Silver Brocade'*, Campanula lactiflora, C. persicifolia *'Alba'*, Catananche caerulea *'Blue Giant'*, Chrysanthemum superbum *'Alaska'*, Geranium × oxonianum *'Claridge Druce'*, Hemerocallis *'Angel of Light'*, Nepeta *'Blue Beauty'*, Phlox paniculata *'Bright Eyes'*, Scabiosa caucasica *'Blue Perfection'*, Thalictrum aquilegifolium; ***Annuals:*** Cosmos bipinnatus, Campanula carpatica *'White Clips'* (half-hardy perennial); ***Bulbs:*** Gladiolus *'Impressive'*, Lilium *'Casa Blanca'*.

artists refer to as color values. Those safe and proven pastel combinations always work because all the colors are of the same value; they have the same relative weight. What this means is that delicate, baby pink is balanced and not extinguished by baby blue, though it would be visually erased by cobalt. Even colors that generally look nice together, like pink and purple, can destroy each other if their relative values are off. Put a shell pink phlox next to a rich, midnight purple one and both plants look terrible. Change the pink for rose, or trade the purple for lavender, and both plants are enhanced. Color

theory as it relates to gardening is a complex topic (treated in thorough and telling detail by Penelope Hobhouse in her masterwork, *Color in Your Garden*), however, a brief summary may clarify its main, practical points. What artists call "hue" is the color itself; red or green, blue or yellow, orange or purple. Most colors are really a mixture of two or three others—what we call loosely "red" might be tomato or cherry, while "purple" might be a blend of reddish blue tinged with green, like a leaf of purple smokebush. "Value" is the degree of that color, whether paled by white into a tint, or deepened with

Potent Pastels *Transformed into a mixed border, the planting gains form and year round presence. Its gentle color scheme gains considerable impact when its chalky tints are supplemented with deeper shades of the same colors. The additional plants are:* **Trees:** *Weeping apple (*Malus *'Red Jade');* **Evergreen shrubs:** Kalmia latifolia, Pieris japonica, Leucothoe fontanesiana *'Scarletta';* **Deciduous shrubs:** *Fothergilla gardenii 'Blue Mist',* Rosa *'Reine des Violettes';* **Perennials:** *Aster novi-belgii 'Ada Ballard',* Echinops ritro *'Taplow Blue',* Geranium cinereum *'Ballerina',* G. psilostemon, Thalictrum aquilegifolium *'Thundercloud';* **Annuals/biennials:** *Black hollyhocks (*Alcea rosea *'Nigra');* **Bulbs:** *Acidanthera murielae,* Lilium *'Pink Perfection';* **Vines:** *Clematis 'Hagley Hybrid',* Ipmoea purpurea *'Kniola's Purple-Black' (annual);* **Grasses:** *Hordeum jubatum (annual),* Pennisetum *'Burgundy Giant' (half-hardy perennial);* **Ground covers:** *Coleus varieties (annual), polka-dot plant (*Hypoestes phyllostachya *(annual)).*

black into a shade. High values are light and luminous colors, while low values are dim and subfusc. The intensity of a color refers to its saturation, or weight. Spectral colors are pure, completely saturated and of high intensity. A pastel red can be of high intensity, as in the daylily 'Vermilion Clouds', while a strong red, like that on the back of a rhubarb leaf, is of low intensity, because it is tempered by a good deal of gray or black.

When colorists speak of hot, heavy colors, they mean strongly pigmented colors in the warm end of the color spectrum—reds, oranges, golden yellows, and purples. Cool, light colors are their opposites; a soft tint of clear citrus yellow, say, or sky blue. Green is neutral, the garden equivalent of beige, because it goes with everything. Many a harsh color is tempered by surrounding greenery, just as a retiring color may be boosted to prominence by its foliar companions. The texture of a leaf, whether matte or reflective, can affect the color value of the

Odd shades and muted colors are excellent palette extenders, gentling vivid shades and waking up dull ones. Gaillardia *'Burgundy' is one of the best, blooming from early until late, and as lovely in bud as in flower. The tall mahogany plant,* Sedum maximum *'Atropurpureum Honeysong', is another good mixer, its dark stems and rosy flowers complementing blues, reds, and purples or coppers, bronzes, and golds with equal eclat. Author's garden. Photo: Mark Lovejoy*

flowers it accompanies every bit as much as its own shade of green. Soft yellows, whether creamy or greenish, buffy or chalky, are almost universally useful blenders, but white is tricky, for though it sparks up a high valued combination, it will break up a low valued one distractingly. The importance of color values is not technical but practical; they help us figure out why certain combinations work, or teach us how to remedy those that fail. When brash colors clash, we can look for cooling solutions

among their analog shades, dimming their fire with calming, cousinly colors. When pastel mixtures prove dull, we can give them zest by spiking the mix with more intense hues of the same colors, or by adding hotter, contrasting colors, then bridging the gaps with intermediate shades.

In the garden, successful combinations often result when complementary contrasts are tempered with plenty of secondary and tertiary shades. If a blue-and-orange combination—perhaps of calendulas and cobalt blue pansies—comes off as harsh or insistent, an infusion of yellows will mellow the effect, particularly when some of the yellows used are as strong in value as the central blue, while others are milder and softer. A small amount of white will clarify and add sparkle to our group, while a lot will significantly lower its visual temperature. Now most of our colors are high and bright, making a gay but still rather flat composition. To add depth, we introduce a number of related blues; slate and French blues, ocean blue and muted midnight. These brother blues will moderate the electricity of the cobalt, toning down any tendency to harshness. Next we add sherbet oranges, peach, and chalky salmon to link the crayon orange to the gentling yellows. What we have now is no longer an obvious pairing, but a color run, a textile term used by weavers and knitters to describe their extended color palettes.

Transitions between border sections with incompatible color themes are also worked this way, incrementally and in graded steps of color. Intermediate colors, including lots of greenery, can forge visual links that reduce jarring clashes to stimulating contrasts. In my kitchen border (overlooked by the big kitchen window), an elderly shrub, *Weigela florida*, opens its warm pink blossoms in May, just in time to skirmish unpleasantly for pride of place with the deepening copper and red-gold of *Spiraea × bumalda* 'Gold Flame'. The colors are utterly unsympathetic to each other, and the shrubs only ten feet apart, so this is not a disagreement that can easily be overlooked. Foliage provides the first buffer, with strong vertical accents coming from tall species iris and stalks of late-blooming lilies. Blue rue, sage, and lavender quietly divide the scrapping pair, while more positive transitions are worked with colors sympathetic to both pink and warm yellow. Bronze fennel looks richly metallic behind the spirea, yet takes on purplish shadows near the weigela. The yellowy green flowers of cushion spurge, *Euphorbia polychroma*, and the creamy yellow-and-green leaves of *Euonymos fortunei* 'Silver Queen' strengthen the ties woven by foliage greenery, and echo the spirea's gold in moderating, yellower tints. Wine-purple and warm blues work equally well with the coppery gold and the strong pink, so tall columbines in these colors are woven throughout the group, and a haze of forget-me-nots clouds the lower reaches of both shrubs. Certain murky reds can also swing both ways, complementing warm pink as nicely as they do red-gold, and the backdrop of red sand cherry, *Prunus* × *cistena*, and purple smokebush, *Cotinus coggygria* 'Velvet Cloak', serves to further unify the border.

The result of these transitional plantings is surprisingly harmonic, leading the eye in convincing steps from one color run to the other without any visual jolts. In a new border, the potential for strife could have been eliminated more simply by replacing the pink weigela with 'Java Red', which has purple leaves and red flowers. In this case, however, the weigela is a venerable one that fit very nicely into the border scheme as it was first conceived. When I first assembled this border, all its components were pink and purple or blue. However, as so often happens, the border gradually altered as I started playing with new colors. Before I knew it consciously, that tasteful pink and purple had become a fascinating and far more complex run of copper, bronze, and purple, with a good deal of blue and red in it. I do have a 'Java Red' weigela tucked away in a nursery bed, and in another year, it will be large enough to replace the elderly pink shrub. Though planning ahead might have avoided this particular situation, it is a good example of the way gardens are apt to change, and a reminder that a knack for making effective transition plantings will prove at least as valuable as one for putting together enticing combinations.

Artful gardeners are often asked how they come up with border combinations. Some, of course, are planned on paper, but even more are spontaneous, inspired by a garden visit or a new acquisition. Many border colorists get ideas from a popular matching game, like plant lotto, in which possible combinations are bandied about by the contestants. A breathtaking combination will trigger a round of matchmaking, with each person trying to top the previous suggestion, and everybody goes home with a headful of ideas to play with. Seeing a mat of creeping *Acena* 'Blue Haze' beneath dark leaves of *Lobelia* 'Happy Returns' in a friend's garden made

Many combinations are based on color, but the best give equal importance to contrasts of shape and texture. In the Withey/ Price garden, the variegated Phlox paniculata *'Nora Leigh' is paired with a foamy, periwinkle blue everlasting (*Statice *species) which picks up the rather pallid pink of the phlox's flowers and disguises its sparsely furnished knees. Photo: Peter Ray*

me realize how well it would lift the black leaves of *Ophiopogon planiscapus* 'Dark Knight' or the dim bulb *Ranunculus ficaria* 'Brazen Hussy', with leaves so dark as to be dirt colored, into prominence. Another friend's combination of the yellow-leaved *Caryopteris* 'Worcester Gold' with a golden *Carex elata* 'Knightshayes' and *Geranium wallichianum* 'Buxton's Blue' inspired me to underplant my 'Worcester Gold' with vivid tufts of *Deschampsia flexuosa* 'Tatra Gold' and *Veronica prostrata* 'Trehane', a low grower with similarly golden leaves and blue flowers. Excellent partnerships may be suggested by small details we notice when we carefully study our plants. Many flowers have golden eyes or creamy yellow throats that we can echo effectively with similarly colored companions. Stalk and stem are often tinted pink or red or purple, which may be matched more subtly in background and ground-cover plants. Where minor colors are too strong to repeat pleasingly, replace them with pastel tints or use stepped down shades of the same color. Such details don't radically alter the overall effect of a composition, but they add depth and polish, just as lovely earrings or a jazzy hanky lend finish to an incomplete ensemble.

Some of the very happiest combinations evolve from chance juxtapositions in the nursery bed, which has to rank among the colorist's most useful tools. All new and unfamiliar plants find an immediate home here, rather than straying into the border proper before we really know how to place them well. A good nursery bed also holds garden staples, plants that could be worked into nearly any color scheme. Mine holds a good number of daylilies, which I collect by the dozen, because when I need specific colors to round out a preplanned scheme, daylilies are very apt to provide the perfect shade of tomato red or pewter or salmon or plum. Since catalog descriptions (and indeed, personal interpretations of color) vary a good bit, it's a good idea to visit daylily nurseries to choose with your own eyes. I also make a point of buying nearly every interesting plant I see, because you never know when it might be available again, and it can always find a temporary home in the nursery bed. At season's end, when perennials are marked down to bargain prices, I buy extras of favorite all-purpose filler plants; purple sage (*Salvia officinalis* 'Purpurea') with dull purple leaves that go with everything, floppy rose and purple *Sedum* 'Vera Jameson', dark red *Gaillardia* 'Burgundy'. (Years ago, when my garden was a sea of silver and pastels, my staples were artemisias, clary sages (*Salvia sclarea*), and white-variegated hostas.) This way, whenever I want to share a good workhorse plant, freshen up or rearrange a combination, or replace a winter casualty, there are plenty of options right at hand to choose among.

Most of us begin building combinations in pairs, using flower color as our first criterion, then gradually working in texture and form. As our skills increase, success with simple combinations encourages us to attempt more challenging ones. Each triumph increases our confidence; we begin to ask more of our combinations, and learn how to get it. We manage to pull off longer lasting pictures, matching trios and quartets. These develop into vignettes, the striking, complex combintions that make a garden memorable. Few people leave a garden marveling over its hedges: it is the sight of pale yellow 'Prairie Moon' peonies tumbled with a sheaf of creamy *Clematis recta* 'Purpurea', underplanted with blue hostas and overhung by a gray leaved *Rosa glauca* that lingers long in the memory. Such groups may become the core of a whole border section, with each component linking to neighboring plantings. At their best, such vignettes encompass contrasts of plant form and flower color, of leaf size and pattern, with the main flower tints being echoed by underplantings as well as matching outright with those of secondary players.

For the smitten colorist, the creating of combinations must rank among the most satisfying of the lively arts. No matter how advanced or experienced we grow, there is always more to learn, more to attempt, more to pursue. The very process of growth and education contributes largely to our pleasure, yet wise gardeners rely less on rules and color charts than on discovering the full scope of their personal taste. No matter how refined or effete, no genuine expression of taste will ever succeed in pleasing everybody, but it is enough if they please us. To be right, our color combinations need only be made with conviction and delight, and, like folk art, they will have the strength of authenticity.

Some of the best combinations arise when we study our flowers with care, discovering hidden tints and shades. 'Apricot Beauty' tulips are not only apricot, but contain sherbet orange, salmon, bronze, and dull red, as well as buttery yellow and green. By choosing companions in any of these colors, we can emphasize the tints we prefer and subdue those we dislike, or combine them all in a complex color run. Photo: Mark Lovejoy

Annual squirrel tail grass, Hordeum jubatum, *spills its pink and gold feathers through a tumble of catmint,* Nepeta 'Six Hills Giant'. *Given the chance to ripen its seed, it self-sows reliably each year. Author's garden. Photo: Mark Lovejoy*

Chapter Six

ANNUALS AND BIENNIALS IN THE MIXED BORDER

*M*ixed borders are gardens of permanence, intended for long-term enjoyment. Their planning and making may take a year or many years (depending on how much pleasure one takes in process). In either case, their polished maturity belongs to the future; mixed border makers soon learn to reckon progress by decades as well as days. Annuals, evanescent creatures that complete their life cycle in a single season, and biennials, with only double the life span, might not seem to belong in such a setting. For a variety of reasons, they don't command a noticeable amount of respect in horticultural circles. Serious gardeners are often rather scornful of annuals, associating them with the gaudy, mass produced floral gewgaws found in supermarkets and low end garden centers. Annuals are widely touted as quick-fix plants for busy people. To neophytes leery of long-term commitments, annuals are presented as idiot-proof, toss-away plants. Impatient gardeners are urged to make an instant splash with them. Annuals brighten the summer rental cottage, the vegetable patch, the sidewalk strip. If annuals are ever recommended for border work, it is generally to fill spaces reserved for the eventual needs of youthful perennials.

That is an unquestionably valuable role, particularly in mixed borders, where the young woody plants demand ample space all to themselves if they are to develop properly. However, short-lived annuals and biennials have strengths that earn them, in their own right, a secure place in some of the world's oldest and most distinguished mixed border gardens. Annuals are famous for adaptability and endurance. There are appropriate annuals for any climate, any soil, any situation. Their floral persistence makes them the backbone of the cutting garden, and it is worth noting that varieties which last well as cut flowers will also be lastingly productive in the garden. Besides coming in every imaginable color and shade—including some better left unimagined—annuals offer a range of textures unsuspected by casual nursery browsers. The silver lace of fine-cut dusty millers; the broad leaves, like velvet-napped hearts, of fruit sage (*Salvia dorisiana*); the ruffled and veined foliage of scented geraniums; the wiry, netted mounds of 'Irish Lace' marigolds (*Tagetes filifolia*) bring refreshing textural variety to the border. Though the average bedding plant is not especially shapely, annuals can vary as much in form and size as in color. Fast growing castor beans (*Ricinus communis*) and annual hibiscus (*Hibiscus manihot*) fill their spaces as effectively as a good-sized shrub. The biennial sea holly called Miss Wilmott's ghost (*Eryngium giganteum*) and the magnificently prickly dyer's teasel (*Dipsacus fullonum*) are dramatically sculptural. No fragrance garden would be complete without annual sweet peas, honey-scented alyssum, the purple leaved heliotrope that smells of ripe plums. Sunny days awaken the mysterious, stirring perfume of mignonette as warm summer nights call forth the elusive violet scent of sweet rocket and the sumptuous, teasing scents of flowering tobaccos, stocks, and evening primroses.

With such a catalog of virtues, ardent gardeners would want to grow these plants no matter what difficulties were involved. Happily, annuals and biennials are by and large an unassuming lot, responding to the simplest care with exuberant, long lasting gratitude. Even those with briefer bloom and decided cultural preferences can become border mainstays if we consider their quirks as strengths rather than drawbacks. In the cool Northwest where I garden, tropical heat lovers like zinnias and hibiscus rarely perform with the zest they show where summers are hotter. However, spring wildflowers like farewell-to-spring (*Clarkia* species) and baby blue eyes (*Nemophila*) that bloom only briefly in their native California may do so for months in Seattle, where even summer temperatures are relatively low. Despite the lack of heat, the Northwest seldom enjoys significant rainfall between May and October, so prairie dwellers—and even some desert flowers—which dislike excess summer water may grow nicely in our dry gardens. Shy woodlanders that demand shade and shelter in hot climates revel in the open under our overcast skies, their gentle tints emphasized by the pearly gray atmosphere that local painters call "oyster light."

In gardens where summer heat is fiercer, extending into sultry nights, equatorial exotics that only sulk in my garden will bloom with generous abandon. In southerly gardens, trailing browalias, snapdragon vine (*Asarina* species or cultivars like the rosy 'Victoria Falls'), nasturtiums, and the *Abelmoschus* Mischief series (a hibiscus relative) begin to blossom a month before my plants do. Given the accumulated hours of heat they crave, such annuals may ripen their seed and sow themselves into persistent colonies as they never would for me. Many heat loving tropical annuals demand a good deal of supplemental water if they are to remain productive over many months, making them less attractive choices where summer watering is restricted. However, annual dryland flowers like portulaca, spider-

flower (*Cleome*) and gilia hybrids (*Leptosiphon*) will thrive and bloom in those hotter gardens despite drought. As long as we don't make the mistake of trying to grow the same things no matter which part of the country we inhabit, annuals can be found to fill virtually any ecological niche, natural or otherwise. If annual asters and sand verbenas can bloom in the deserts of the Southwest, the reflected heat that makes summer deserts of tiny urban gardens will hardly daunt them. The same is the case for annuals which bloom in seaside gardens (such as blue daisied felicia, California poppies, and gazanias); they are often tolerant of both the drought and air pollution which plague many urban gardens. Where the usual tropicals don't grow well, look to native wildflowers or related genera for annuals which can appreciate what your garden has to offer.

Although annuals and biennials may be found in every kind of natural habitat, from sandy seasides to bogs to mountain meadows or stony, barren peaks, it isn't always so easy to find them through ordinary garden plant sources. Some are available as seed through large mail order catalogs such as Stokes or Thompson & Morgan. Specialty growers like Prairie Nursery and Plants of the Southwest offer plants and seeds of regional natives, often including annuals. Uncommon but gardenworthy annuals are frequently listed in the seed exchanges of various plant societies. However, unless you know what you are looking for, the unfamiliar Latin names rarely capture the eye of the casual catalog cruiser. In order to reap the cream of the harvest, a little educational research is required. This can begin at your own garden book shelf, but will probably expand to local and even regional libraries if you really get hooked. Many community libraries are part of larger networks, and if they have little to offer in their own collections, the librarians may be able to get specialty books for you through regional university or larger city libraries.

Once you begin looking for such information, it is interesting to find how seldom the provenance of a given plant is mentioned. Sometimes a country or geographic area will be indicated, but this can be of limited use when the area in question is geologically varied. "South America" might, after all,

Where summers are hot, bulbs and perennials may bloom and fade in a matter of days, leaving the garden short on color. Annuals carry on happily, taking heat and drought in stride, providing endless flows of blossoms in exchange for weekly deadheading. Fletcher garden, Los Angeles. Photo: Cynthia Woodyard

mean the high plains of Patagonia, the rain forest of the Mato Grosso, or the rocky slopes of the Andes. Most of the time, more exact information isn't really necessary, but at times, it makes the difference between success and failure. If we know, for instance, that a given plant is from South Africa, we may assume it will like a warm, dry position. A little more research, however, might tell us that it grows in boggy mountain meadows in South Africa, which is a different story all together.

When I first grew interested in raising uncommon annuals, I began gathering wildflower books from all over the world. Until recently, the pickings were slim, limited mostly to amateurish pamphlets or pithy tomes more heartwarming to the botanist than the gardener. However, the current popularity of meadow and wild gardens has improved the selection, and now one can find dozens of illustrated books, both regional and international in scope. Such a collection is a good resource, one which works two ways. When I first leaf through them, I write the name of any fetching creature that catches my attention on my wish list, from which I make up my plant and seed orders each year. Later, when I spot an intriguing annual in a catalog or seed list, I search out references for it. Sometimes I can't find an entry for the species I can get seed for, but by reading up on other members of the family, I get a good idea of what conditions the plants will enjoy.

Well illustrated seed catalogs can whet plant lust with glimpses of enticing unknowns from all over the world. Few, however, tell you much about their cultural requirements and dislikes. A simple dictionary of plant names can help, especially one which adds a few facts beyond the mere names. I like the one by Allen J. Coombes (published by Timber Press), which offers a bit of information on the source or meaning of the name, and gives the country of origin. Though nonspecific, this does present valuable clues. For instance, if a plant hails from New Zealand, I assume it will grace my garden for a few years, but be lost sooner or later to a harsh winter. If it comes from Japan, or China, chances are excellent that it will grow for me. The plant name itself may hold further clues, particularly when the specific refers to habitat. A little Latin is a help here, and there are plenty of good books on botanical Latin if you escaped school without learning any. After pawing through these primers, even the Latinless will have gathered that *rivularis* refers to streamside plants, that *maritima* means ocean or beach, *montanum* is for mountains, and anything *pratensis* is a meadow dweller. It doesn't hurt to similarly designate portions of your garden; here is the hot sun and reflected light of the oceanside, here, the dripping hose makes a constant bog (sometimes it's easier to roll with things than fix them . . .). Over here is a well-drained, gritty area that will do duty as a mountain scree, and here is the rich, evenly moist soil of the alluvial plain. By choosing flowers that enjoy the conditions they must face, we can make their environmental adaptations work to the advantage of our gardens.

These lessons absorbed, we can confidently place annuals like creeping zinnia, *Sanvitalia procumbens*, at the front of the border, guided as much by the Latin name as the common one. Toadflax, *Linaria maroccana*, a Moroccan wildflower, and *Ageratum mexicanum* both appreciate sunny spots reminiscent of their home climates, while the Greek root, *helios*, in annual sunflowers, *Helianthus annuus*, tips us off to its similar proclivity for sunshine. Sweet alyssum,

Lobularia maritima, is a maritime or seaside plant that will take drought in stride, while *Reseda odorata*, or mignonette, earns a place near bench or window through the promise of pleasing odor or fragrance, which it amply fulfills. While provenance is not a surefire clue to a plant's needs, it can provide valuable clues: the annual purple bell vine, *Rhodochiton atrosanguineum*, doesn't offer any cultural tips in its name, but coming as it does from southern Mexico, we can make an experimental assumption that in northerly stateside gardens, it will appreciate sun and reflected heat (as indeed it does).

Their multiple virtues make annuals compellingly attractive garden plants, yet they do have a few drawbacks. Unless they are deadheaded fairly often, many will simply cease to bloom. After all, an annual's job is to raise a healthy crop of seed, then die. Some modern hybrids are sterile, bred to be everblooming whether you deadhead them or not. These set no death triggering seed, yet unless groomed periodially their clustered dead become unsightly, and mar the living buds and blossoms. Overfed and watered, many annuals will swamp young perennials and even shrubs, smothering them beneath armloads of lush, rot-prone vegetation. The very strengths that win our appreciation can become deadly when unleased without safeguards.

If annuals as a class have a fault, it is overabundance. It may manifest itself in the ways described above, or it may arise through technical inducement, as when plant science encourages an superabundance of blossom, out of proportion to the overall size of the plant. Though many annual species do bloom with abandon, selection and hybridization programs have exaggerated that natural trait until the poor petunia or begonia becomes an overblown caricature with all the charm of a plastic plant. This fault has been emphasized by the recent interest in dwarfism, for when an undersized plant is decked with huge flowers, the result is not happy. Grotesquely enlarged flowers most often occur when a propensity for doubling of petals or gigantism is encouraged through breeding programs designed to create floral novelties with mass market appeal. African marigolds the size of grapefruit and dinner plate dahlias are cases in point; what can one *do* with such plants

Dusky purple heliotrope is remarkably long blooming and its fragrance is strong enough to offset the old sweatsock smell of giant sea kale, Crambe cordifolia. *Garden of Peggy VanBianchi, Kingston, Washington. Photo: Mark Lovejoy*

urally elegant annuals out there, waiting to be admired for exactly what they are. Gardeners who dismiss these charming ephemerals as vulgar are missing a world of pleasure. A more thorough exploration of the field will reveal heartening numbers of annuals without such damning defects of style and form.

Some of the most charming annuals are little detail plants, far from showy, yet able to enliven cracks and crannies too small to house more demanding plants. They fit neatly between prim balls of clipped box and the brick edgers that outline a formal border. They are equally at home along a stone path winding through an informal mixed border. They can encircle young border trees with a scented froth of flowers, or underplant a patch of lesser bulbs you want to highlight.

Consider the retiring violet cress (*Ionopsidium acaule*), a minute crucifer that is quite easy to overlook in a border setting. Only a couple of inches tall, it spreads in a film of faint lilac and fresh green wherever you choose to sow it. It needs no thinning, and with repeated sowings will bloom almost nonstop all through the year. Many times, seedlings that sprouted in November will bloom during the first thaws of January. All winter long, a string of mild days brings these tiny flowers into bloom. Though they prefer a bit of shade during the warmer months, during the autumn and winter they bloom best in the sun, which coaxes forth a subtle scent like a ghost of the sweet breath of their cousins, the wallflowers. I like to sow violet cress near the winter-blooming hellebores, in a spot which is shaded during the summer and open to the sky all winter, yet protected from winds by the background shrubs. Most years, I grow it to appreciate from autumn through late spring, for in summer such subtlety is hardly noticeable.

Another fragrant cousin, sweet alyssum (*Alyssum maritimum*) pours generously out of the cracks between edging stones in my big border. This old-fashioned favorite is a useful spreader which covers a good deal of ground, though its crown is small enough to tuck between bulbs or among perennials. It, too, is almost everblooming where winters are mild, and even where they are fierce indeed, this

in a garden setting? Surely they exist only to amaze. This is not to say that hybridizing is bad in itself; many unadulterated species are graceful and long blooming, yet others—like petunias, geraniums, and impatiens—have benefited enormously from selective breeding programs. However, the general clamor for everblooming plants that don't need staking has led past refinement to some rather dubious "improvements." Fortunately, the huckstering catalogs which promote novelty plants don't have the entire market sewn up. There are hundreds of nat-

modest creature will reappear, spilling cascades of lacy green leaves and rounded heads of clean white florets over path or covering the bare earth between wakening perennials come spring. Early in March, I dig up clumps of seedlings and spread them around the garden, weaving a lacy white edging to delight the bees and cover up the crumpled leaves of retreating crocus. In another spot, the pinky purple alyssum 'Rosy O'Day' seeds itself throughout a sunny bank carpeted with various thymes and other Mediterranean subshrubs, where its honey scent mingles with the pungent ones of rosemary and sage and lavender.

There are many places within mixed borders where other diminutive annuals can make a splash. The hedges that back deep borders are usually divided from the border proper by a narrow pathway designed to allow the gardener access to groom and guide the border back through the summer. Such spots are generally drab, since unseen, but I like to drape mine with colorful scarves of pastel annual candytuft (*Iberis*) or blue rivers of lobelias or cup flower (*Nierembergia caerulea*). Though never noticed by most visitors, these glowing ribbons reward my eye when I do duty at the border's back. I use the hidden access paths in my mixed borders as testing grounds for annuals which I suspect will do well in the border. These decorative details serve a double purpose, for I learn how they will react with competition while the maintenance paths take on the quality of a secret garden.

After a hard winter has carried off my little hedges of shrubby New Zealand hebes (something that happens with depressing regularity), I replace them with splashy annuals. By summer's end, I usually decide to try more hebes—their textures are too alluring to resist—but in the meantime, the border front has been awash in deep sea blue flaxleaf pimpernell (*Anagallis linifolia*) and ruffled white Virginia stocks (*Malcolmia maritima*), interrupted at intervals with some of the less retiring pansies, like the vivid masks of 'Imperial Joker', burnt orange rimmed in violet, or 'Imperial Gold Princess', clear, sun yellow with a blood red heart. Where I have extended beds, or ripped out large areas of something I'm tired of, and am not quite sure just how to proceed, I might

cover the ground for the summer with sheets of the silver-variegated nasturtium 'Alaska', which I have been coaxing into a selected seed strain with mostly apricot- and melon-colored flowers. If the open area is midborder, I may use the tendril-less sweetpea, 'Snoopea', which produces chunky, almost shrubby little plants two to three feet high, covered with compact clusters of blossoms in a warm but soft color run involving pinks, salmon, murky purples, and a good clean white. (I remove the white flow-

*In their native habitat, California poppies (*Eschscholzia californica*) are spring bloomers, but where summers are cool, well groomed plants will carry on all summer. Generally seen in bright shades of orange and yellow, the cream-colored strain at the statue base has been carefully developed and preserved. Garden of Margaret Ward, Bainbridge Island, Washington. Photo: Mark Lovejoy*

ering plants to tubs or containers, for the mixture is a better border blender without them).

In partial shade, *Linaria* 'Fairy Bouquet' produces clouds of minute snapdragons in clear pastels touched with white. The fine-textured foliage is a slightly grayed green, and a generous sowing produces an unbroken sheet of fluffy plantlets only ten to twelve inches tall. Where a bit more height is wanted, mountain phlox (*Linanthus grandiflorus*) will make foamy cloudlets of palest pink and cream twelve to fifteen inches tall. This does as well in partial or filtered shade as in fuller sun and, once established, tolerates considerably drier conditions than its frail foliage and gossamer petals would suggest. Sunnier spots are filled temporarily with a strain of California poppy (*Eschscholzia californica*) called 'Thai Silk'. In its original state, this seed mix runs to coppers, bronzed reds, and shimmering golden browns, as well as fuchsia pinks and a vibrant, metallic rose. Though all are lovely, there are few places in the borders where such a wide range is really welcome. Over the years, I have selected my own sub-strains, encouraging the brassy browns and coppers in one area, and favoring warm pinks, butter, and cream in another. Since I want seed to run fairly true, I am ruthless about roguing out anything that doesn't fit my goals. Within a few seasons, it is possible to develop a strain that runs heavily to your preferred colors. Now, if I want a patch of clear rose poppies, I can be fairly sure of getting them.

In hot, dry positions, before much soil improvement has gone on, I might spread a hot, sun-colored poncho of dwarf annual gaillardias, the tousled, lustrous 'Red Plume' and the lemony 'Yellow Plume', masses of silky, party-colored portulaca and creeping zinnia (*Sanvitalia procumbens*), with its hundreds of tiny, brown-eyed golden daisies. This heady mixture makes flat, drought-resistant carpets of sheer, snapping color, from which the broad foliar swords of yuccas and New Zealand flax (*Phormium*) emerge in bold, sleek curves that balance the floral bravado.

Larger annuals make wonderful midborder fillers, covering gaps left by early bloomers. Foamy flowers suitable for drying can be especially useful sequencing plants in warm, sunny gardens, billowing out just as the flowers of June start to falter. *Limonium aureum* 'Supernova' boasts multitudes of papery florets on multi-stemmed heads that build like golden cumulus some three feet high. This and other dryable flowers will benignly overlap with resting columbines or lungworts left exhausted by spring. The rather shorter *L. sinuatum* is an amiable airhead, fluffy and insubstantial, yet capable of filling in reliably for spent dwarf iris without robbing them of light or air. 'Sunset Shades' is a lovely mix for hot borders, with a full range of muted reds stepped down through amber, apricot, sand, and salmon to soft golden yellows. This and several other species come in a good number of plain colors as well: clean or ivoried whites, yellows brash or chalky, clarion pinks or faded lavenders, and some very good blues. In warm climates, *L. caspium* 'Filigree' will unfold its electric blue lacework in a frothy mound a good yard high and more across. In my garden, it runs smaller, and never persists as a perennial, as it may where winters are very mild. None of these dry land flowers enjoy shade or damp feet, and once they have settled in, they grow rapidly with little or no supplemental water.

Cosmos, airy yet space filling, can follow tatty oriental poppies, which always look like the remains of a cat fight once the glorious blossoms are gone. Happily, you can cut poppies back clear to the ground, give them a refresher of compost, and they will obligingly leaf out again, more compactly this time. Tuck some cosmos in between the poppy crowns, give them a share in the compost, and they will cover for you nicely. *Cosmos* 'Sea Shells' is a tall strain (three to four feet), with curled petals like tiny horn-shaped shells. This gives the flowers more distinction than the flat, daisy-shaped kind, and they come in an appealing run of pinks and lavenders, with a fair bit of white thrown in. If white is what you want, you cannot do better than the old standard, 'Purity', which also stands tall and carries an abundance of large, sparkling white flowers above netted foliage. A shorter cosmo, 'Versailles Tetra', stands two and a half to three feet tall and carries deep-toned flowers of pewtery rose tinged with black, an excellent mixer with dark purples and powdery blues. The Sensation series includes several

Vibrant reds and hot pinks, metallic coppers and bronzy oranges make up the glowing, sari-silk tints of the 'Thai Silk' strain of California poppy (Eschscholzia californica). By selecting seed from favorite plants and growing them in isolated patches, one can develop personal strains in favored colors. Photo: Mark Lovejoy

distinct shades of red or dark pink, as well as the extremely floriferous 'Sonata White', which replaces 'Purity' where height is not wanted. The long-blooming 'Ladybird' comes in primary yellow, red, and orange and, at not much over a foot, it makes a fluffy front row filler in hot borders.

The larger annual poppies make striking mid-border plants, ably distracting the eye from past glories. Opium poppies (*Papaver somniferum*) are usually sold as "peony flowered" (even to the point where some catalogs list them as *Papaver paeoniflorum*). This nomenclature squeamishness may have something to do with the odd fact that while it is legal to buy and sow the seed of opium poppies, it is not legal to grow them. They flourish in older

gardens in my part of the world, despite the activity of the vice squad. In Seattle, these tough guys used to descend on the garden of my elderly neighbor and pull up all her opium poppies, huge double purples with ruffled, slightly fringed petals. She would shake her fist and squawk at them, fuming publicly, but the minute they left, she would laugh in triumph, saying, "They never seem to wonder what I'm growing out back!"

A more delicate annual version of the robust oriental poppies, opium poppies have shimmering blue-gray leaves, scalloped and cut. The stiff, upright plants have an heraldic look about them, like something on an ancient shield. They stand two to three feet tall, with multi-branched stems rising from the leaf nodes. Drooping, heavy buds rise as they open, the crumpled petals ironed smooth by the sun, their flimsy silk crisping with new vitality as they unfold. To keep a succession of flowers coming, snip off each spent blossom; you can even cut the whole plant back by a third, and new buds will spring from every leaf node. A typical batch of seed will produce plants with flowers in shades from white to purple and red, all with a characteristic black thumb mark at the base of each petal. Most are single, a few loosely double, some packed tight, with frilled or fringed tips. Opium poppies have been much selected for color and form, and seed swapping has brought me every shade of purple from plum-black through grape with a bluish luster to clear lavender. My favorite is crushed raspberry, though a big, silky one with palest pink petals and a smudgy black thumb print gets a lot of attention. I am always passing out seed of this plant, mindful of those stern federal regulations. What can one do if a seed packet accidentally rips just above a large, well prepared hole in the border? Accidents do happen, every year without fail.

A novelty form of opium poppy called 'Hens & Chicks' is an admirable border adjunct, both in blossom and in fruit. Each large flower is encircled by tiny ones, tightly clustered about its base. These extras don't show much when the flower is open, but once it falls and the pod begins to swell, they form a decorative fringe of podlets reminiscent of the fast multiplying sedum for which it is named. I let many plants of this and the ordinary kind go to seed, not just for the harvest, but because the dried heads are exceptionally handsome. They are shaped like swelling urns, subtly textured like hammered bronze. As they age, they fade from green to grayish bronze, and develop a mottled patina of verdigris and black.

The common field poppy of Europe (*Papaver rhoeas*) has given rise to any number of pretty seed mixtures. My favorite, 'Mother of Pearl' (also sold as 'Angel Wings') was selected by Sir Cedric Morris, whose painterly eye produced this lustrous, subdued strain of slate and lavender, antique pink and mauve. It makes a garden miracle when grown with the biennial money plant, *Lunaria annua*, an early

*Opium poppies (*Papaver somniferum*) are illegal to grow, though the seed may be freely bought and sold, which may be why they are often called peony poppies. Their silvery foliage and wonderful color range—from midnight purple through shell pink and clean white—make them popular despite their illicit status. Photo: Mark Lovejoy*

bloomer that changes its blossoms into coin-shaped seedpods. Come fall, these are silvery, but in summer, the ripening pods and the leaves are infused with purple and pewtery gray. Both do well in sun, but accept a bit of filtered or light shade, and neither cares for extra water, making them excellent coverage for early bulbs and resting hellebores.

Bishop's flower (*Ammi majus*), like a refined version of Queen Anne's lace with rather better foliage

Even annuals must be considered as whole plants rather than merely colorful flowers. In May, the silvery green foliage of opium poppy contrasts elegantly with the gray-green of sea holly, Eryngium alpinum superbum. *By July, the sea holly bracts will deepen to a bright, steely blue. Garden of Peggy VanBianchi, Kingston, Washington. Photo: Mark Lovejoy*

Once they have paid their way with a good burst of bloom, I replace them with bedding chrysanthemums. Though there are many hardy chrysanthemums, the stunners that show up in late summer at the nurseries are mostly bred from tender species and strains. The newer hybrids are so glorious in color, in texture, in sheer bloom power, that I consider three or four dollars a bargain for a burgeoning gallon potful. I cordially detest the huge "football corsage" flowered mums, and am not much excited by the fat little button types, either, but I am a sucker for those with midsized flowers, especially the flaring spoons and the dainty spiders. Last year, I grew 'Bravo', a rusty red sunburst, the tawny brown and copper 'Rodeo', several delicate spiders like the silky purple 'Lancer' and pinky rose 'Tinkerbelle', and a knockout in almost metallic pink, flushed rose and brown, called 'Grenadine'. These were all so good, I overwintered them in the unheated sun porch, pulled them to bits in the spring, and enjoyed them a second season before losing every one to a sudden freeze in mid-November.

Where early daylily or iris foliage stands flowerless, annual larkspur (*Consolida ambigua*) will send up delicate spires in lovely runs of lavender and white, blue, and rose. This is one of my favorite annuals, and one of the few that cohabitates gracefully with greedy iris. Slim stalks and thready leaves make them less competitive with the iris, which are apt to resent the presence of luxuriant companions. 'White King' is especially handsome, its porcelain pale petals aristocratically veined in milky blue. There are some dozen single colors available, a good range of clear or cloudy pinks, lavenders, blues, and a soft salmon that blends wonderfully with rich reds, wine purples, and slate blues. The larkspurs must be sown in situ, or in the very deep, narrow pots used for tree seedlings, for they hate transplanting, and are very apt to die off in resentment if their long roots are crowded. The seedlings may be thinned somewhat if they seem over close, but they are sturdy independents which don't need much assistance to give their best. When the main stalks are spent, cut them back carefully, and every side shoot will produce buds at the leaf nodes. These secondary flower stalks are smaller than the first, but lovely

and manners, makes a good mask for post-bloom lupines. These are so unattractive, even when cut back, that they really cry out for a covering plant to hide their shame. I usually treat lupines as biennials rather than perennials, tossing them after their second year. Though some people have better luck with them, in my garden they have never been worth the considerable space they require once their first bloom is past. They just get bigger, not better.

nonetheless, and often continue blooming until hard frost.

Bells of Ireland (*Moluccella laevis*) is another spiky one with scalloped green flowers arrayed on chubby turrets. Long-lasting and handsome even unto death, this annual flower dries attractively in or out of the garden. Where springs are cool, it is wise to start bells of Ireland indoors, for when sown in the open they can be slow to develop, and may not come into bloom until the tail end of autumn. In warmer climes, it will bounce into bloom by midsummer, lasting in the border till late frosts collapse its browning towers. Up to three feet tall when well suited, bells of Ireland make a good follow-up for mid-border forget-me-nots and tulips. Similarly spire-like, but far broader at the base are the red Italian brussels sprouts called 'Rubine', which rise from young rosettes of silvery blue into tall spikes of heavy burgundy, their three-foot stems studded with blackish red leaves and sprouts. The chunky taproots will fit between clumps of summer-dormant *Geranium tuberosum*, or patches of bulbous, spring-blooming iris. An unusual statice called *Limonium suworowii* 'Pink Pokers' is a low, creeping plant that sends up surprising spires of hot pink, some of them straight, others amazingly sinuous. Like all its clan, it dries well; if you want to take advantage of this, sandwich statice between spring bloomers and late summer achievers. It will cover for the first, then you can harvest it as the second is coming into power.

Vase-shaped midborder annuals require very little foot room to support an expansive aerial display lasting several months. The most obvious example, annual baby's breath (*Gypsophila elegans*), is a slow starter, but by late summer it is ready to cover for early perennials that have lost freshness. This makes it a natural to pair with delphiniums or early veronicas. 'Snow Fountain' is a strong-growing selection that may reach two feet in height and rather more in girth, its large florets giving the plant more impact than the filmy haze of the perennial sort. 'Pink Fountain' is a chalky pink, 'Red Cloud' warm pink rather than red. More odd than pretty, *Bupleurum rotundifolium* 'Green Gold' fascinates flower arrangers with its greeny gold flower heads. With

*Moon seed, or money plant (*Lunaria annua*), blooms well in dry soil, and looks especially pretty in shade, where its silvery seedpods gleam attractively. It is seen here against a red barberry, Berberis thunbergii 'Atropurpurea', sharing ground with honeysuckle, Lonicera periclymenum 'Graham Stuart Thomas', and lavender-blue Geranium tuberosum. Author's garden. Photo: Mark Lovejoy*

leaves like a honeysuckle, and the flower of a euphorbia, this oddball annual produces as many of its curious, green-bracketed golden blossoms in shade as in sun. It sends up airy, multibranched stems two to three feet high in good soil, though the plants tend to be more compact in drier, hotter sites. Red-stemmed Swiss chard also makes a handsome, if nonfloral, statement in such a position, as do the frilly edible kales like the gray-green 'Scotch Curled' or the bluer 'Winterbur'.

Flowering tobaccos (*Nicotiana*) come in a variety of sizes and shapes, some making good place holders for dormant plants, others best as border infill. All have tubular flowers ending in a starburst of petals, little trumpets sending out their heady perfume like floral music. *Nicotiana alata* (synonym *affinis*) has yielded a multitude of short, bushy bedders in many colors, pastel and bright, including white and green. The Nikki series offers some of the best colors, but the plants have little or no scent. The Sensation series has the familial seductive fragrance, but comes only in a color mixture. This doesn't matter so much if you buy blooming plants at a nursery, where you can pick the colors you want, but is annoying if you want to grow your own from seed; you must raise them under glass to bring them into early bloom before placing them in the garden. 'Fragrant Cloud' is a big, clean white that blooms well in sun or partial shade, releasing its insinuating night scent as twilight falls. Where tall plants are wanted, the meadow nicotine, *N. sylvestris*, fills the bill, rising as high as six feet, with large, spoon-shaped leaves and great swags of elongated white blossoms. Its scent is light, suggesting woods and meadows rather than the boudoir. My own favorite is *N. lansgsdorfii*, its short-belled trumpets a bright ripe olive green with a navy blue eye. Airy and many branching, it can reach five feet in height, weaving companionably through more solid companions.

Certain annuals are surprisingly substantial in appearance, with more structural effect than many perennials. Snow on the mountain, an annual euphorbia (*Euphorbia marginata*), rises in cool looking peaks, like green alps dusted with fresh snow. In late summer, it is tall enough at four feet to mask bevies of dilapidated early beauties. A dwarf form, 'Summer Icicle', makes sturdy-looking hummocks some eighteen inches tall and across for the border front. The mallow family is full of long-lasting annuals which are excellent border candidates, for most couple pretty, simple flowers on substantial-looking plants with small root systems and slim central stems that allow them to snug in between resting bulbs or retiring early bloomers. *Malva moschata* 'Alba' is an ardent self sower with lacy green foliage, handsome in itself, and an excellent foil for the many two-inch

blossoms of chalk white, brightened by feathery pink stamens. A taller cousin, *M. sylvestris* subsp. *mauritiana* may reach five or six feet, but is such a slim creature that it looks best in groups of three or five, all decked with small single flowers of rich purple veined in black, the petals tinged with a sheen of fuchsia pink. *Malope trifida grandiflora* is seldom more than three feet tall, but is similarly splendid in coloring, with saturated purple flowers shimmered with red. The variety 'Vulcan' is satin red veined black, the more dramatic for the familial green star that marks its heart. 'White Queen' carries silky white flowers, while those of 'Pink Queen' are sugary pink threaded with rose. The flaring petals of their cousins, the lavateras, are ruffled and open in the lavender-pink *Lavatera cachemiriana*, a slender three footer, or broad and glossy as a hibiscus in *L. trimestris*. This last boasts several pretty mixes, but several named varieties are more suitable for border work. Most are various shades of pink or rose, but 'Mont Blanc' carries huge flowers of shining white on relatively short stems, making it the best choice for a front border position.

Even more substantial in appearance are the chunky amaranths, ornamental forms of an edible grain. By midsummer, it's hard to believe that 'Joseph's Coat' (*Amaranthus tricolor*), a stately two- or three-foot tower of parrot feather scarlet and yellow, could ever fit into a four-inch pot. There are several similar forms with darker leaves, such as the crimson-and-maroon 'Molten Fire', or the emphatic, desert sunset tones of 'Illumination', which bring a truly exotic note to the border, blending well with the oversized foliage of hydrangeas, fatsias, and ornamental grapevines. Annual amaranths of all kinds are quick growers, making sizable and dramatic (or even melodramatic) border characters. The weeping, oxblood red ropes dangling from love-lies-bleeding (*A. caudatus*) are not to everybody's taste, but the form called 'Green Thumb', in which the bristling bloom spikes are more upright and vividly green, is much admired by flower arrangers, and brings interesting textural variety to small-leaved shrubs and perennials. Both of these run two or more feet tall, but 'Pygmy Torch' is an upstanding dwarf variety with protruding spikelets of bur-

The cherry pink blossoms of Malope trifida *have green windowlike translucencies at their heart, giving them a starry-eyed look. This annual does very well in dry soil, and blooms generously in light or filtered shade. Photo: Mark Lovejoy*

gundy-black, a wonderful antidote to smooth border front tussocks of herbs and little grasses.

A few annuals qualify as statuesque, queenly creatures that will grace the border's deepest reaches. These are most useful when a large, important player has been lost to winter or old age, leaving an unsightly gap. These oversized annuals also lend height to young borders, a quality that will later be supplied by shrubs or vines or perennials. In warm gardens, *Hibiscus manihot* 'Cream Cup' brushes the sky at eight feet. Each stem is laden with heavy buds that unfurl like the eye of a camera into huge, dark-

eyed flowers the color of heavy cream. Where summers are cooler, these fast growers need a jump start under glass if they are to reach half this height, but however tall they become, they are generous and long bloomers, producing buds and flowers well into October. The annual hibiscus makes a big plant with many outstretched arms, fitting cozily between established shrubs or filling up an empty hole all on its own. Where ground space is limited, a fascinating garden variant of edible orach (*Atriplex hortensis* 'Rubra') may be preferred. Orach can exceed seven feet in height, and its willowy stems trimmed with long, drooping, triangular leaves give it an unusual silhouette that contrasts well with bulkier plants. There are several strains with colored leaves, one chiefly in coppers, bronzes, and golds, others in reds, maroons, and burgundy. The seed of either strain is variable, but since the seedlings show hints of their future color very early, it is easy to pot up like tints together for later garden use, culling out any drab duds along the way. Those with golden or copper foliage bring a gleam of light to dull corners among dark-leaved rhododendrons, or brighten the dusky purple of hazel or smokebush (*Cotinus coggygria*). The somber spires of the darkest red forms make a sumptuous background for apricot-colored roses like the opulent tea 'Just Joey', or the coffee-and-cream blend of 'Climbing Butterscotch'.

Annual sunflowers (*Helianthus annuus*) make wonderful temporary hedges or fences, rising in solid-looking walls that easily top six feet in good soil. The 'Autumn Beauty' strain yields hand-sized flower heads in shades of gold and copper, bronze and warm maroon. For more controlled effects, use single-color hybrids like the elegant 'Italian White', with ivory petals tinged faintly apricot and centered with meltingly big brown eyes. 'Velvet Queen' boasts black-eyed flowers with lustrous, deep-napped petals of a murky, saturated red so dark as to be nearly black, while 'Lemon Queen' is a clean citric yellow. Another hedge candidate is the castor bean, an outsized exotic with the improbably opulent look of Victorian wrought iron. Of the several species available in the seed trade, *Ricinus communis* offers the most distinctive forms. The tallest may exceed ten feet when grown in good soil in a warm sheltered spot. Among these are 'Zanzibarensis', with tremendous, long fingered green leaves as much as two feet across, and 'Black Beauty', in dusky eggplant purple. The relatively compact 'Carmencita', with glossy mahogany leaves and brilliant carmine buds, or 'Impala', with bronzed red foliage and soft yellow flowers, are powerful-looking plants despite their mere four or five feet in height. All have weird, bobbly flower heads in shades of red from screaming pink to a subdued mahogany. In youth, they look like curtain trims, maturing into seedpods that resemble fringed sea creatures. Though definitely odd, they are curiously attractive, and must be kept out of children's reach, for **castor beans are deadly poison in every part**. Tucked away at the border's back, they can't be considered an attractive nuisance. In any case, children who frequent your garden should be taught that picking and tasting fruits or flowers must only be done with your guidance. If greater height or mass than castor beans can provide is wanted, we must turn to annual vines, which are covered in chapter 7.

BIENNIALS

Biennials differ from annuals in having a two year life cycle. In their first season, they produce a leafy rosette, but will not bloom until the following summer. Forget-me-nots and sweet William, wallflowers and foxgloves are familiar cottage garden biennials that frequently self-sow into long-lived colonies. By introducing yearlings two years in a row, such colonies can present a perpetual supply of bloom sized members. Young biennials are often undistinguished in appearance, best isolated in a nursery bed until wanted in the borders. A special few are exciting even in their rosette stage; an escapee from the kitchen garden, *Angelica archangelica* is an uncommonly striking herb, great in form and size alike. In its first year, it makes ruffled tussocks of toothed leaves up to a yard long. The following summer, it sends up thick, ribbed stalks topped with

gigantic umbels of greeny white florets six or eight feet high. *Verbascum bombyciferum* 'Arctic Summer' fattens into great cabbages a yard across, each pointed leaf made of silvery velours. The bloom stalks rise a good five or six feet above this, in branching tapers, but I often pinch out the flowering shoots for a year or two, just to enjoy the leaves longer. (This effectively prolongs the life of the plant, for verbascums rarely die before setting seed.) An even more exciting one is called 'Silver Lining'; this form has the largest leaves of any verbascum I know, darkly silver and embossed with pewtery veins, the leaves stretching as much as three feet in length. Once it blooms (in tall, branching candelabras twinkling with little yellow flame flowers), it is history, so I ruthlessly prune its heart out, keeping it juvenile as long as possible.

The arching, heart shaped leaves of the ordinary money plant (*Lunaria annua*) become stunning when liberally dusted with silver freckles. (Though the specific *annua* implies annual status, it is indeed a biennial.) The form 'Variegata' has purple flowers held over well powdered foliage, while the even splashier 'Stella' has white flowers and more heavily patterned leaves. Both are apt to be plain green for much of their first year, so it is best to grow these in a nursery bed, roguing for unmarked plants before setting them out in late fall. Even then, the variegation may show only as a thready white line at the outer edge of the leaves. This looks unprepossessing, but spring will develop their coloring fully, and by midsummer the plants will be queenly creatures three and four feet high, impressive even out of flower. Plants in shade hold their silver longest, lasting well into fall. The plain-leaved species offers quite a few color forms, with flowers of reddish purple, pale lavender, washy pink, and clean white. By keeping distinct colors well apart in the garden, one can develop very pretty strains that seed mostly true to form. The leaves and seedpods of plants grown in sun will take on numinous tints of purple, slate, and lead as they ripen. The late Kevin Nicolay, well known botanical artist and gardener extraordinaire, grew money plant with the hazy, silvery 'Mother of Pearl' poppies (*Papavar rhoeas*), making an unforgettable picture which I often duplicate in my own borders.

Where thistles thrive, gardeners are wise to be cautious in introducing what could be serious pests into their borders. If field thistles are ubiquitous in your part of the world, it is worth calling the county extension agent for advice before going in heavily for ornamental thistles and unwittingly unleashing an agricultural horror. However, most of the showy horticultural thistles are milder mannered than their lowly field brethren, self sowing modestly if at all. In my garden, the nearby fields are purple with Canadian thistles, but their border kin have yet to seed themselves in the crowded beds. Bristling Scotch thistles (*Onopordum acanthium*) form ominous, spiny rosettes, as leathery as the backs of young crocodiles in their first year, spreading as much as three feet across. When they rise, they may top six feet, their branched candelabra of arms alight with fat, rosy flowers. Arabian thistles (*O. arabicum*) are taller and larger in every part, more silvery of leaf and rather darker in flower. Milk or Mary thistles (*Silybum marianum*) spread from demure, white-veined rosettes into spiny giants, the rippling little leaves expanding into armed killers two or even three feet in length, the many-branched flower stalks rising six or seven feet in height. Seed sown early in spring will produce flowering plants by mid- to late August, but late sown seed will rest over the winter, returning to flower the following summer. Though the young rosettes look tame enough, this is not a plant to place anywhere you think you might want to be yourself. Weeding under or near milk thistles is memorable, but not pleasantly so, and I still have a scar from the year I tried to mow them with the Lawn Boy. The little spines that edge the infant thistles are as sharp as slivers of glass, and they get equivalently fiercer as the plant enlarges. This doesn't mean they must be banished to the back of the border—I like to use milk thistles three or four feet back from the border's front edge, to draw the eye from fading perennials at summer's end. In September, when the thistles are in their glory, the surrounding foliage is a muted tapestry, a quiet backdrop for those majestic, mottled leaves and flower laden spires. Just don't

The huge, sculptural foliage of the hybrid biennial Verbascum *'Silver Lining' contrasts powerfully with purple hazel leaves. Author's garden. Photo: Mark Lovejoy*

plant them where an unwitting visitor can brush against those wicked spines.

Hollyhocks are perhaps most familiar as perennials, old-fashioned flowers that persist in farmyard and urban alley alike, long after the garden that spawned them has vanished. However, where the disfiguring rust disease is prevalent, it works best to treat them as biennials, growing them to size in a nursery bed, then transferring second-year plants to the borders. Though statuesque, hollyhocks have gawky knees that are best hidden away at the back of the border, even where rust is uncommon. It is intriguing to notice how healthy the wildling hollyhocks in abandoned yards and alleys look, with never a trace of rust. Bring their offspring into the garden, however, and within a few seasons the tell-tale red pustules show up. I find this is less apt to happen when hollyhocks are grown in lean, well-drained soil, without close neighbors. Unfortunately, I have no border spot which matches those needs, so I settle for replacing my hollyhocks every year. Besides eliminating rust problems, it gives me the chance to try different selections. Current favorites are a clear, straw yellow (from a city alley), and the rich inky red one called *Althaea rosea* 'Nigra'. Both are singles, according well in form and color with the rather difficult pinks of old roses. A sheaf of black hollyhocks also makes an unforgettable backdrop for the oversized *Geranium psilostemon* with its snapping, black eyed magenta blossoms, and calls out the ruddy undertones in murky daylilies like 'Decatur Dictator' and 'American Revolution'.

Purple and white foxgloves (*Digitalis purpurea*) have naturalized in many parts of the country, growing freely at woodland edge and in overgrown meadows. Given partial shade and a slightly acid soil, their lancelike bloom stalks may reach six or seven feet. Foxgloves are marvelously structural plants, bringing height and firmness of line to blobby borders which have not yet found their destined shape. They do well in crowded borders, accepting the squeeze with convivial pleasure. They were favorites in the overflowing Victorian cottage gardens, where they lived cheek to cheek with strawberries and wandering pea vines, so it is not surprising that they would find mixed border life to their taste. By ruthless roguing, one can produce fairly consistent strains of these field flowers—clear purple, richly spotted pink, unmarked white—within five or six years. Several wonderful old strains are commercially available, such as 'Sutton's Apricot', a warm, pinky golden shade, and the clean, chalky yellow 'Sutton's Primrose'. Seed from a lovely plant you buy at a nursery is likely to yield an assortment of colors, but if you have the space, you can devote a nursery bed to foxgloves, growing seedlings and choosing the color or shades you want until your own strain is born. In the garden, I allow a chosen few plants to go to seed each year, saving some of the seed for swaps and trades and scattering the rest in situ. The silvery seedlings act as markers

for large sweeps of autumn crocus (*Colchicum* species) which run through the back of several borders. Though overly abundant, they are easily thinned, and extras can be potted up for plant sales or trades. (The apricot and pale yellow foxgloves are always in demand.)

Sweet William (*Dianthus barbatus*) is another cottage garden biennial that works well in mixed borders. The yearling leaves are long and leathery, very dark green, and often stained with reddish tints. Though usually sold in color mixtures, several pure colors are available, among them 'Dunnets Dark Crimson', an excellent red. Here, too, it is easy to make your own selections from mixtures, and I have devloped one that tends to black stems, ruddy leaves, and blackish red flowers. It would be just as simple to select for pastels or eyed pinks or pure white, if your fancy led that way. Other border worthy biennials include Brompton stocks (*Matthiola incana*), gray and long of leaf, almost like culinary sage. They are rather shrubby in form, with ruffled semidouble flowers, usually in shades of rose or pink or salmon. My favorites are creamy white, with the pronounced family fragrance that earned them their traditional place beneath the sunny kitchen window in cottage gardens. I grow them beneath lead-colored dwarf purple willows (*Salix purpurea* 'Nana') in a small mixed bed near the back door, where we get full advantage of the lovely scent.

Well armed teasel (*Dipsacus fullonum*) is a princely plant that looks equally at home in wilder "natural" borders or in architectural modern grass gardens. Its spidery, bristling seedpods were used long ago to smooth the nap of woven cloth, but now they are prized by flower arrangers and border builders alike. The greenish, thistlelike flowers are not remarkable, but the dangerously spiny rosettes are awe-inspiring, maturing into five or six feet of prickly magnificence. Their skeletal remains have a strong, sculptural beauty that lasts well into winter. For me, they self-sow modestly, but I take care to root out unwanted seedlings young, before they sink their sturdy taproots too far into the rich border soil.

Perhaps the most extraordinary—and certainly the least pronounceable—biennial in the trade is *Michauxia tchihatcheffii*, a campanula relative from Turkey. (Said properly, it sounds rather like a sneeze, according to Graham Stuart Thomas.) This is one of a handful of plants that can truly be called traffic stopping. It prefers well-drained soil, but tolerates anything from full sun to dappled shade, so long as it has shelter from strong winds. The rough, rather frumpy rosette is hardy to at least 12 degrees Fahrenheit, but may be even hardier with deep snow cover. Where it survives, summer will produce a tough, wiry stem five feet high, with numerous stiff and branching arms. Each branch is clustered with large, lantern-shaped buds that open into improbably huge flowers. Narrow, reflexed petals are centered with elongated, almost baroque sexual apparatus. I used to think of them as starbursts of white, but ever since a friend remarked that they look like an octopus in heat, the thought has stayed with me. Though its glory lasts but a single season, michauxia is a flower that haunts the memory, its very brevity an important part of its charm.

TEXTURAL HERBS

Annual herbs offer the mixed border builder a full palette of ornamental leaves, their flowers a pleasant dividend rather than the main event. Fuzzy, crinkle-leaved borage (*Borago officinalis*), with its drooping clusters of cobalt blue flowers tinged with pink, is a wonderful foil for a host of white 'Regale' lilies when they bloom, and an able screen for their retreat from the scene. Although borage self-sows relent-

A stellar but weird biennial, Michauxia tchihatcheffii*, long a rare and coveted collector's treasure, is increasingly available from commercial seed houses. Photo: Mark Lovejoy*

lessly, its hairy seedlings are immediately recognizable, and are very easily removed in first youth. Both purple basil and red perilla are available in ruffled-edged versions, as well as the usual flatleaf forms. They come in several heights, too, and are good fillers amongst young perennials and small, midborder shrubs. Parsley offers half a dozen kinds of leaf, from flat to intensely frizzled, and a variety of heights. The ordinary kitchen variety bolts too early to win it border placement, but in my garden, parsleys with more complex leaves have proved slow to bolt and seed. They can be discreetly harvested as well, which keeps fresh young leaves in production, but excess use unfits them for decorative duty.

The luscious smelling fruit sage (*Salvia dorisiana*) is grown for its felted silver-green leaves that release their enticing fragrance to the summer sun. The slim wands of dusty red flowers are a bonus in warm gardens, where they prove most attractive to hummingbirds. Bushy clary sages (*S. horminum*) have coarse, broad leaves and long stems tipped with papery bracts of pink and lavender, blue and white. The seed strain called 'Claryssa' is especially good, with oversized, very long-lasting bracts. One can buy three sumptuous single colors of this, including a deep, midnight blue stained with violet, light fuchsia pink veined purple, or chalk white netted in green. The usual bedding salvias (*S. splendens*) are a harsh fire-truck red, a challenging color to work into most border schemes, but a new one called 'Laser Purple' combines a compact shape and very long-lasting bracts with a throbbing, broken heart purple that works with a hundred shades and tints. The ordinary culinary sage (*S. officinalis*) is perfectly hardy in my garden, where winter temperatures seldom plummet into single digits. However, the several decorative forms are less hardy, and though they look convincingly shrublike, I generally treat them as replaceable annuals. The shrubby little 'Purpurea' has long, velveteen leaves of silvery purple, darkest in the new growth, paler in mature foliage. 'Tricolor' has rougher textured leaves of celadon green and gray, splashed with cream and rich pink. Here, too, the young growth is the brightest, but the mature bush holds a good deal of quiet color. 'Ictarina' is also tricolored, but its leaves are painted in shades of lemon and lime. Like the others, this makes into a good-sized bushlet by summer's end, and the leaves, though less pungent than cooking sage, may be gathered and dried for wreaths and edible holiday decorations.

TENDER PERENNIALS

Some plants sold as annuals are actually tender perennials that may persist for several years in warm gardens. *Helichrysum petiolare* is one such, a pewtery little immortelle that weaves long arms studded with round, felty leaves into neighboring shrubs or perennials. There are several other forms and species in the American nursery trade, notably the lemon-and-lime-colored 'Aureum' (also called 'Limelight'), darling of the English, which has pale greenish gold foliage. It is a cheerful worker, and brings a lovely lightness to plantings of larger leaved shrubs and perennials. I prefer the more subtly colored 'Variegatum', its gray leaves softly splashed with cream and celadon green. Both of these variegated forms deliver their best color in light shade, but need a warm, sheltered place to grow luxuriantly. *Helichrysum microphyllum* is a daintier cousin often used in hanging baskets, its slim, wreathing stems decked with tiny, rounded leaves shaped like little mouse ears, and similarly covered in silvery gray fur. When grown against a fence or wall, any of these weavers will push themselves three or four feet upward in open filigree patterns, the lower stems stiffening and thickening in support. If you want one to climb a bit midborder, simply place a stout stake or tripod behind a young plant, and lightly tie the central stem upright to make a leader. This way, they develop into little weeping trees, providing valuable contrast of habit and leaf form amongst more solid plants.

The deadly angels' trumpets (*Datura* species) are greenhouse shrubs in much of America, yet where summers are warm, they will bloom in their first season, and when they do, few flowers can match these supernal concoctions. *Datura meteloides* makes a shrubby mound of blue-gray leaves a good yard high and at least as much across, all covered with flaring white goblets big enough to drink from (though that would be a serious mistake, for daturas are virulently poisonous in every part). They have an intense night fragrance that makes them a must in a moon garden where all the flowers and much of the foliage is in shades of white and silver. In the border, they insist on a warm, sheltered spot without root competition, but given rich soil, they will romp into bloom in short order. In my cool garden, they do best with the assistance of a garden greenhouse umbrella, a handy portable gadget made of clear plastic which creates a warm, moist environment for exotic plants. A smaller hybrid called 'La Fleur Lilac' has pastel lavender flowers and glossy, lobed leaves of bronzed green in a shrublet under

two feet in height. If seeds are sown early, this one will come into bloom in July. *Datura suaveolens* has enormous, dangling white flowers with tiny waists flaring into swirling skirts—pure Ginger Rogers. If you have any place to winter them over, this datura can grow to a great size. I know one couple who have zealously carried a plant through ten seasons, coddling it indoors all winter, then arranging its rather lanky arms (now more than eight feet long) over a trellis for the summer, where it drips down curtains of scented white flowers like heavenly rain. There are quite a few daturas about, many of them in sumptuous shades of violet and Tyrian purple, soft or bright pink, even apricot. Most, however, don't reach blooming size for at least a year, and all need indoor shelter for half the year if they are to be carried over for other seasons.

Dahlias are tender bulbs, often treated as annuals. This black-leaved hybrid, 'Bishop of Llandalf', is definitely worth the trouble of lifting and wintering over in a safe, dry spot.
Photo: Peter Ray

Like other nominal annuals, many common houseplants such as coleus can broaden the palette of fascinating foliage plants for the border. Think of the variety offered by this clan alone—there are leaves of every color and shape, many of them every bit as colorful as any flower. In warm spots, the green-striped, red-backed tradescantias usually grown as dangling pot plants will weave gently through plain leaved neighbors. Purple heart (*Setcreasea pallida*) will spill its alternating tiers of bronzed purple leaves, folded like nesting origami boats, over the border edge, and in hot gardens may even open its glowing pinky purple flowers. Fancy angel wing and rex begonias will enliven shady gardens, their wide, winglike leaves spreading in marbled contrast to the bold foliage of spent peonies or quiet groupings of hosta and fern.

If you enjoy them enough to make the bother worthwhile, tender perennials may be lifted at summer's end and sheltered in the house or greenhouse or carried on by cuttings. Most of my cuttings are struck in August and September, when the plant stems are half ripe but not yet woody. Bedding geraniums (*Pelargonium*), immortelles (the shrubby *Helichrysum* species), and many of the tender salvias will root readily, most in open-textured mixtures of bagged soil and vermiculite mixed with sharp sand or grit. A small amount of steamed bone meal can be blended in to keep the young plants going until they are ready to pot up. I root most cuttings in gallon cans, mixing a spoonful of hydrated hydrophilic polymer into the bottom third of the soil mix in each before sticking the cuttings. You can pack cuttings quite tight, as many as fifteen or twenty to the gallon, so long as the leaves are trimmed enough not to touch each other. When struck in late summer or early fall, they often leap into new growth, putting on roots in just a few short weeks. However, unless they are in singleton pots (four-inch, usually) I have found it best not to disturb cuttings by potting them on too soon; when divided and repotted before the winter solstice, many healthy cuttings will falter and fail. Apparently, they need the encouragement of longer days and shorter nights to trigger recovery from potting on. I keep them in an unheated sun porch, though the hardiest often survive our usually

moderate winters in a large cold frame, surrounded by dry leaves for extra insulation. Pot them on in late winter or early spring, and the plants will be ready to return to the garden by May.

PLANTING TIPS

Growing annuals in mixed borders is much like growing them elsewhere, with a few exceptions. Many annuals have fine, fibrous root systems, quite unlike the plump, tough roots of many perennials. Annuals are often shallow rooted as well as lacking in reserves, which makes them vulnerable both to drought and to root crowding in mixed borders, where the more permanent denizens are already well established. If annuals are to grow well, they need adequate root space, which can be a challenge in a well filled mixed border. Many annuals may also need more moisture than surrounding plants, at least until they, too, are firmly established. Even drought-tolerant annuals will rarely perform well if stuck into dry, rooty soil and ignored—nothing is truly foolproof. No matter what the setting, situation, or plant involved, annuals that are given a good start in life will perform best.

In beds of their own, in window boxes and hanging baskets, cosseted annuals will bloom with zeal, thanks to ceaseless watering and grooming. The best annuals for mixed borders are less needy, sturdier of constitution, and, if not self cleaning, at least capable of continuous bloom even when not frequently deadheaded. Since they won't get daily attention, give them the benefit of good soil and ample water when first planted. When I plant perennials in the border, I take out whatever formerly filled the space, dig a deep hole, and refill the spot with fresh compost and some rotted manure or aged, shredded bark. I add a handful of grit or coarse sand for drainage (my soil is tight clay), stir it all up, then set in the new arrival. Where annuals are to grow, I do much the same, adding a good sprinkle of steamed bone meal and a tad of slow release, pelleted fertilizer as well. (Soil which is designed to feed

*Fragrant annuals can be planted directly in the borders or grown in pots and moved about as more color is required. Flowering tobacco (*Nicotiana alata*) and sweet alyssum (*Lobularia maritima*) are among the most potently perfumed. Garden of Peggy VanBianchi, Kingston, Washington. Photo: Mark Lovejoy*

shrubs and perennials slowly and consistently is not always rich enough for annuals, which don't have time to linger over their food.)

All newly planted annuals are watered in well, no matter how drought tolerant. Since my mixed borders are only watered once a month through the summer, the annuals—and other new additions— are hand watered at least weekly as needed until vigorous new growth appears. After that, they are fed and watered individually only when a severe grooming leaves them looking a bit thin. If August

finds them past their prime, I may replace them with new plants, or simply cut them back hard and give them a boost of water, fertilizer, and a fresh mulch of compost. Nearly always, this is enough to encourage another month or two of flowers.

The hardest trick in a full mixed border is to find enough clear ground to introduce annuals. There may be plenty of space above ground, between large, slowly expanding perennials or under the skirts of newly leafing deciduous shrubs, but below ground, it may be a different story. One solution is to introduce tap-rooted annuals, like California or Shirley poppies, many mallows, and certain sea hollies. Another is to excavate serious holes each spring, root pruning the surrounding permanent plants in the process, then refurbishing the soil as outlined in chapter 2. Eventually, the annuals will get crowded out, but that, after all, is part of how border succession works. A third option is to establish permanent spots where annuals are to grow each year. This is easy to say, but it can be hard to remember come fall, when the borders are cleaned and replanted. If you are an impulsive planter, it pays to mark these designated places as soon as you remove their summer occupants. Set up short canes and string or labels—whatever it takes to remind yourself not to plant there during the off season. This marking need not be unsightly, so long as it triggers thought before action. It can be done very unobtrusively, using birch twigs and black thread, or by covering those areas with mulch of a slightly different color or texture.

The most practical technique for me involves sinking empty, oversized pots between those large perennials or on the outskirts of shrubs. These "pot holes" become places to insert tubs of annuals (and other things), guaranteeing them enough root space. You don't plant in the empty pots, but rather use them like reservoirs to hold filled containers. When you stack up empty pots after a big planting session, you will notice that containers which are nominally the same size—usually one, two, or five gallons— come in a plethora of shapes. Set aside those which are slightly oversized—a bit wider than the others— to use as pot holes. The slightly smaller pots will slide in and out of these big ones, and you can change the display very easily. In dry or difficult parts of the border, as where old, established shrubs and trees have already laid claim to most of the soil space, it works well to use a pot hole a full size larger than your planting pot, and pack the interstices with wet sphagnum moss, which helps keep the inner pots moist. This means that where I want to use a one-gallon container, I sink an empty two-gallon pot. If I want to use a five-gallon planter, I sink either a ten-gallon can or one of the many odd-sized containers that fill the potting shed, saved for just such an occasion. To prepare the inner pot for planting, toss in an inch or so of coarse gravel or small stones, to prevent the drainage holes from blocking up underground. Next, mix a handful of hydrated hydrophilic polymer in the bottom half of the soil in the inner pot before inserting the plant. Once the potted plants are rooted in, this keeps them fresh between waterings, and often frees you from extra waterings all together. I also use compost and aged manure, both of which are water retentive, rather than bagged soil, which tends to be very light. Commercial soils often have a high percentage of peat moss in them, which dries out quickly and is very hard to rewet.

Many annuals can time-share border accommodations with bulbs, particularly when bulbs that bloom in late winter or earliest spring are coupled with summer annuals. It takes a bit of local research to learn which bulbs will adapt best to this technique in your own borders. Begin by observing which have withered sufficiently by late May or early June to allow total removal of their leaves. The sooner and more completely they go dormant, the better candidate they make for sandwich plantings. Species crocus or the smallest daffodils, Grecian windflowers (*Anemone blanda*), and species tulips like the starry little *Tulipa turkestanica* or sunny *T. tarda* have all proved long-lasting sandwichers in my gardens. To smooth the transition from spring into summer, interplant late spring bulbs—May-flowered tulips, hyacinths, and alliums—with spring-blooming annuals that carry on into early summer. Forget-me-nots are a traditional choice, for they froth delightfully about the bulbs, hiding their faults as they fade, then carry on for the several weeks it takes to ripen the

bulb foliage properly before removing it. Forget-me-not seed can be bought in white or sugar pink as well as several shades of blue, making them workable in any number of color schemes. They start as little rosettes that fit snugly between sheaves of daffodils and tall tulips, then expand like rising bread, covering the browning bulb leaves as they go. Fried egg flower, *Limnanthes douglasii*, is another cheerful early bloomer that helps disguise the passing of small, finer textured bulbs like *Fritillaria michailovskyi* or hoop petticoat daffodils (forms of *Narcissus bulbocodium*). The glowing yellow ribbons of Bowles' golden grass (*Milium effusum* 'Aureum') pair nicely with fragrant, bulbous, *Iris bucharica*, a dainty thing with diaphanous petals of yellow and white.

Pairing annuals with bulbs demands special techniques to reduce the likelihood of damaging the bulbs. The bulbs must be planted deep, and should rest on a thick floor of sand or coarse grit to ensure quick drainage. Many gardeners plant bulbs in mesh baskets to protect them against mice and moles, but such baskets are an equally good safeguard against an errant shovel or trowel. Planting sandwiched bulbs in baskets makes it difficult to slice them all in half when preparing soil for the next plant layer.

ANNUALS FROM SEED

Raising annuals from seed expands your selection enormously, and frees you from the tyranny of the garden center. Most are very easy, sprouting freely and growing on with the most routine of care. A single seed packet will generally produce plenty of plants, enough to have and to share. Before I had children, I grew hundreds of plants from seed each year. Now that my time is more limited, I get together with a few friends before ordering seed. We decide which annuals (including vegetables) we can't live without, then each of us raises a manageable number (usually a few dozen kinds) and come spring, we swap seedlings.

If a whole flatful of seedlings is more than I want or need, I sow a few in a tin or tray of heavy aluminum foil. Though these trays are made to be tossed away, they can be recycled for several seasons. Josephine Nuese, author of that neglected classic, *The Country Garden*, mentions in it an excellent trick, which is to poke small holes in the sides of these pans. This allows the roots plenty of air, and makes for terrific seedlings, chunky and well-rooted. Check for specific instructions on each seed packet; some seeds like light, and need no covering, while others like a mere dusting of vermiculite. A few prefer total darkness in order to germinate, which can be arranged by covering the seed flat with a black plastic bag. Certain tropicals need bottom heat to germinate, which is easily supplied with a preset heat cable. My seed pans live in the unheated sunporch, where they are kept moist till germination with jackets of heavy duty plastic cling wrap. Once seedlings emerge, they theoretically get misted every day, but, lest I forget, which I often do, I spread a thin layer of hydrated hydrophilic polymer over the bottom of the seed tray before filling it. Once the young seedlings root into it, they have a reservoir against drought. It doesn't make up for the lack of frequent watering entirely, but it does buy the forgetful some time.

When the first true leaves appear in the seed trays, you can slice the seedlings apart, each with its own soil block, using an old kitchen knife. Pot them up at once, using moist potting medium, setting the little things into two-inch plug pots if they are tiny and frail, or four-inch pots if they are sturdy and vigorous. (Small seedlings get lost in oversized pots, and can be overwhelmed by an excess of water. Again, mix some hydrated polymer into the bottom half of each pot. Give them some shade for several days after this, either using shade cloth draped over the nearby windows or with old screens. These can be made free standing by adding a prop made from thin wooden slatting mounted on a hinge. Such screens are cheap and simple to make, and travel outdoors with the plants when they are ready to harden off, then again when they are placed in their final garden positions. In every case, shade the plants during the hottest part of the day for two or three days, increasing exposure to direct sun slowly.

Quite a few annuals can be sown directly in place in the garden, which saves all the fuss and bother. However, until they are familiar to me, I find it best to sow them in flats or pots, even if those containers are left in the garden. This prevents me from thoughtlessly wiping out a whole colony of something by mistaking it for a weed. This isn't as silly as it may sound, for a great many garden flowers have wild and weedy counterparts. Indeed, the apricot foxgloves are indistinguishable from the commoners in the first-year rosette stage, and unless they are marked, I can't tell whether the seedlings have been deliberately sown or have insinuated themselves into pot or plot. Ornamental grasses are especially tricky, and I always raise these in well labeled flats and pots. They look so much like regular old weed or lawn grass, it is almost impossible to remember their worth during the vigorous spring cleaning of the borders. I have a fatal tendency to rip them out, then remember in dismay that all that thick, green stuff isn't grass, it's Grass, elevated by horticultural fiat to ornamental status.

Status is exactly what annuals are short on these days, but as we have seen with ornamental grasses, horticultural fashions do change, though often slowly. Annuals may be out of favor, yet the moment we look beyond the commonplace annual offerings so readily available, we discover a host of handsome, hard-working plants that earn their way into our borders on solid merits. Their ardent generosity gets them into young and empty mixed borders, but their long-lasting good looks, adaptability, and steady performance keep them in established ones, where they may ably fill a dozen niches. In mature mixed borders where large scale changes are few, annuals refresh and renew color blends and combinations and allow the gardener scope to continue experimenting even when the garden's formative years are past.

Nodding blue tassels of Clematis macropetala *'Blue Bird' decorate the lower branches of purple hazel,* Corylus maxima *'Purpurea', in my mixed borders. Photo: Mark Lovejoy*

Chapter Seven

VINES AND CLIMBERS
IN THE
MIXED BORDER

Climbing plants are generally overlooked and undervalued in American gardens, yet if thoughtfully used, they can contribute some of the richest effects to be found in the mixed border. Well placed climbers will make sheets and curtains and spuming fountains of blossom and foliage, while taking up only a fraction of the ground space required by a shrub of similar size. Mixed borders present the gardener with a multiplicity of likely settings in which vines and other climbers might shine. Perimeter plantings of shrubs and small trees, often supplemented with stout fencing, can support magnificently oversized climbers, while the borders themselves offer hosts in a splendid variety of sizes, shapes, and heights for less demanding vines. Indeed, even the smallest border plants may be paired with climbers in combinations which display both participants to advantage.

Perhaps it is because we are most accustomed to growing our honeysuckles and clematis on trellises or walls that we so seldom let them appear in less formal roles. This is a pity, because more natural settings suit many climbers better than artificial ones. Trees and large shrubs may act as living arbors for lusty climbing roses and ornamental grapevines. Shrubs of any size offer a provocative diversity of forms, colors, and textures against which more moderate climbing plants may be arrayed. Lesser climbers, often classified as scramblers, can decorate subshrubs and weave amongst sturdy perennials. Trailing semiclimbers like nasturtiums or delicate *Clematis × durandii* can clamber through tall ground covers or brighten the carpet on the garden's floor.

The fact that garden climbers are usually seen trained on flat surfaces reinforces the unspoken notion that these plants are two dimensional by nature. However, like water, they adapt freely to the shape of their holder. A clematis that makes a thin sheet of color on a wall appears exotically different when threaded through the great, saw-toothed leaves of a lacecap hydrangea. Small honeysuckles can creep through a stout rhododendron, while vigorous ones will hang in loose, perfumed nets from the boughs of a tall fir. A leggy rose like 'Alchemyst' that looks incurably stiff on a trellis will lean comfortably into the embrace of a small pear tree. Lax, multi-branching climbers like *Rosa souleiana* loosely lace tree to shrub, veiling the border's perimeters with cascading curtains of blossom and vivid hips.

Though the largest, heaviest climbers are best placed in mature trees or on sturdy fences, nearly any ornamental shrub will make a good host for modestly sized vines. To see where climbers might fit into your own borders, browse through nurseries, books, and other gardens and assemble a working list of climbers that thrive in your area. When you make the garden rounds, look for quiet corners or hedges that could use a touch of floral embroidery. Before planting, however, a number of factors must be taken into account to insure that host and guest are appropriately paired. Relative size is primary, for a climbing companion should always enhance the host, and must never overwhelm or harm it. A diminutive rockrose or daphne would be swamped by a vigorous trailer, while a dainty alpine clematis would disappear into a bold-leaved maple. To maintain balance of scale, large, architectural shrubs are better paired with vines that pour in solid rivers of color than with airy wanderers. A gold-spotted acuba looks gloriously brazen bearing a broad sash of purple-leaved grape, yet even a large-flowered clematis looks like a fussy detail against the complicated shape and pattern of the shrub's foliage. Bare-twigged shrubs such as 'Moonlight' broom or winter-blooming jasmine make natural hoops against which flurries of small-textured vines like 'Antique Fantasy' sweet peas or a chocolate-flowered morning glory may be excitingly displayed. The same shrubs would be crushed to insignificance if laden with massive swags of bittersweet (*Celastrus orbiculatus*) or a climbing hydrangea.

Playing with contrasts of color is another major consideration, for vines offer unparalleled opportunities to emphasize background foliage and plant forms which might otherwise be overlooked. A murky red sand cherry (*Prunus × cistena*) that quietly echoes the darker tones of border flowers will be brought into prominence by ribbons of coral-pink 'Climbing Shot Silk' roses or fat rosettes of the ashy pink double *Clematis* 'Belle of Woking'. A multi-trunked elder, *Sambucus nigra* 'Marginata', with large, white-edged leaves becomes a visual feast when wrapped in lacy yards of canary creeper, *Tropaeolum peregrinum*, with its golden, birdlike flowers. Bright flowers can bring out the hidden beauties of subtle foliage, as when strands of rose-red *Rhodochiton atrosanguineum* are woven through the silvery feathers of bushy *Artemisia absinthium* 'Huntingdon' to heraldic effect, or when the orange peel clematis, *Clematis orientalis*, is grown through the pleated copper foliage of the weeping purple beech, *Fagus sylvatica* 'Purpurea Pendula'. Close shadings of similar colors can also create lovely vignettes, as when the ruffly double *Clematis viticella* 'Purpurea Plena Ele-

gans', with two-toned blossoms of violet and purple, is wound through a group of ornamental sage, *Salvia officinalis* 'Purpurascens', with its long velvety leaves of silvered purple. Combinations of the same color can be showstopping, as when a golden mock orange (*Philadelphus coronarius* 'Aureus') is simultaneously covered with both its own white, gold-stamened flowers and the double white rosettes of *Clematis* 'Duchess of Edinburgh'.

Contrasts of texture and form suggest themselves readily when we are carrying young plants in nursery pots about the garden, looking for likely settings. However, further research is definitely in order before planting, since the ultimate rather than the present size of the climber must determine its garden position. Should we want to pair the leathery, rust-backed leaves of *Vitis coignetiae*, an ornamental grape that colors stunningly in autumn, with the long, fuzzy gray-green leaves of *Hydrangea aspera*, it is essential to provide significant secondary support such as a sturdy fence or a sixty-foot maple for the vine, which will otherwise swallow the ten-foot hydrangea in one gulp. Height and mass of vine alone are not the only determiners, however, for the intricate little bells of *Clematis viticella* 'Betty Corning' fade to inconsequence against glossy, ornate fatsia leaves, despite parity of plant size. Thread the same clematis through a tall white Spanish broom (*Cytisus multiflorus*) and both vine and shrub are improved by the connection. The relative density and weight of the vine must also be considered, for while both a climbing monkshood, *Aconitum volubile*, and a climbing nasturtium relative, *Tropaeolum tuberosum* 'Ken Aslet', may achieve ten or twelve feet in height, the first is airy enough to be permitted to weave among the slim, rather brittle stems of a golden cutleaf elder (*Sambucus racemosa* 'Plumosa Aurea'), where its soft blue flowers drip enchantingly through the elder's green-gold foliage. The tropaeolum, in contrast, produces luxuriant masses of lush, rounded foliage that would smother all but the hardiest host. It looks wonderful cradled in the curving lower arms of a silvery blue spruce or a stout fir, where its tubular orange-red flowers show up vividly and its abundant growth will be strongly supported without harm to its host.

Large, vigorous vines require substantial support and will quickly overwhelm an insufficiently sturdy host. Golden hops, Humulus lupulus 'Aureus', runs up its tripod of stout stakes by May, scrambles into the laburnum behind by June, then scales a pair of blue spruces at the border back. At its feet is the Siberian iris 'Summer Skies'. Author's garden. Photo: Mark Lovejoy

The dwarf shrubs that make up the mixed bor-der's midborder islands may also serve to carry climbers. *Daphne odora* is rather plain in summer, but can be made to bloom again with a few strands of a rosy flowered Persian everlasting pea, *Lathyrus rotundifolius*. A silver-leaved, pink-flowered little scrambler, *Convolvulus elegantissimus* brings a second wind to a lavender-blue 'Minstead' broom, while its annual relative, *C. tricolor* 'Heavenly Blue', makes a charming accent for shrublets of spring-blooming *Genista lydia*. The intense indigo of *Caryopteris* 'Dark Knight' is cooled by tendrils of the creamy yellow, long-armed *Viola* 'Beshlie'. Gaudy little *Spiraea* 'Goldflame' burns even brighter when infiltrated by deep orange 'Padparadja' pansies, named for the fa-bled crown jewel of Sri Lanka.

Though evergreen herbs like sage, rosemary, and lavender are not commonly thought of as hosts for climbers, mature specimens can make excellent showcases for small, slow-growing, or delicate scramblers. An upright 'Tuscan Blue' rosemary will hold lacy ropes of magenta-purple *Acerina* 'Victoria Falls', while the extra long stems of a plump, low-growing lavender, *Lavandula intermedia* 'Fred Bou-tin', will support a delicate tracery of creeping *Fuch-sia procumbens* with its tiny green-and-purple trumpets. The common culinary sage, *Salvia officin-alis*, has a number of handsome garden forms with leaves of purple and pink, green-gold, or furry gray. All make good-sized subshrubs which will support the smallest scramblers, like *Viola cornuta* in its many forms, half-hardy *Sandersonia aurantiaca*, with its globular orange lanterns, or wispy threads of the tender perennial *Codonopsis viridiflora* with its char-treuse-and-purple bells.

We tend to forget that certain climbers also make excellent ground covers. Glossy ivy, bird footed or heart shaped, spangled with gold dust or silver stars, can carpet as well as climb. A few variegated climb-ers insinuated into a mass ground cover planting will wake up a boring bank of plain pachysandra or vinca. Beds solid with prostrate junipers are im-measurably enriched by bright strands of clematis, which will as happily run sideways as up or down. Evergreen climbing euonymous, perhaps in a var-iegated form, can mingle with perennial sweetpeas

(*Lathyrus latifolius*). Broad border edgings of woolly lamb's ears (*Stachys* species) can carry annual *Thun-bergia fragrans* 'Angel Wings' with its snowy, scented blossoms.

In order to prolong visual interest, pair climbing plants which perform especially early or late with hosts having opposite tendencies. Many early bloomers, like broom and forsythia, lilac and spirea, are undistinguished in form, offering little more than bulk and greenery during the summer. Part-nered with summer-blooming climbers, whether annual or perennial, such shrubs can actively con-tribute to the border's beauty for many months. A rhododendron which is glorious in spring could be kept visually alive all summer by a lacy *Eccremocarpus* covered with flowers shaped like fat little goldfish. Hollies that were bright with berry all winter could remain showy from May through November if laced with a cream-splashed annual hop vine, *Hu-mulus japonicus* 'Variegatus'. Perennial climbers might seem the most logical candidates in mixed borders, yet in places where naked, woody-stemmed climbers might impair the looks of the winter garden or mar the dashing display of spring, annual or ephemeral vines work best. Woody vines with permanent stems, like Dutchman's pipe (*Ar-istolochia durior*), climbing hydrangea, and wisteria, are often too large in scale and aspiration for the border proper. These are reserved for the garden's perimeters, where they find support from the largest trees and shrubs. Smaller woody vines, like varie-gated kiwi, certain honeysuckle, and some species clematis can be hidden beneath the evergreen foliage of shrubs like rhododendrons, kalmias, pieris, and conifers until their time to shine arrives.

Exact combinations of hosts and climbers will vary from garden to garden, for both timing and bloom sequence may alter as much due to specific conditions as to variables of region and climate. Finding perfect mates is easier in the garden than in the human world, yet even so, a good deal of tink-ering and experimentation may be necessary before utterly satisfying results are achieved. You may begin, as I did, by pairing a soft yellow forsythia with early flowering *Clematis alpina* 'White Moth'. This made a charming though brief picture, but the

Vines may ramble as well as climb, lacing through small shrubs and perennials at the border's front, and even playing the role of ground cover. Clematis 'Ville de Lyon' pours through a stand of hellebores to decorate the rippled, black leaves of Ajuga pyramidalis *'Metallica Crispa' in the Withey/Price garden. Photo: Lynne Harrison*

uary. My shrub, *Forsythia suspensa*, colors well in autumn, which strengthens the show with a backdrop of copper and scarlet foliage for Lady Betty's periwinkle-purple blossoms. The handsome witch hazel *Hamamelis vernalis* 'Sandra' would do much the same thing, if no forsythia were handy.

All this is not to say that there is no room for architectural elements in the mixed border. Indeed, vines and creepers trained over trellis panels, hoops, arches, or special shaping forms—whether geometrical pyramids or fluffy bunnies—can make wonderful focal points where borders are formal in design and feeling. However, in informal, naturalistic borders, traditional architectural supports can look artificial and out of place. Rustic supports may seem more at home, whether unpeeled, shaggy logs shaped into a summerhouse or pergola, rugged treillage fashioned from irregular tree branches, or woven lattice panels of willow wands or fruit tree prunings. Tepees or tripods made from sturdy straight branches serve to elevate sweet peas or honeysuckle above the summery froth of border perennials in long-lasting vertical exclamations.

These last are especially valuable, since they look handsome and can be made in minutes by a ten-year-old child, let alone a middle-aged gardener with few woodworking skills. Tripods, not surprisingly, are made from three sturdy sticks or branches, tied firmly together at their tops. You can do this with twine, which looks very nice but rots; with wire, which hardly shows at all if it isn't the shiny kind, but rusts; or with plastic stretch tie tape, which lasts forever, but is usually a regrettable shade of green that goes with nothing. I usually opt for twine, and reinforce the join each year, sometimes even before the tripod collapses. To use a tripod, spread the three legs as broadly or shallowly as seems appropriate, then dig little holes with your trowel for each foot. If the sticks are slim, as might be right for annual sweet peas or a little *Clematis macropetala*, only a few inches of stick need to be buried, and the tripod will hold just fine. Where a lusty *Clematis* × *jouiniana praecox* is involved, choose stout branches at least eight feet tall, place them well apart, and set them at least six inches deep. To encourage plants to climb, wrap the tripod's legs with bands of twine,

vine required a thorough clean-up each fall in order that dead leaves and stems not clutter the shrub's bare branches all winter, and detract from the grace of the swelling buds. Trading 'White Moth' for late summer- and fall-blooming *Clematis* 'Lady Betty Balfour' greatly increased the forsythia's midseason value, which was otherwise negligible. Since this clematis likes a hard pruning in late winter, there are now no straggling old stems to hide come spring, and I don't have to worry about mauling the vine when I cut forsythia branches for the house in Jan-

wire, or even green willow twigs, which look prettier than the twine or wire. Long strands of weeping willow, cut before the leaves emerge, can be loosely woven about the tripod legs, then tucked back upon themselves to secure the weaving. These dry in a few weeks, and are surprisingly strong, sometimes lasting several seasons.

Tepees are very similar to tripods, except they may have as many legs as you like. These are the traditional support for runner beans (which, by the way, look just as striking in the mixed border as in the vegetable garden).

Where wire supports like tomato cages or plant hoops draw the eye, you can disguise their gleaming metal with bands of willow, woven around each tier just as you wove them around the tripod legs. Prunings from other vines can be used to guide large vines with long internodes (the spaces between leaf buds) up their supports; thick strands of grapevine, honeysuckle, or rough hop vines can be wrapped around wooden poles, tall stumps, and even tree trunks. Black plastic netting or chicken wire, similarly wrapped, and well secured at either end, can also support a lot of vine.

Many gardeners admire the romantic look of a treeful of roses or a living drapery of wisteria, yet are uncertain how to reproduce such scenes. When a host shrub is not furnished to the ground with branches, or when the chosen tree branch is out of easy reach, the gap between the climber and the climbee must be artificially but unobtrusively bridged. Plastic pea netting, tough and all but invisible, can be draped in loose swaths or cut into narrow ropes and laced into the host, its lower ends pinned to the ground with tent pegs or forked twigs. Coarse, loosely twisted ropes may be slung into the tallest trees, their ends, weighted with heavy knots, making dangling paths for twining vines (leave plenty of slack to allow for the play of wind). Twiggy sticks (such as alder, hazel, or birch) can be poked into the soil to guide questing climbers onto fences, lower tree limbs, or shrubs.

Natural climbers are equipped with twining stems or tendrils, aerial roots (like the sucker feet of ivy), hooks and prickles, or similar mechanisms for attachment. Most are readily trained into almost any position on a living host, needing far less intervention than they would on architectural supports. Wall grown clematis requires weekly training during the spring in order to keep their stems well spaced. Grown on a shrub or up a tree, clematis tends to sprawl out naturally. Intertwined or errant stems are simply separated, their twisted tendrils cut away, then wrapped gently under or through the branches of the shrub; no ties are needed. Honeysuckle and jasmine, sweetpeas and morning glories will scramble attractively into a shrub or tree with just an occasional bit of direction from the gardener. Climbing hydrangea and varieties of *Euonymus fortunei*, like ivy, are often nonclimbing for the first few years after planting, while they establish strong root systems. After that, they will climb with goodwill, though their first long shoots generally need to be encouraged or even gently tied into position.

Most so-called climbing roses need significant assistance to get aloft, though many will stay put nicely once they grow into place. Climbers and ramblers are apt to throw out long, supple stems even in the first year after planting, and these may be lightly bound to host branches with stretchy plastic tie tape. Being flexible, tie tape holds the canes securely in place, yet allows them to move slightly in wind or with growth, reducing stress breakage of the climbers' main stems which become the permanent framework for the plant. Certain roses, like *Rosa soulieana* or the creamy old rambler, 'Wedding Day', need only a few ties when young, for they quickly develop an extended network of well-armed and multi-branched canes that cling tenaciously to their host. Within a few seasons, the ties may be removed entirely. Brittle, stiff-legged hybrid climbing roses like 'Climbing Shot Silk' or 'Handel' will need to be staked permanently into position, again bound with stretchy ties. Repeat bloomers tend to be slower growing than the once-blooming species and hybrids, and even after they put on generous growth, their hold on their host may be tenuous. Such roses usually require a good deal of tying in, but the abundance and long season of their bloom makes the extra effort worthwhile. If necessary, any pruning out of older canes must be done in stages, removing three- or four-foot sections at a time in order not to damage the healthy canes. Generally, however, established climbers need little annual pruning. Indeed, in some cases, it is scarcely possible; by the time a vigorous *Rosa filipes* 'Kiftsgate' has scaled fifty or sixty feet up a tall fir, only the prissiest of gardeners is going to worry about accumulated deadwood. Where smaller roses fill shorter trees, pruning may be carried out as needed from the relative security of an orchard ladder.

CULTURAL NEEDS

While rarely as exuberant as their equatorial counterparts, some of which grow measurably each hour, hardy climbers are generally quick growers. This productivity makes them especially welcome in young gardens, where fast results are appreciated, but again it is important to match the vigor of a climber with the strength of the host. Where an energetic vine like wisteria is to be paired with a sturdy but slow-growing tree or shrub, it is better to plant the host first, giving it the advantage of several years' growth. A less lusty placeholder— perhaps an annual morning glory or variegated hops—can take the wisteria's position until the intended host is strong enough for the job. Since a serious mismatch made early in a woody plant's life can cause permanent damage, patience in the formative years pays off. In order to reduce the waiting time, one can grow the climber in a nursery bed, perhaps encasing the roots in a grow bag. (Favored by field growers, these bags are made of heavy plastic, sometimes lightly coated with copper. Like a pot, but larger and deeper, grow bags confine root growth, directing it down, rather than out, and greatly reduce transplant shock.)

Any good garden soil will suit most climbers. In the mixed border, the greatest difficulties arise where trees and shrubs have been in place for a long time. The result is nearly always dry, rooty soil, which must be loosened and well amended before young climbers are introduced nearby. A handful of hydrated P4 hydrogel mixed into the planting hole

Most clematis require a sunny situation, but 'Silver Moon' blooms abundantly in partial or filtered shade. The shapely ostrich ferns, Matteuccia struthiopteris, *are aggressive spreaders, but their young croziers may be harvested for the kitchen. Withey/Price garden, Seattle. Photo: Mark Lovejoy*

will help climbers establish quickly and decrease their dependency on supplementary water. (For a one- or two-gallon plant, use about half a cup of hydrated gel, and about one-quarter cup for smaller plants.) A layer of horticultural barrier cloth may be placed around the mature woody plants to discourage their questing roots before heaping on up to eight inches of good topsoil to support perennials and climbers. Care must be taken to protect the crowns of established plants by sloping the added soil away from their trunks. The sloped soil may be bound in place with mannerly ground covers such as small-leaved vinca or slow-growing ivies.

The only caveat with climbers is that once one begins to use them excitingly, the effect is heady. The danger lies no longer in ignoring climbers, but in swinging too far in the opposite direction, until no surface goes undecorated. Though splendidly baroque, such an excess of detail can be as distracting as too little is boring. There are times when I wander through my borders, new clematis in hand, looking for a likely site, only to find that every possible vertical already has a hopeful young vine nestled at its foot. Fortunately, hard winters, moles, fighting cats, and errant dogs continually thin the ranks, leaving only a label in memorium. Years ago, such losses caused me endless heartache, but maturity and the acquisition of far too many plants have convinced me that here, as everywhere else, moderation is the key to gardenly happiness.

The following is a sampler of climbing plants which are appropriate for mixed border situations. There are dozens, indeed, hundreds more which thrive in various parts of the country. To develop your own palette, visit other gardens, contact plant societies, and read widely. Above all, experiment freely; many a sheltered garden holds microclimates one or two zones warmer than might be supposed. In addition, many of the zones indicated are best guesses, based on performance in England and the maritime northwest. Once better known here, we may well find that our hot American summers extend the climatic limits for these and other climbers considerably.

PERENNIAL CLIMBERS

Clematis are among the most familiar flowering vines, yet only a handful are commonly grown in our gardens. The family deserves a closer look, since it offers bloomers for every season of the year (in mild climates, at least, for winter bloomers like *Clematis cirrhosa* and *C. c. balearica* are hardy only to Zone 7). There are dozens of early performers, vigorous species like the honey-scented *C. montana*, with four-petaled flowers rather like dogwood blossoms; the airy scrambler, *C. alpina*, with curving, open bells; and the fluffy, double-skirted forms of *C. macropetala*.

The small-flowered and species clematis are sadly overlooked, outshone by the buxom, brazen summer bloomers. The named summer beauties are indeed irresistible, but it is well worth exploring less common plants rather than using the ubiquitous *C. × jackmanii* or 'Nelly Moser'. The ruffled, double florets of midnight purple 'Vyvyan Pennell' look smashing waltzing through a red barberry. The elegant, curling bells of *C. texensis* 'Duchess of Albany' in creamy rose, or the scarlet ribbons of *C. t.* 'Gravetye Beauty' will wake up a slumbering weigela in midsummer. The spidery, ivory 'Huldine' or doe-eyed single *C. viticella* 'Alba Luxurians' does magical things for white variegated euonymous. (Even *C. × jackmanii* can look stunning when looped through a variegated shrubby dogwood.) Fall bloomers include the sweet autumn clematis, *C. dioscoreifolia*, looking like a fragrant white cloud, so profuse is the bloom on an established plant. There are many late or repeat bloomers, such as 'Lady Betty Balfour', purple with a lemon yellow heart, or the china blue 'Will Goodwin', that bloom till hard frost. All fall bloomers appreciate a warm, sunny position on an open, airy shrub like forsythia or lilac.

Gardeners who find clematis frustrating may feel better when they realize that these plants generally need three to five years in the ground before they hit their stride. Once they achieve sufficient root growth, they will continue to perform well for many years, so they are well worth the wait. However, where a large area is to be covered, it helps to use more than one plant; in the Purple Border at Sissinghurst, no fewer than five *Clematis* 'Ville de Lyons' are grouped on the famous wall, making a stupendous spectacle that one plant could never match. Where clematis are growing very slowly, the most likely problem is lack of food, for clematis are gross feeders. Like roses, they appreciate feeding mulches every spring, and hybrids in particular need frequent supplemental boosts during the growing season.

Clematis may be as handsome in seed as in flower. Flossy seed heads of Clematis tangutica *decorate a sleek mound of blue rue. Author's garden. Photo: Mark Lovejoy*

(Doses of tomato food in liquid form give very satisfactory results.) Siting can also lead to problems, for while most people know that clematis like their heads in the sun and roots in the shade, they sometimes forget that tucking a vine too close to their host or protective shrub can cut off their water supply. Dry shade is anathema to these vines, which thrive in deep, rich soil. Hydrated P4 hydrogel mixed into the root zone will help enormously, for clematis are big drinkers, too, and will perform far better if given an extra gallon or two of water each week in dry spells (open ended plastic pipes set into the soil direct the water to their root zone, so noth-

ing is wasted in runoff). Deep mulch will conserve moisture, keep clematis roots cool, and discourage competitive weeds.

Aconitum volubile (Zone 7, growing ten to fifteen feet) is one of several Asian climbing monkshoods, none of which are common. *Aconitum volubile* is easily grown from fresh seed, which sometimes appears on seed exchange lists. It is a vigorous, twining vine with rather small, deeply lobed leaves and purple to blue and green hooded flowers in small clusters, appearing in late summer and continuing until hard frost. This is an excellent companion for showy fall foliage shrubs or small trees, particularly witch hazels, parottias, and other members of the Hamamelidaceae. It grows best in rich, moist soil and partial or filtered shade, but tolerates quite dry conditions once established, thanks to fat, almost tuberous storage roots. This plant benefits markedly from the addition of P4 hydrogel in its root zone, and appreciates an annual feeding mulch of aged manure and compost.

Actinidia kolomikta (Zone 4, to fifteen feet) is a vegetable valentine. Its heart-shaped leaves open bronzy red, turning to green as they mature. The unfolding buds elongate into hand-sized leaves, their pointed tips liberally brushed with white and pink. Variegation will be most pronounced in full sun, but develops nicely in partial or high, filtered shade. This vine looks glamorous laced through a hedge of copper beech or clambering into an open-branched red maple at the border's edge.

Adlumia fungosa (Zones 7 to 8, to fifteen feet), is native to the eastern woods, where it is known as mountain fringe. This dainty climber is light enough to run through a border, decorating perennials and ground covers with its pale green lace. It will toss its ferny foliage and tubular, heart-shaped flowers in off-shades of cream, purple, and green among hostas and true ferns, or wend its way up dogwoods or fruit trees with equal good will.

Akebia quinata (Zone 5, fifteen to twenty feet) is a handsome scrambler with five-lobed leaves as long as fingers. The species offers dusky purple—or rarely, white—flowers that smell like grapes and stand out attractively against a light colored background, as when romping through a silvery blue spruce or a golden holly. The sparsely set fruits, which look like purple pickles, are edible, if not especially tasty.

Ampelopsis brevipedunculata is too vigorous a plant for the mixed border, but its diminutive variegated form, 'Elegans' (Zone 5, eight to twelve feet), is modest both in manner and stature. The stems are fuchsia pink, the leaves richly marbled with cream, sage, gray and pink, and though its flowers are virtually unnoticeable, it offers sprays of lovely berries in fall, in every tint between foam and ocean blue. Let this one twine through a hydrangea, over a sprawling juniper, or lace through a sheet of plain green ivy. There are several forms circulating under this name, some more variegated, others with lacier though rather plain leaves, but all are worth growing.

Aristolochia durior (Zone 4, to thirty feet) or Dutchman's pipe, a woody vine native to the eastern woods, has bold, rounded leaves and bulbous, purple-and-green flowers that resemble curving, fat-bowled tobacco pipes. Not a vine to toss casually over a slender young dogwood, this noble plant brings a lush, exotic look to the garden, and turns a chain-link fence into a solid wall. It can be trained over a summerhouse wall, encouraged to climb a clustered tepee of very sturdy poles, or looped into the arms of a strong tree.

Billardiera longiflora (Zone 8, to eight feet), Tasmanian climbing blueberry, is a tender perennial that is well worth coddling in a greenhouse each winter, just for the sight of its fat berries spangling a golden cutleaf elder or a flaming smokebush in fall. Vines grown from seed may fruit white, rose, or even purple, but in the most common garden form the berries are a saturated cobalt blue. The slim stems are rather sparsely leaved, and light enough to roam through front line perennials and ground covers, where the greenish bellflowers are easily examined.

Decumaria barbara (Zone 8, to thirty feet), native to southeastern America, is a hydrangea relative with sinuous, twining stems that carry it easily into a large shrub or small tree. Semi-deciduous, it has shiny, pointed leaves that linger longest in a sheltered position in half or filtered shade. In such spots, the shrubby vine will produce hundreds of small clusters of white, fluttering flowers. In gardens, the shady woodland spots it prefers are often too rooty and dry for its taste, and a generous helping of P4 hydrogel at the root zone will prove beneficial. The gel may also extend the hardiness zone by providing a measure of frost protection as well as moisture conservation (the gel freezes and holds the soil temperature at 32 degrees Fahrenheit, while air temperatures may be considerably lower).

Humulus lupulus (Zone 6, to twenty feet), the hops that contribute to beer making, also contribute to fine garden making. The best form in the border is 'Aureus', its leaves bright gold in youth, darker in maturity, paling to soft yellow autumn. Like many golden leaves, these tend to scorch in full sun, and color best in partial or filtered shade. Perennial golden hops will happily scale a laburnum or birch, and look gorgeous pouring through a copper beech hedge.

Hydrangea anomala petiolaris (Zone 4, to fifty feet). Think carefully before planting this handsome, woody climber, because it does not move with grace. The thick, brittle stems adhere to tree trunk or fence by means of tough little rootlets, and though it can take a year or two to settle in (during which time it may display no climbing tendencies), once well rooted, this plant can cover a good deal of territory in a year. It works wonders on chain-link or strong wooden fences, where it may be espaliered in fans or informal patterns. It also makes a striking covering for tall, high limbed trees, where a long expanse of bare trunk can look out of scale with border plants, and will dramatically clothe a prostrate log or fallen tree in woodland borders.

Jasminum officinalis (Zone 7, twenty to thirty feet). Lacy of leaf and flexuous of stem, this hardiest of the climbing jasmines will wind luxuriously scented wreaths of clean white flowers over arch or bower all summer. It will also climb into an open-limbed tree, but dislikes the shade and dry soil associated with such conditions, and is too vigorous a companion for most shrubs. It will do far better on a fence or draped over a large and sturdy tepee of branches. *Jasminum nudiflorum* (Zone 5, to twelve feet) is an arching, rather formless shrub that can be tied in to a wall (or the supportive trunk of an old fruit tree) and convinced to grow, if not climb, upright. Trained in this manner, it may reach ten to twelve feet, and produces its almost scentless golden trumpets very freely during any warm spell between November and March.

Lathyrus latifolius (Zone 5, to ten feet), the European everlasting pea, is a twining climber that will wander through a large hydrangea or spill over a steep bank unsupported. It looks very pretty grown midborder with its bottom growth confined in a tall

Woody climbers need permanent and sturdy support and plenty of room. This lusty Hydrangea anomala petiolaris has been scaling the house walls in the Withey/Price garden for several decades, and has become large enough to host in turn smaller clematis and annual climbers which decorate its lower reaches. Photo: Mark Lovejoy

hoop or tomato cage, from which it will cascade abundantly. The scentless flowers are usually rosy pink, magenta, or clean white, but pretty pink and white bicolor forms also occur. It has a number of attractive relatives which are worth seeking out for mixed border positions.

Lonicera × *americana* (Zone 5, to thirty feet). The honeysuckle clan is full of climbers, both evergreen and deciduous—far too many to detail here. However, this hybrid is an outstanding example, having vivid purple stems, glossy green leaves, and intensely fragrant flowers that are red in bud and white to creamy yellow in flower, appearing from April through June.

Parthenocissus tricuspidata (Zone 4, to sixty feet). The smallest of the Boston ivies, *P. t.* 'Lowii' has tiny enameled leaves the size and color of tree frogs. In my garden it spills in a starry shower from a slim fingered maple, *Acer pentaphyllum*, enlivening its somber red foliage with a sparkling autumn display of brass and bronze. A mild mannered Virginia creeper, *Parthenocissus henryana*, retains the rich purple-green tints of its new foliage when grown in shade, each leaf deeply veined in silver. This vine flashes scarlet in fall, a lively companion for *Tropaeolum speciosum*, the flame flower, which sends heavy swags of dull red flowers up shrub or tree come late summer. Both partners look wonderful against yew hedging or dusky fir boughs.

Rosa species and hybrids. Quite a few of the two hundred rose species are climbers or scramblers, armed with stout thorns and flexuous canes. Species roses, which seldom needing pruning and are largely self-supporting in tree or large shrub, are perhaps of most interest to the mixed border maker. Lady Banks' rose, *Rosa banksiae* (Zone 8, to thirty feet), is popular in southern gardens, where both its double white, violet-scented form, 'Alba Plena', and the double yellow 'Lutea' are trained on sunny walls or into elderly, multi-branched trees. The Cherokee rose, *R. laevigata* (Zone 7, to twenty feet), with large, white single flowers above glossy, semi-evergreen foliage, is a strong grower that produces whiskery red hips against pale gold foliage in autumn. *Rosa filipes* (Zone 6, thirty to one hundred feet) offers masses of creamy, fragrant little flowers

A feast for eye and nose, the climbing rose 'Alchymist' is wound through with strands of potato vine, Solanum crispum *'Glasnevin'. In small gardens, climbers may be thoughtfully paired to take fullest advantage of any available space. Garden of the late Kevin Nicolay, Seattle. Photo: Kevin Nicolay*

in loose clusters up to eighteen inches long in June and July. It is best known in its ultravigorous form, 'Kiftsgate', named for the garden in which a single plant covers the aerial equivalent of a quarter of an acre. This is a plant for large gardens, or gardens in which a very large tree needs significant decoration. Grown as a shrub, *R. soulieana* (Zone 7, twenty to fifty feet) seldom exceeds twelve feet, but trained into a tree or over large shrubs, it quickly spreads into an airy network, each arm of which may grow twelve feet in a single season. The stems are lax and light enough to be threaded through tall lilacs or over big viburnums, but it is perhaps most spectacular when grown through a weeping or umbrella

pruned fruit tree. It produces hundreds of corymbs of white, scented flowers up to ten inches long in July and August, followed by glossy little red hips. Check with local rose fanciers and societies to find hybrids and other species that will perform well in your own region.

Solanum crispum (Zones 7 to 8, to fifteen feet). Potato vine is too plebeian a name for this aristocrat with its sheets of smoky, grape-colored flowers. It needs a sunny position to flower well, and is usually grown on a south facing wall, but will pour over a large aucuba or through a shrubby purple elder without harm to its host. The dark-flowered form, 'Glasnevin', is slightly hardier than the species, and is worth carrying over the winter in a greenhouse where the vine is too tender to be grown out of doors.

Vitis species. When the eastern woods are ablaze with foliar fire, thick ropes of wild grape turn soft gold, glowing like pale sunshine through the trees. In the border, a number of grapevines can provide a similar effect, for all are decorative if not always fruitful. *Vitis vinifera* 'Purpurea' (Zone 6, to thirty feet), a dark-leaved form of the wine grape, has young leaves of deep red that turn almost black in maturity. The grapes are tiny, black, and bitter, with a powdery bloom on them. *V.* x 'Brant' (Zone 4, to twenty feet) has fat palmate leaves like chubby, short-fingered hands. They color with astonishing brilliance in fall, taking on rich shades of copper, red, and mulberry. 'Brant', a hybrid between two table fruit grapes, bears small but fragrant and flavorful grapes. *Vitis cognetiae* (Zone 5, to sixty feet) is potentially the largest of the bunch, though it can be kept within bounds by pruning if need be. Where space permits, few sights are more spectacular than a great fir laced with this vine. Its big, rounded leaves are deep forest green, backed with cinnamon fuzz. In fall, they make a glorious cascade of crimson, punctuated with clusters of purple black grapes. In my garden, *V. vinifera* 'Purpurea' springs up between clumps of silver blue fescue. A few stems are trained along the ground, but others climb through *Buddleia* 'Lochinch' with soft sage gray leaves and Wedgwood blue flower spikes, on their way into an old birch tree. The purple and copper vine against the green and butter gold of the birch leaves is one of the loveliest sights in the garden.

EVERGREEN CLIMBERS

There are only a handful of evergreen climbers hardy enough for American gardens. Euonymus, often underrated, is among the few which perform well in most parts of the country (in some form or other). The various selections of *Euonymus fortunei radicans* (Zone 5) are among the most reliable climb-

ers. Some will hoick themselves as much as forty feet into a tree, though all are easily held at a moderate eight to ten feet by pruning or the vagaries of winter. Variegated forms can lighten dull corners, while the plain green ones, though not distinctive in appearance, are obliging background plants against which more dazzling companions may shine. Like ivy, euonymus flowers only when it reaches the top of its support. The blossoms are bitty nothings, but the seedpods, lined in sharp pink with orange seeds, are pleasant bits of brilliance in fall.

Strong climbers can hold more than one companion. The back fence in the Withey/Price garden is draped with a thick sheet of purple grape, Vitis vinifera 'Purpurea', *which in turn holds a hardy kiwi,* Actinidia arguta, *as well as the summer-blooming* Clematis 'Comtesse de Bouchaud'. *Photo: Mark Lovejoy*

Purple grape colors richly in hot summer sun, growing redder as autumn approaches. Kevin Nicolay enjoyed the contrast of the matte, nearly black foliage laced through silvery Artemisia ludoviciana. Photo: Kevin Nicolay

Hedera species. Ivy, though often used, is equally undervalued in American gardens. This willing worker offers many attractive leaf forms as well as a good range of colors and patterns. The common, coarse varieties are generally unfit for border work, but gems like the sage gray and white 'Little Diamond' or the glossy golden 'Buttercup' make demure ground covers, or slink slowly up a stout hedge for a decorative winter accent.

ANNUAL CLIMBERS

Smaller and lighter in weight than their perennial counterparts, many annual climbers can be given the run of even a young border. Growing shrubs that might be damaged by a weighty *Ampelopsis* species will accept the gentler embrace of 'Purple Podded Stringless' runner beans, with their dark, lustrous pods and black stems. Slim ropes of canary vine (*Tropaeolum peregrinum*) can wreathe through the forming branches of a young shrub or small tree without harm. Annual vines make decorative additions to plain climbers, as when variegated Japanese hops (*Humulus japonicus* 'Variegatus') is set to mingle with green ivy or euonymus. Cathedral bells (*Cobaea scandens*) with its big, winged bells in purple or greenish white will brighten a somber juniper or yew hedge. North of Zone 5, many of these tropical plants will not perform well unless set out rather late in a warm, sunny site, sheltered from wind and protected against unseasonal frosts.

Asarina barclaiana (Zone 8 as perennial, to fifteen feet). Snapdragon vines of several sorts are sold as annuals in America. This one, with velvety pink or purple flowers, is sometimes sold as *Maurandya*, but under either name, it is a productive, floriferous scrambler that will partner with small shrubs or large perennials charmingly.

Cobaea scandens (a fitful perennial in Zones 7 to 8, to fifteen feet; soundly hardy in Zone 9, to forty feet) is generally treated as a reliable and productive annual. Its chubby cup-and-saucer flowers open from lime green buds into creamy green flowers that quickly deepen to purple, sprouting like fluted trumpets from the lacy calyx. (*Cobaea scandens* 'Alba' matures to a clean, green-tinged white.)

Dolichos lablab, the hyacinth bean (Zone 9, to fifteen feet as a perennial; ten feet as annual), looks rather like an exotic runner bean, with long, narrow racemes of mauvey purple blossoms (occasionally white forms occur). These are followed by plump beans, often flushed a ruddy purple. The trifoliate foliage deepens to dusky, greenish purple in fall, against which the bright beans glow sumptuously.

A self-sown annual pumpkin vine adorns a red barberry, where its fluted, golden blossoms glow against the dusky foliage. The vegetable patch offers the border builder many such cross-overs. Author's garden. Photo: Mark Lovejoy

The big, lusty-looking vines melt away at first frost.

Gloriosa rothschildiana (Zone 9 as perennial, four to eight feet). Glory lilies, of which several species are occasionally offered through mail-order nurseries, need a good deal of heat and light to flower well, but where summers are hot, these tropical climbers make spectacular ornaments for border shrubs. The wiry vines are scantily clad in narrow, shiny foliage, and the curly, reflexed flowers, brilliant red and yellow, look as exotic as parrots against border flowers. They partner well with fatsias or other large-leaved shrubs, and may also be threaded up an ivy-covered fence to startling effect.

Humulus japonicus 'Variegata' (to twenty feet) has palmate, lacquer green leaves strongly variegated in fresh white. This vigorous vine needs a sturdy host, but makes a wonderful contrast to somber conifers, glossy holly, or matte-leaved rhododendrons.

Ipomoea. The morning glory clan is a tremendous one, packed with wonderful annual (and perennial) climbers. Old-fashioned favorites like 'Heavenly Blue' are mostly forms of *I. tricolor*. Newer hybrids draw from the tropical gene pool, resulting in spectacular creatures like 'Roman Candy', clear rose with a white picotee edge and silver-dusted leaves, and the enormous browny red flowers of *I. imperialis* 'Chocolate', a smasher when grown up a purple smokebush. A tender perennial sweet potato, *I. batatas* 'Blackie', is becoming popular among garden colorists, thanks to its lacquered black stems and leaves with the purple-black luster of ripe eggplant. (In my orange, black, and purple border, it winds through a gold-leaved Mexican orange shrub, *Choisya ternata* 'Sundance'.) Though its pink flowers are few in cool summer areas, it is worth growing for the foliage alone, even where its plump tubers need wintering over in a warm greenhouse.

A thick but lightweight rope of *Rhodochiton volubile* (perennial Zone 9, to fifteen feet, six to ten feet as annual), laden with parasoled flowers of rich fuchsia purple, will waken the slumbering pink tints in a purple leaved cotinus or purple hazel. This heat lover needs a warm, sunny spot to bloom well, but when suited, rewards the least care with generous bloom until frost.

Green-streaked Tulipa viridiflora *'Spring Green' gleam beneath a white Portuguese broom,*
Cytisus multiflorus. *Author's garden. Photo: Mark Lovejoy*

Chapter Eight

BULBS
IN THE
MIXED BORDER

*S*ince the distant days when tulipomania swept Europe, westerners have been seriously smitten with bulbs. Tulips are still among the most beloved of garden bulbs, with a host of others at their heels. Narcissus and anemones, liles and dahlias all have their passionate admirers. Minor bulbs like snowdrops and baby blue puschkinias are grown and loved by passionate collector and easygoing amateur alike. Rare is the garden that holds no bulbs, but rarer still is the garden that uses them to the fullest capability. Like roses, bulbs are probably least attractive when segregated in ghettos of like kind. With their multitude of strengths, bulbs deserve thoughtful border placement so their many excellences can be fully appreciated. Bulbs both hardy and tender can enrich every color scheme and every season. In the milder regions of North America, it is possible to assemble an ongoing sequence of bulbs to bloom from New Year's back to Christmas. Where winters are severe and snow cover lies deep, the latest and earliest bulbs are most likely to be enjoyed on a sunny indoor windowsill. However, through much of Zone 6 and in protected pockets northward, some of the hardiest bulbs will bloom through the winter despite frost and snow. Pools of cupped crocus and nodding fritillaries rouse the sleepy spring borders to ardent life. Great, trumpeting lilies and fluted spires of gladiolas enliven subtle tapestries of midsummer greenery. Flaming masses of crocosmias will ignite a flagging border in late summer, followed by the misty lavender goblets of autumn blooming colchicum and a steady succession of hardy winter bloomers.

Much as they enhance the garden year, however, bulbs which bloom outside of the high summer season are not often well suited to use in traditional borders. When the first aconites and snowdrops make their appearance on the tail of winter, they nearly always bloom alone, unaided by any supportive companion. In earliest spring, most perennials are at their worst, scarcely fit company for delicate fritillaries and bulbous iris. Minor bulbs are often naturalized under trees and shrubs in large gardens, but it is a challenge to find just the right niche for bulbs in small urban yards, where a single garden area must serve the gardener all through the year. The mixed border offers a distinct advantage over traditional borders in presenting a number of suitable environments for bulbs, both hardy and tender. The sturdy framework plantings of perimeter shrubs and tapestry hedges can be threaded with thick ribbons of early and late bloomers to brighten the garden when the border plantings are quiet. Minor bulbs which lie dormant all summer can be housed beneath the skirts of deciduous border shrubs, where they will receive plenty of winter light and find protection from excess summer moisture. Midborder islands of evergreen shrubs make excellent backdrops against which massed bulbs are displayed to advantage from late autumn until midspring. In each case, the bulbs' beauties are supported by carefully chosen companions. When they fade, their withering foliage is hidden by the rising crowns of perennials and the maturing leaves of deciduous shrubs.

CARE AND CULTURE

Though tulips and other spring bulbs continue to be planted by the millions each year, most are treated as annuals. Big border tulips and narcissus are particularly unreliable in traditional border settings, and gardeners who want to recreate specific effects each year accept the fact that they must replace these bulbs periodically, if not annually. If bulbs seldom persist in traditional borders, it is most often because their cultural needs, simple but strong, are not met. Perhaps foremost is their need for elbow room. Even those that tolerate companionable interlayering with the bulbs of other seasons or interplanting with perennials may resent being smothered by lush foliage. Most bulbs need free access to sun and air during all stages of growth, from first shoots to final ripening. The early stages of development are usually unhindered, but the accelerating growth of neighboring border plants and the exigencies of the impatient gardener may interfere with the last and least attractive phase. If they are to persist, bulbs need time and space to ripen properly, which means their leaves need to fade and dry up naturally before being removed. Braiding, bunching, or tying them serves only to speed them on their way to plant heaven. Careful placement can minimize the visual impact of browning bulb foliage by screening it from view behind rising companions. When this is not enough mitigation, bulb foliage that is limp and discolored but not yet dry can be gently pulled to the ground (though never broken) and tucked out of sight behind a shielding neighbor. If need be, leaves that are close to dry can be lightly covered with a loose mulch like shredded bark. Sometimes unusual

weather patterns can alter garden timing so that a bulb companion develops too quickly, crowding out the bulbs before they are ready. When this happens, it usually suffices to remove a few large leaves which overlap the bulb's air space, and to encourage the bulb foliage to lean away from the intruder while it finishes drying.

Bulbs in active growth need plenty of room, yet dormant bulbs may actually do better with close companions which can keep them from getting more water than they really want. Though most bulbs need a steady supply of moisture while in active growth, few of them appreciate wet soil during their dormant phase. Many, indeed, will rot if kept wet during dormancy, yet the dry, open soil conditions they like are seldom found in summer gardens or herbaceous borders. In mixed borders, there are a number of situations in which dormant bulbs can safely rest. In deep borders, where the background or perimeter hedges are divided from the border beds by narrow access paths for weeding and maintenance, the modest strips of soil at the base of the hedges and shrub belts can hold hundreds of bulbs which bloom from autumn through spring, their browning leaves neatly concealed by weed-suppressing ground covers. Any or all of the many deciduous border shrubs, large and dwarf, will host hordes of early bloomers that have finished their cycle by the time the shrubs leaf out. Small border trees may provide similar shelter, their bare branches allowing in plenty of winter light, their leafy canopy shutting out the summer rain. When the soil beneath the shrubs and trees is kept well mulched, it tends to be open in texture despite the great quantity of roots. Lacy ground covers like *Vinca minor* 'Miss Jekyll's White' or purple-leaved Labrador violets, *Viola labradorica*, are fine shade-tolerant place holders. In sunnier sites, blue leadwort, *Ceratostigma plumbaginoides*, or creeping *Veronica repens* will cover bulbs without smothering them.

Midborder island plantings of dwarf evergreen shrubs are often the focal points of the mixed border in winter, their contours forming natural niches in which to position bulbs which bloom from early winter through midspring. In order to protect the bulbs' air space, the gardener creates pockets around

The mixed border provides numerous niches where bulbs may thrive, protected by shrub and tree or basking in summer sunshine. Clusters of neighboring perennials will disguise leggy, naked stems and screen dying bulb foliage from view. Woodyard garden, Portland, Oregon. Photo: Cynthia Woodyard

each island which will hold only bulbs and ground covers. Large scale perennials which themselves demand a considerable uninterrupted space if they are to achieve their best form can be placed around the bulb space to avoid a gappy appearance in the border interior. You can also play up the topographic differences by adding an eye-catching ground cover like golden creeping Jenny, *Lysimachia nummularia* 'Aurea', and a few shapely ferns about the base of the host plant, making a simple but attractive vignette to be glimpsed through the veil of taller growth at the border's front. In many cases, the winter and early spring bulb pockets can be shared with summer bloomers like alliums and galtonias that have compatible life cycles and similar cultural needs, which helps keep the area interesting after the early plants have faded.

Hardy lilies, giant fritillaries, and other large, rot-prone bulbs can be placed in the bays between background shrubs where they won't be disturbed. In heavy soils, their planting pockets should be very deep and well amended with grit or coarse sand to insure the quick drainage they need. Placing such bulbs with a bit of tilt, rather than straight upward, and topping each bulb off with a mulch of grit can significantly prolong their lives, for bulb rots commonly begin at the neck or collar. As the dying stem collapses, rainwater accumulates in the stem hole at the top of the bulb, leading to the decay of the entire bulb. Tipped bulbs will still bloom upright, thanks to the plants' ability to correct direction, yet excess water will run off freely, leaving the bulb dry.

Frost tender and borderline hardy bulbs coax their way into many a mixed border with a winning combination of beauty, fragrance, and exuberant bloom. In my own garden, several problem spots between long-established trees have been given permanent "pot holes." These are large, empty pots sunk into the ground, to be filled through the year with a succession of potted plants. Surrounded by tough ground covers, these pot holes host tender bulbs like gladiolus and dahlias, freesias and pineapple lilies (*Eucomis* species), all of which do far better in pots than they would in the dreadful, rooty soil around them. A handful of Broadleaf P4 hydrogel in the bottom of each pot keeps watering needs low, and it is far easier to lift and dry out an entire pot for off-season storage in the unheated sun porch than to dig and bag and label and store each set of bulbs individually.

Many bulbs and rhizomes that could be hardy and long-lived in border settings fail to thrive or increase because of repeated disturbance. Pot hole plantings are one solution, but won't do where we want to encourage large, natural-looking colonies to spread. Dormant bulbs lost from view are often lost indeed when sliced to bits by an errant shovel or trowel. Simple labels are rarely adequate, since even if we actually read and heed them, they do little more than indicate the general area where the bulbs were introduced. In mixed borders where bulbs spread freely, making permanent place markers that outline dormant midborder bulb colonies will greatly improve the odds of their survival. To be effective, such markers must be obvious to one who is looking for them, yet unobtrusive enough to escape the attention of the casual viewer. They must be movable, so that their range can be expanded or reduced with the bulb colony. Each season as the bulb shoots first appear, the markers are moved to indicate the new limits. This way, when the gardener is roaming the off-season border looking for an empty place to drop in a new plant, the little markers remind us of what lies underground, and show us exactly where we may safely dig. I employ a variety of such markers in various settings, which range

from small rocks to short sections of bamboo or plain sticks set upright in the ground. Ground covers can also be used, by trimming back plants which exceed the bulbs' range or resetting fresh divisions just past expanding boundaries. It helps to similarly indicate the fullest reaches of deciduous shrubs when in leaf, for it is easy to forget that such plants are still growing. A subtle row of stick markers will show you how far you can plant new bulbs without infringing on border plants, and will act as a pruning guide should you wish to keep shrubs to a certain size.

Where moles, mice, squirrels, and other varmints take their toll on border bulbs, the gardener can enlist modern technology as an aid to preserving the peace. Horticultural barrier cloth keeps moles at bay as well as roots; I have had good luck in keeping especially tasty bulbs untouched for years by wrapping groups of them in large underground packets. To do this, dig out the area where you want the bulbs to a depth of at least eighteen inches. Line the planting hole with an oversized piece of barrier cloth and add six inches of soil (mixed with coarse sand or grit if drainage is a problem). Position your bulb groups, then top them off with more soil. Any loose edges of cloth can be trimmed away, rather than lapped over, for the top layer must be left open so that the stems can find their way up through the soil unhindered. If squirrels are digging down to the bulbs, cover them with a few inches of soil, then place a flat piece of coarse wire mesh or screen over the bulbs before piling on the remaining soil. The mesh must be wide enough to let stems grow through without constriction; for little things like crocus, species tulips, and puschkinias, even quarter-inch mesh will not present any difficulty, but larger bulbs with fatter necks will need half-inch or larger mesh. This may mean that a determined mouse can still reach the bulbs, but a handful of old-fashioned mothballs or flakes (the smelly, naphtha kind) mixed into the top few inches of soil is often an effective mouse deterrent. (It also seems to discourage cats from regarding the freshly disturbed earth as a lovely litter box).

In favored sites, bulbs may become all too comfortable, multiplying even better than we might

Throughout the Platt garden, bulbs naturalize freely beneath the sheltering shrubs. Narcissus *'Peeping Tom' was planted by the dozen and divided when crowded, but the white dogtooth violet,* Erythronium *'White Beauty', colonized with assistance from Mrs. Platt. With careful placement and partnering, even finicky wildlings can be persuaded to increase in mixed borders. Photo: Cynthia Woodyard*

wish. Where this happens, it is easy to control their spread either by heavy mulching, which prevents the sprouting of seed, or by removing the extra bulbs. It is often recommended that bulbs be moved when dormant, and it is true that they do not resent or even notice disturbance in this state. However, bulbs out of sight are equally out of mind; it can be all but impossible to find them come late summer or fall, even if you should happen to remember that you wanted to move them last spring. Fortunately, nearly all bulbs can be safely moved after they have bloomed. Indeed, bulb fanciers like to order their precious snowdrops and rare scillas "in the green," meaning that the plants will be shipped while the

foliage is still lush. If you don't want to wait for bulbs to finish blooming, simply snip off their blossoms to enjoy in the house. Whenever possible, it is best to take a chunk of soil along with the bulbs, to reduce the shock of relocation. However, where bulbs are tightly intertwined with turf, neighboring perennials, or ground covers, this can be quite difficult. In these situations, one must carefully insert a shovel at a safe distance from the bulbs and gently lift the clod upward, preferably without breaking it free. The bulbs can be gently pulled out backward, their tops sliding through the loosened soil, and potted up immediately in prepared pots full of compost or rich potting soil. The clod with its attached green-

Browning bulb foliage is tucked beneath burgeoning neighbors where it does not mar the approach of summer. Photo: Jean Atwater

ery is then reset, firmly tamped into place, and watered. If you work fairly fast, neither bulbs nor the disturbed plants ever look back. The extra bulbs can be labled and ripened off in the pots, a nursery bed, or set directly into a new garden location. They may show signs of shock, wilting, and browning off before the rest of the colony, but so long as the bulbs were not damaged, they will reappear next year in fine shape.

A few bulbs, like autumn crocus (*Colchicum* species), certain bluebells (*Scilla* species), and many grape hyacinths (*Muscari* species), can only be admitted to mixed borders with a caveat. They must be very well positioned, or their abundant, smothering foliage will be a distinct liability. Colchicums can be awkward plants to work with, for their flow-

ers are generally short stemmed, and don't carry visually over a long distance. In autumn, one wants to see them up close, yet their foliage—lovely, lush cabbages in spring—becomes horrid, smothering masses of rotting greenery in early summer, not exactly a welcome presence in a carefully arranged close-up planting. The solution is to find places where they will be visible in September but not in June. In my garden, a large colony of *Colchicum autumnale* is grouped at the back of a ten-foot-wide border. They are arranged between 'Fabia Tangerine' rhododendrons, along with a vigorous lungwort, *Pulmonaria longifolia* 'Roy Davidson', a form with very long, narrow foliage richly sprinkled with silvery spots. In spring, the cabbagy colchicum foliage looks pretty between the building clumps of pulmonaria. By early summer, the lungworts have expanded to completely cover the dying colchicums. In late summer, the pulmonarias begin to look tatty, so they get cut back and fed with refreshing manure tea. By autumn, there are gaps in the borders where perennials have come and gone, leaving a clear vista through to where dozens of colchicum bloom between the newly tidy pulmonarias, whose spotted silvery foliage makes a lovely backdrop for the bulbs' lavender-blue blossoms. In another area, colchicums are tucked at the border back beneath some beautyberries, *Callicarpa* 'Profusion'. These begin

to drop their golden bronze leaves in September, displaying masses of tiny violet-blue berries on every twig. The purple colchicums rise above a carpet of *Vinca minor* 'Aureo-variegata' to echo the brilliant berries above.

Most scillas do objectionably well in my garden, and I treat them with very little respect, hacking their lank, lush foliage off close to the ground the moment it threatens to flop over neighboring plants. This daunts the bulbs not at all, except in curbing their propensity to overrun any and all companions. Muscari, too, can become pests rather than pleasures. Some species and forms are rather slower to increase, and since these are usually popular with visitors, I usually pot up the clumps at the fringe of each colony as giveaways. Even so, muscari may increase too rapidly, so I both trim them as soon as they finish blooming to prevent their going to seed and rigorously thin the colonies every few years.

Scilla may multiply all too well when given garden room, but they can be kept in their place by cutting the foliage back hard immediately after bloom. The lush colchicum foliage on the right still looks fresh, but by June, when it becomes unsightly, both colchicum and scilla will be hidden by a thicket of perennials at the front of the border. Photo: Mark Lovejoy

SEASONAL SUGGESTIONS

An astounding number of bulbs, more or less hardy, adapt well to the mixed border setting. Below is a very partial discussion of how bulbs might be used in a mixed border. It is anything but definitive, partly because sheer numbers make such lists daunting, but also because what works in one garden may or may not succeed elsewhere. Where winters are mild, a continuous succession of bulbs can provide a whole year of bloom. Most of the following bulb combinations would be practical in Zone 5, but no matter where you live, it is always worth experimenting to learn the limits of your particular garden. By pushing those limits, and tinkering a bit with whichever conditions can be altered or controlled, the gardener can often find a way to encourage some surprising plants to take hold. Some, perhaps most, of your experiments may fail, but every success will help to expand your garden palette at both ends of the garden year.

LATE WINTER

January and February can be bleak and gray, making any bit of garden cheer doubly welcome. In a Zone 5 garden, the new year might be greeted with a glad-hearted group of snowdrops, *Galanthus elwesii*, which bloom during spells of open weather despite snow and frost. In my garden, great clumps of snowdrops run beneath an evergreen *Viburnum davidii*, the curving arch of the grayish snowdrop foliage repeated in the deeply grooved viburnum leaves. In a sunnier spot, the English snowdrop, *Galanthus nivalis*, blooms some weeks later, tucked between the protective arms of a creeping Oregon grape, *Mahonia repens*. This has winter-bronzed leaves which find an echoing warmth in buttercup yellow aconites, *Eranthus hyemalis*, which generally appear some time during the first month of the year. The long-blooming aconites, with their fringed green ruffs, make a splendid surrounding for an early perennial, *Hacquetia epipactis*. This charming tussock-former blooms in February and March, opening pincushions of tiny golden flowers surrounded by large, brilliant green bracteoles. Both plants do very well in company, and will thrive beneath the sheltering branches of deciduous shrubs or small trees.

Nearly every garden has a sun trap or two, places where even the shy winter sun shines first and lingers longest. This is the place to put an all-weather bench, and to pack the ground with winter bloomers. Golden trumpets of winter jasmine, *Jasminum nudiflorum*, are almost leafless, yet the lustrous, brilliantly green twigs look fresher than most winter foliage. The little flowers open from red-tinged buds during every thaw and warm spell, egged on in my garden by shaggy clumps of *Iris unguicularis*, both 'Winter Treasure', with clean white flowers, and the deep-toned 'Oxford Blue', at their feet. In less favored climates, sheets of crocus would do the trick just as nicely.

Snow crocus, a group of species and related hybrids which often pierce the snow to bloom at the turning of the year, brighten the late winter garden at the first thaw. These are best planted in great sweeps and sheets, for their narrow, grassy foliage is unobtrusive even as it fades, and the small bulbs can be planted tight by established shrubs and perennials alike without harm. Many of them seed freely, multiplying over the years into enormous colonies. They do not increase as quickly in lawns, where their foliage is often mowed before it is really ripe. Lovers of tidy lawns will do better to thread these small creatures liberally through their borders, for if they are to do well in grass, the first mowing must often be put off until mid-March or early April. Yellow *Crocus chrysanthus*; white or lilac *C. sieberi*; bronze-brushed, golden *C. ancyrensis*; and the lavender-blue *C. tomasinianus* are among the most common members of the snow crocus clan. There are many named forms as well, which can be used to play up quiet winter beauties of bark and blossom. The Chinese witch hazel, *Hamamelis mollis* 'Pallida', has soft yellow, intensely fragrant ribbon flowers which appear in late January or early February. Mine is underplanted with *Helleborus torquatus*, a Balkan species with green and silvery plum-purple flowers, and masses of *Crocus sieberi* 'Violet Queen' to wake up the highlights in the somber hellebores.

EARLY SPRING

By March, the garden is awash with tulips and daffodils and a host of less familiar minor bulbs. The first flowers of spring often look slapdash rather than dashing when strung through beds of wakening perennials, but the evergreen, shrubby islands within the mixed border give them a firm setting. *Narcissus* 'February Gold' rarely earns its name by appearing before the end of that month, but it is nearly always in bloom by the first of March, followed a few weeks later by a similar little one, 'March Sunshine'. Both may be circled with ruffles of long-blooming windflowers, *Anemone blanda*, in clean white or snapping sea blue. These willing creatures emerge while the ground is still frozen, their frizzy, parsley green foliage red with cold. The flowers open over a long season, and they tend to reseed abundantly when well suited. The seedlings are easily moved about the garden, so an initial investment of a hundred bulbs can be returned manyfold over the years. Since windflowers die down completely by early summer, they can be massed under deciduous border shrubs which leaf out late, like smokebush, *Cotinus coggygria*, and those with rather airy foliage, like golden ninebark, *Physocarpus opulifolius* 'Dart's Gold'.

The first soft, springlike days bring on the fragile-looking flowers of a clump-forming Juno iris, *Iris bucharica*. Its foliage looks rather like that of dwarf corn, and the flowers, with their tissue-paper-thin petals of chalky yellow and ivory, are intensely fragrant. These contrast very nicely with the rounded, leathery leaves of *Bergenia* 'Beethoven' and the rough, sage gray foliage of *Rhododendron* 'Ptarmigan', both of which have white flowers.

Certain bulbous iris are also terrific mixed border candidates, especially the indigo blue *Iris reticulata*, which unfurls its tightly rolled blossoms very early on. A number of named forms offer a wide range of blue shades, all more lasting in the garden than the golden *I. danfordiae*, very similar in form and timing. The slim little bulbs tuck easily between grasses and border perennials, and their long foliage is so fine as to be almost invisible once the border begins to fatten up in late spring.

MIDSPRING

Several species tulips grow very nicely in mixed border settings. *Tulipa turkestanica* opens sprays of splayed ivory stars on slim, drooping necks in midspring. Its strappy little leaves persist into summer, yet are easily hidden beneath neighboring coralbells (*Heuchera* species) or sprawling catmints. *Tulipa tarda* squats low to the ground, its wide, flat

The bulbs of spring bloom in cheerful array in my mother's garden, tucked between perennial herbs and flowers. Photo: Jean Atwater

blossoms looking like yellow-yolked eggs from especially cheerful chickens. Planted in groups of ten or twenty, these can be spaced rhythmically along the front of the border, their foliage soon hidden by companionable tumbles of *Sedum* 'Ruby Glow'. Short and sassy, the hot pink *Tulipa pulchella* opens plump goblets a few weeks later, emphasizing the pinky overtones in red-backed sorrel, *Oxalis oregana*, and the hairy, red-stained leaves of mother-of-thousands, *Saxifraga stolonifera*. (This striking house plant will grow willingly out of doors south of Zone 5). Purple-leaved Labrador violets, *Viola labradorica*, make an exciting underplanting for *Tulipa pulchella* or the tiny red *T. linifolia*.

De Caen anemones (Zone 5), the ruffled, silk petaled florists' flowers, begin to blossom now, often continuing into early summer. Besides the usual color mixtures, these can be had in individual colors, which makes them far more useful for the arranger of floral symphonies. 'Lord Lieutenant' is an intense cobalt blue which accords well with the heavy, hot colors of many border tulips. 'The Bride' is of course white, a wonderful thing to lavish beneath a weeping, white-flowered 'Red Jade' crab apple. 'Hollandia' is an electric red, larger and even brighter than the species, *Anemone* × *fulgens*, which is slightly grayed in tone and has a black throat. 'St. Brigid' is the common mixture of doubles, many of them tattered in form and nearly as lacy as zinnias. These are best used in the cutting garden, for their form is too varied to be useful in deliberate compositions. 'St. Bavo' is a much handsomer doubles mixture in which the petals are whole and only loosely doubled. These, too, can be grown in the nursery bed for a year, sorted and labeled for color, then placed in garden groups.

The broad, dappled leaves of dogtooth violets are beautifully reflective, bringing light to the shady areas they prefer. Where white-striped *Lamium maculatum* 'Roseum' circles the shoots of the tall peony 'White Innocence', groups of pink trout lilies, *Erythronium revolutum*, make a delicate accent to the shell pink lamium flowers. *Erythronium* 'Pagoda' has saucy, reflexed petals of warm yellow, with red eye markings that pick up the ruddy tints of *Euphorbia amygdaloides* 'Rubra', which expands its green-gold

balloons (really bracts, rather than flowers) at this season. A weirdly beautiful European species tulip, *Tulipa acuminata*, persists well in crowded borders and tolerates light or dappled shade, making it another good companion for dogtooth violets. Its long, slim petals look like twisting flames, fire red touched at the base with gold, giving them their folk name, "flame tulips."

In sunnier areas, dwarf foliage shrubs like spireas and barberries are leafing out, accompanied by single early tulips, which also adapt very well to mixed border life. In my garden, several hundred 'Princess Irene', a coppery orange flamed with red and bronze, fill the gaps between the copper-red foliage of *Spiraea* × *bumalda* 'Goldflame' and clumps of strawberry blond *Uncinia unciniata*, a punky looking (but tender) mop-head grass which is well worth growing as a greenhouse refugee where winters are wet (it is probably hardy into Zone 6 or 7 in well-drained soil, but it rots before it freezes). Nearby, a hundred 'Spring Green' viridiflora tulips, their ivory petals licked with green, flow beneath a white Spanish broom, *Cytisus multiflorus*, which looks like frozen fireworks.

LATE SPRING

Some of the longest lived bulbs are old favorites from our ancestors' gardens. The tulips known as Darwin or cottage acclimate nicely to border conditions, as will fringed and single lates. A chalk yellow fringed tulip, 'Maja', not only persists but multiplies in heavy but well-drained soils. Its soft coloring makes it a good companion for 'Moonlight' broom, a hybrid of *Cytisus scoparius*. There are more than a few of these dwarf border brooms, which illuminate the early spring garden. 'Minstead' flowers in pinky lavender, a knockout when underplanted with single late 'Menton' tulips. 'Lilac Time' broom, a sparkling burgundy, makes a splendid backdrop for massed 'Black Diamond' tulips. Most of the triumph tulips seem less long lived, but some are so beautiful that they are worth replanting every few years. 'Apricot Beauty' is perhaps the most popular, and deservedly so, for its complex coloring

In the Withey/Price garden, terra-rossa pots of 'Princess Irene' tulips and 'Antique Fantasy' pansies decorate the herb garden in spring. Photo: Peter Ray

makes it compatible with all sorts of color schemes. I use it liberally beneath a huge old quince, *Chaenomeles speciosa*, where the soft red brushmarks on the back of the tulip petals echo the coral of the quince petals.

The same daffodils that naturalize well in grass, including a number of species, can compete successfully in mixed borders. 'Carleton', an older hybrid with tall, sturdy stems, is a reliable performer, mingling attractively with white-variegated moon weed, *Lunaria annua* 'Stella', and golden *Euonymus japonica* 'Gold Spot'. A dwarf daffodil, 'Hawera', opens its sprays of tiny, soft yellow blossoms quite late in spring. These and other multi-flowering daffodils look better in relatively small groups than in great sweeps, because their form is too complicated to read well en masse. Bunches of ten or twelve, interplanted with a golden grass, *Carex elata* 'Knightshayes', look like shafts of sunlight amongst the green of emergent perennials.

Checker lilies, *Fritillaria meleagris*, are usually sold in a delightful mixture of white, lavender, purple, and heather tweed, these last being checked and flecked in bewitching combinations. There are a number of named forms, all larger and lustier than the plain species. 'Alba' is an ivory-white that makes a lovely accent nestled between clumps of creamy variegated figwort, *Scrophularia aquatica* 'Variegata' or threaded through the big, fuzzy leaves of *Primula kisoana* 'Alba'. 'Charon' is a dusky plum which complements the rosy purples of many spring blooming hellebores, and 'Saturnus', darkest of all, is winered, a strange color which nicely emphasizes the glossy red stems and new foliage of Japanese peonies. Once rare, and still unpronounceable, *Fritillaria michailovskyi* is now tissue cultured by the thousands, making this small collector's treasure accessible without fear of buying illicitly gathered wild bulbs. The warm chestnut and dull gold of its curving bells glow rich and medieval looking against clumps of the delicate, gold striped grass, *Acorus* 'Ogon'.

In late April and May, the border's edge is bright with a loose linked chain of dwarf iris, all forms of *Iris pumila* or the short, mannerly hybrid intermediates. These are useful, good little plants which

bloom in a huge range of colors and combinations, making them highly attractive to those who enjoy color play. Many are cheerful, like the rose and garnet 'Bright Button', or the sunny black and yellow 'Bee Wings'. Others may be bold, like the root-beer red 'Cherry Pop', or brazen, like the stunning brown and flaming gold 'Tantara'. A choice handful are incredibly subtle, like the delicate biscuit brown 'Tea Party' or creamy 'Green Spot'. My favorite is 'Seafoam', a whisper of palest green and cream with a soft blue beard, enhanced by the deep blue flowers of the slow-spreading, black-leaved *Ajuga pyramidalis* 'Metallica Crispa' and a matching green columbine, *Aquilegia viridiflora*, with skirts of chocolate and silver-green. These dwarf iris are far easier to use than their oversized bearded counterparts, for they tuck nicely between the ornamental herbs and dwarf shrubs that face down the border edges, multiplying quietly without invading anybody else's ground. Indeed, these demure creatures can be lost if not kept free of expanding perennial foliage later in the season.

EARLY SUMMER

Though summer-blooming border iris are among the most beloved of garden plants, most of the big bearded ones look dreadful as soon as their brief glory has past. Then, too, many are ground hogs, intolerant of neighbors, and demanding the sunniest spots all for themselves. However, a few, like 'Corn Harvest' and 'Golden Encore', are reliable rebloomers where summers are hot, producing two or more crops of blossom if the spent stalks are cut away. Quite a few Siberian iris are similarly remontant, and have the additional benefit of lastingly fine foliage, as good as many an ornamental grass. A tall Siberian, 'Chilled Wine', with flowers the color of a good burgundy, blooms continuously over a long season, as does the diminutive 'Illini Charm', a warmly colored lavender-rose blend. Less long blooming, but utterly beautiful is 'Limeheart', the color of the western sky just after sundown, when the last trace of blue has drained away. Backed by the lacy leaves and plumy cream flowers of *Aruncus*

'Zweiweltenkind', 'Limeheart' is memorable indeed. Long blooming or not, Siberian iris earn their positions with an elegance of line and strength of form that make them worthy companions for oversized perennials like the stately peonies and substantial shrubs like lacecap hydrangeas.

The great onion clan is well represented in early summer, and many of these willing bulbs make excellent border members. In June, the twelve-inch globes of dark, metallic blue *Allium christophii* dwarf their two-foot stems. Placed midborder, the shimmering globes rise like alien spacecraft between smooth sheaves of 'Prairie Blue Eyes' daylilies. *Allium giganteum* stands far taller, on four-foot stems,

Siberian iris earn their place in mixed borders with graceful flowers and foliage as good as any grass, upright and firm through the summer and often fading to dull gold in autumn. This is 'Summer Skies' with golden hops behind. Author's garden. Photo: Mark Lovejoy

but the flower heads themselves are a mere six or eight inches across. This one is quite at home at the border's back, nestled between arching stems of red-leaved *Rosa glauca* and the little pink hollyhocks of *Lavatera thuringiaca* 'Barnsley'. It is also effective placed toward the front of the border, where its foliage can be hidden but its lanky stems and bobbing lavender blue heads are easily admired and touched. Perhaps the most dramatic border onion is *Allium schubertii*, which carries its enormous rosy heads on foot-tall stems. These glow like gazing balls at the border's front, and look especially striking when grouped with blue-armed sprawls of *Euphorbia myrsinites* and tall *Sedum maximum* 'Atropurpureum'. The seedlings place themselves with imagination, appearing at the base of a wine-red butterfly bush, *Buddleia davidii* 'Burgundy', or amongst clumps of fire pink valerian, *Centranthus ruber*. *Allium aflatunense* is an especially adaptable species, which holds its orange-sized pinky purple puff balls on yard-tall stems. It takes crowding with equanimity, and associates attractively with almost any color. At Barnsley, Rosemary Verey mingles it with the chalky rose bottlebrushes of *Persicaria bistorta* 'Superba', (formerly *Polygonum bistorta* 'Superbum', and still sold that way in several catalogs). I like to thread it between the lower branches of purple smokebush, *Cotinus coggygria* 'Velvet Cloak', or blend it with sulfur yellow *Thermopsis caroliniana*. The dark maroon drumsticks of *Allium sphaerocephalum* are terrific blenders, mixing excitingly with bronze fennel and warm-colored daylilies like the apricot 'Three Bars' and salmon-peach 'Sing Again', which repeats its bloom over a long season.

Maturing mixed borders offer a good deal of shade, which means there is plenty of room for special woodlanders like *Arisaema triphyllum*, the native jack-in-the-pulpit. This handsome New Englander loves moist, humus-rich soil and needs a fair amount of shade, making it a good candidate to place beneath the wide canopy of an old fruit tree. (A handful of hydrogel worked into the root zone will help this and other moisture lovers establish quickly.) Jack-in-the-pulpit transplants poorly, and should only be collected from the wild when threatened by the bulldozers of development, for it rarely survives the

Allium *'Purple Sensation'* blooms over several weeks, then continues in good looks as its great seed heads ripen and dry. Its broad, pale blue foliage is a lovely foil for the bronze Cordyline australis. *Author's garden. Photo: Mark Lovejoy*

experience. Fortunately, it is easily grown from seed (often available through plant societies and seed exchanges, as well as a few commercial catalogs), reaching blooming size in four to six years. Striking, long-fingered foliage earns this quiet plant its place, for it contrasts marvelously with round-leaved *Boykinia major* and the long-spined umbrellas of the mayapple, *Podophyllum peltatum*. Its curiously striped little flowers are an added bonus for those who like to view the garden from ground level (they are a nice treat for anybody trimming the border edge grass on hands and knees). Our native has a host of very exotic-looking relatives, all with wonderful foliage. *Arisaema sikokianum* is easily raised from seed, and well worth the years of waiting for the slim brown spadix, with its glowing white heart, to appear between its broad, divided leaves. Mouse plant, *Arisarum proboscideum*, is a pretty little cousin of the big aroids which carpets shady ground with shiny, arrowhead leaves. The bizarre flowers look exactly like long-tailed brown and white mice diving for cover between the foliage, a sight invariably enchanting to children.

A group of California lily relatives will tolerate high or dappled shade, building into tidy colonies in good border soils. A charming ten incher, *Brodiaea laxa* opens diminutive deep blue bellflowers in alliumlike sprays, while those of 'Queen Fabiola' are a clear, light blue. Brodiaeas bloom earlier in sunny spots than in light shade, where it may be mid-June before they open. They consort nicely with small ferns and hostas, and will thread their way through ajugas and vincas with ease.

HIGH SUMMER

The lilies of summer are legion, and most of them are rock hardy. Many fit comfortably into the mixed border, enjoying the moist, rich soil, though, like tulips, most lilies appreciate good drainage. They bloom generously in full sun so long as their roots are well shaded by lower growing plants, but most lilies perform equally well in high or dappled shade, making them valuable additions to maturing mixed borders. In small borders, they may be grouped in threes or fives, (even numbered groups tend to look unbalanced), but where there is room for extravagance, lilies should be lavished. Planted in dozens or by the hundred, tall Aurelian trumpet lilies can fill the bays between shrubs at the border's back to make a staggering display. Shorter, upfacing Asiatic hybrids can run in rippling ribbons between shrubby midborder islands. The new dwarf pot lilies are usually sadly ill proportioned, with giant blossoms on stumpy little stems, but when planted in light shade, many will stretch to a more seemly height, making lovely accents between tree peonies or the huge dinner-plate leaves of *Darmera peltata*.

Swirling spikes of narrow lily foliage are striking from first emergence, and they support a host of early bulbs before their own buds are even formed. Large groups of border tulips interplanted with summer lilies will deliver an effortless extra season of color at the border back. With their great variety of shape and color, lilies invite themselves into endless fetching combinations. In my garden, white 'Regale' trumpet lilies grow between smoky masses of bronze fennel (*Foeniculum vulgare* 'Purpurascens') and the dwarf red-leaved sand cherry, *Prunus × cistena*, which emphasize the mahogany-red gloss on the lily buds and the rusty red stamens of the open flowers. A stand of 'Mabel Violet' trumpet lilies brings out the lively undertones in the murky foliage of a purple hazel bush (*Corylus maxima* 'Purpurea'), while starry pink and white oriental hybrids emphasize the pink and cream foliage of the variegated dogwood 'Cherokee Daybreak'. White and gold *Lilium auratum* are breathtaking when emerging from a sea of silver *Artemisia × latiloba* 'Valerie Finnis' and sapphire blue borage, *Borago officinalis*. Serene 'Lady Anne' lilies rise in elegant columns of peachy pink between creamy gray *Lysimachia ephemerum* and the ivory-gray inflorescences of white snakeroot, *Eupatorium rugosum*. The hot, heavy shades of up-facing Asiatic lilies, like cherry-colored 'Monte Negro' or the orange-and-red blend 'Barcelona', combine tellingly with heleniums, inulas, and other sunny flowers. Once brassy low lifes, hardy tiger lilies now come in a muted, mysterious pink as well as cream, caramel, and copper to enliven understated color runs.

Though most lilies are extremely hardy, many other summer-blooming bulbs are not. Where they are tender, they may be treated as splendid annuals, or grown as pot plants. These can be placed in permanent pot holes, or sunk in the border, then lifted in autumn, pot and all. Bold-leaved cannas are wonderfully tropical looking accents among big perennials like *Salvia involucrata* 'Bethelli', with foot-long, velvety foliage veined in fuchsia pink. A few five-foot spikes of *Canna* 'Red King Humbert', with bronze-red foliage and ember red flowers, add snap to an otherwise tasteful foliage border, as will the magnificent 'Pretoria', its warm orange flowers nes-

tled above enormous leaves neatly striped with cream. Tender gladiolus are favorites with colorists, because they provide an amazing range of tints and tones, and their spikes make a solid counterpoint to soft sweeps and gentle mounds. Most mail-order catalogs offer a handful of rather obvious looking creatures, but a good specialist can provide a literal rainbow of subtle, most unusual colors, from ink-violet to café au lait. 'Zigeunerbaron' makes smoky, four-foot spires of lavender-gray, hot pink, and amethyst that look stunning against a 'Rosy Glow' barberry, with its touches of pink and cream and sage, or the plain purple of a smokebush, *Cotinus coggygria*

Many lilies are narrow enough to tuck easily between clumps of perennials, resulting in fleeting but fabulous pairings like this one. Withey/Price garden, Seattle. Photo: Mark Lovejoy

'Royal Purple'. The bronze-and-coffee tints of 'Zuni Brave' are a sumptuous complement to the gingered apricot tea rose, 'Just Joey', while delicately verdant 'Spring Green' is a knockout against a sheaf of 'Green Goddess' calla lilies.

My kitchen border (not only full of herbs, but overlooked by the kitchen window) has a two- to three-foot strip at the front which is devoted to annuals and tender bulbs. That way, there is always room for the special delights which turn up unexpectedly, as well as old favorites like fragrant tuberoses and freesias. Spidery white Peruvian daffodils, *Ismene festalis*, appear in high summer, their curling, icy petals a delightful contrast to clumps of blue rue and purple sage. Pink calla lilies, *Zantedeschia rehmannii*, have long, lance shaped leaves and graceful, curving flowers which remind my son of the big ice cream cones made by folding crisp waffle cookies around a fluting cone form.

Desert candles, *Eremurus bungei*, send up their warm yellow, fluffy spires in salute to the midsummer sun. Brittle, fleshy roots like splayed hands make them very easy to damage, so even where they are hardy (to at least 10 degrees Fahrenheit), growing them in liftable pots may increase the life of these splendid bulbs. Full sun and excellent drainage will also help, for eremurus will rot before it freezes. Several other species and forms are occasionally available from mail-order catalogs, most commonly the Shelford Hybrids mixture. This includes strong yellows and oranges as well as peachy or salmon-pinks. Unfortunately, the colors are not especially compatible with each other, varying widely in weight and value. To work them into color schemes, start mixed bulbs in a nursery bed, then sort and label them by color. If each bulb is planted in a one- or two-gallon pot, it can be used in border pot holes or sunk into the nursery bed. In warm winter areas, these can be transplanted into the border in autumn with very little trauma. The yellow Shelfords are often tinted with a rusty orange that links them to coppery heleniums and marmalade-colored rudbeckias. Pure, soft yellow ones consort well with a dwarf pampas grass, *Cortaderia selloana pumila* 'Sunstripe', while the tawny oranges contrast especially

well with Cape fuchsias like *Phygelius* × *rectus* 'African Queen' or 'Salmon Leap', and 'Gold Band' yuccas. The various pinks work wonderfully in pastel and silver borders, behind lavender clary sages and soft blue *Campanula latiloba*.

Angels' fishing rods, *Dierama pulcherrimum*, is a grassy-leaved plant which extends supple rods six or eight feet above the border floor, curving under their nodding bait of pink- or rose- or plum-colored bells. The only thing they ever catch is the eye of every visitor, all of whom want a piece to take home. A large plant some ten years old sends its drooping wands over a cascade of ruffled, pinky purple roses, the climbing form of the popular 'Angel Face', a combination that never fails to elicit the all-time border triumph, the involuntary "ahhh!" Behind it, under a leafy canopy of pink-variegated dogwood 'Cherokee Daybreak', a stand of white-belled galtonias rises between wheels of white-splashed hostas and the border lacecap hydrangea 'Lanarth White' in a quieter but similarly satisfying combination.

Late summer bloomers include the intensely fragrant peacock orchid, *Acidanthera murieliae*, with elegantly attenuated blossoms of clean white, their throats marked with chestnut and maroon. Whiskered ivory plumes of American bear grass, *Zigadenus elegans*, will blend beautifully with fast gilding ornamental grasses. At the border's front, chubby, honey-colored spikes of the pineapple lily, *Eucomis bicolor*, combine exotically with chrysanthemums in copper and rust and hazy blue asters. A gently tinted Cape fuchsia, *Phygelius* 'Yellow Trumpet', opens its sprays of greenish yellow, tubular flowers as summer declines, and its sturdy, arching stems make wonderful wands for questing strands of a nasturtium relative, the bulbous vine *Tropaeolum tuberosum* 'Ken Aslet'. This form produces its little funnel flowers in burnt orange and red at the approach of autumn, weeks before the plain species thinks about blooming. This is a decided bonus, for in any year with an early frost, the little vines are killed before they can flower. The fat tubers are edible, if not especially tasty, and must be stored like sweet potatoes; they do best in a box of dry sand, kept dry and cool, but never allowed to freeze.

Late summer light turns sheaves of crocosmia foliage to pleated translucencies. Crocosmia 'Firebird' blooms over many weeks, its long buds extending like winged birds above its stiff, wiry stems. Author's garden. Photo: Mark Lovejoy

AUTUMN

As summer slips away, the flames of fall lick through the border, intensifying foliage colors as flower power fades. Though most of the summer bloomers are winding down, a few plants are just hitting their stride. Among them are a number of fine border bulbs, perhaps the showiest of which are crocosmias and related interspecific hybrids. A red-hot five-footer, *Crocosmia* 'Lucifer', blooms from August into October in lovely arching sheaves, each stout stem tipped with sprays of fire red flowers that look rather like freesias. 'Fire Bird' is almost as tall, with brazen, copper-red and orange flowers, and its stiff foliage turns a clear gold as autumn progresses. There are many named hybrids in the two- and three-foot range, including the tender but terrifically long blooming 'Emily McKenzie', with enormous blossoms of hot orange marked with chocolate. The shimmering 'Solfatare', with bronze leaves and gold flowers, looks magical between 'Blue Beauty' rue and a sheaf of × *Solidaster* 'Lemore', a buttery yellow cross between a goldenrod and an aster. Silky kaffir lilies (*Schizostylis*) look like ethereal gladiolus, their narrow blossoms ranged along sinuous, elongated stems above grassy, usually quite untidy foliage which keeps them a few feet back from the border edge.

Kaffir lilies usually begin to bloom in September, and may carry on until March in mild areas. *Schizostylis major* is the earliest, blending its tomato red blossoms with the first fall leaves. Dainty, shell pink 'Vicountess Byng', the larger, glossier 'Oregon Sunset', or the cherry red 'November Cheer' make excellent companions for purple berried callicarpas and shrubby, cutleaf maples with vivid fall foliage. October awakens the glittering pink ribbons of Guernsey lilies, *Nerine* species and hybrids of varying hardiness. *Nerine bowdenii*, one of the toughest, blooms till the first killing frost, jewel bright amongst a sea of silvery, round-leaved immortelle (*Helicrysum petiolare*) and long stemmed, hardy 'Fred Boutin' lavender. 'Cherry Ripe' is a velvet red hybrid of most uncertain hardiness, best grown in a liftable pot for indoor winter storage. In the garden, this one glows with unmatched intensity amid a

flurry of garnet grape leaves from *Vitis* × 'Brant' and the midnight blue flowers of the late-blooming *Scutellaria incana*, its fine-toothed leaves neatly edged in black. A sorrowful beauty, *Gladiolus papilio*, has been opening its smoke gray and lavender flowers, each marked with two green tears, since August, but bulbs grown in light shade at the border's back bloom on through October or November, weaving their long stems through the lower branches of a beautyberry, *Callicarpa bodinieri* 'Profusion', whose every twig is thickly studded with tiny, periwinkle-purple berries.

Beneath the skirts of defoliating border shrubs and trees, autumn crocus unfurl. Lilac and purple checkered *Colchicum agrippinum* glimmers against a cream-washed variegated cress, *Barbarea vulgaris* 'Variegata'. Deep violet 'Lilac Wonder' opens a long succession of large, lustrous blossoms amid thick-stemmed clumps of ruby chard and the dark crinkled foliage of *Ajuga reptans* 'Purple Brocade'. Birch leaves carpet the ground with gold, setting off the white globes of *Colchicum speciosum* 'Album' opening between gleaming tussocks of black mondo grass (*Ophiopogon planiscapus* 'Nigrescens') and a soft gray sedum relative, *Orostachys furusei*. A handful of true crocus bloom in autumn as well, including *Crocus speciosus*, which is variable, flowering in ivory or shades of lilac. It usually appears in September and October, in time to vie with the falling foliage of flaming Sargent crab apple, *Malus sargentii*, and the last of the asters.

Hardy cyclamen, tough little counterparts of the showboat florists' flowers, are being seed grown by a number of responsible nurseries, notably by Nancy Goodwin at Montrose in North Carolina. Though the majority need mild winters, a good number can survive and even thrive well into Zone 5 if their cultural needs are met. These are generally very simple, but they do vary; all like good soil and better drainage, but while most prefer light or partial shade, a few need ample sun to flourish. *Cyclamen cilicium* is a late bloomer with pretty, marbled foliage in its best forms, and delicate white or soft pink flowers which appear from late September until Christmas. This one likes some sun, but seems happy to be nestled close by the big, gnarled roots of an elderly, umbrella-pruned apple in my garden, where it gets full sun from leaf fall through mid-spring, and several hours a day of direct sun all summer. *Cyclamen hederifolium* is also variable, and many collectors have selected for extravagantly lovely leaf patterns, as well as solid silver or pewter. The flowers can be white or several shades of pink, all fine companions for early blooming *Helleborus atrorubens* (of gardens), which opens the first of its green and ruby bellflowers in November.

EARLY WINTER

Winter hardiness is a relative thing: Louise Beebe Wilder was growing an exciting range of hardy bulbs in her New York State garden earlier in this century, including many which are still listed as tender. Various members of the American Rock Garden Society have described their surprising successes (and failures) with winter hardy bulbs in the pages of their society bulletin over the years. Since mixed borders offer a large range of microclimates and site conditions, it is always worth trying a few bulbs of whatever you fancy. In my garden, the South African *Nerine undulata* always works its way out of the soil to sit, half exposed, near the surface. I suppose this is because it likes the summer baking so many bulbs require, but when we suffered overnight drops of sixty degrees one December, the exposed bulbs were frozen solid, then thawed just as abruptly a day or two later. Rather than rotting, they bloomed undeterred the following fall. Plants are mysterious, but their fascinating ways keep us flexible and open to new ideas.

A more reliably hardy bulb, *Crocus goulimyi*, begins to produce its gentle lilac blossoms in October, accompanied by the last gentians and strands of creeping *Fuchsia procumbens*, with its tubular little green and purple flowers. *Crocus speciosus*, a variable species, is not far behind, its white form arriving in time to surround the gilded, tattered glory of a huge *Hosta* 'Sum and Substance' with an aureole of light. Starry white *Crocus vallicola* carries on into December, partnered with *Arum italicum* 'Pictum', which produces its marbled leaves in fall, so they are at

their glossy best in winter, sometimes threaded with plump stalks of tomato red berries. Untidy clumps of slim-leaved *Iris unguicularis* begin to bloom in November, usually led off by the grayish blue 'Walter Butt'. Sunny December days unfurl the tight buds of darker blue 'Mary Barnard' and ivory 'Winter Treasure', which are clustered beneath felted Yakushimanum hybrid rhododendrons and a young autumn cherry, *Prunus subhirtella* 'Autumnalis Rosea', which opens its own pink buds during every warm spell between October and March. The frail, fluttering butterfly flowers of *Cyclamen coum* usher in winter, renewing the cycle of the year as they nod beneath the dusky hellebores.

Iris foetidissima has undistinguished flowers of faded blue, their insipidity redeemed by the brilliance of these autumnal berries which persist well into winter. Photo: Mark Lovejoy

Yellow ribbons of Hakonechloa macra *'Aureola' paired with a smooth hummock of blue rue,* Ruta graveolens *'Jackman's Blue'. This is an excellent example of painting with plants; abstract impressionism in the garden! Withey/Price garden, Seattle. Photo: Mark Lovejoy*

Chapter Nine

GRASSES
IN THE
MIXED BORDER

Ornamental grasses, with their long season of good looks and an exceptional range of colors, shapes, and textures, can be garden workhorses. However, the very differences that set them apart from the common run of perennials make them overpowering when used with too free a hand. Like trees, grasses must be used judiciously if they are to balance and center the mixed border rather than overwhelm it. A few years ago, when grass gardens were all the rage, ornamental grasses were promoted as the ultimate carefree perennial. Their foliar textures and feathery blossoms were widely extolled and Americans went wild with excitement. Urban meadows proliferated, while imitations of pampas and plain dotted the countryside from California to the Carolinas. As the seasons rolled by, rude reality intruded. Many grass gardens began to look distinctly ratty, their elegant lines blurring with age. Time transformed spare pampas to untamed prairie, urban meadow to overgrown lot. Dismayed gardeners discovered that, just as *Rudbeckia* 'Goldsturm' becomes an increasingly shy bloomer when overcrowded, and just as *Sedum* 'Autumn Joy' grows gappy and lax in habit if left undivided for more than a couple of years, ornamental grasses will lose their looks without attention.

In truth, grasses require as much care as most perennials, and more than some. A handsome handful like manna grass, *Glyceria maxima* 'Variegata' or the rich blue Lyme grass, *Elymus arenarius* (*glauca*), can wreak havoc if unleashed in a small border, and can be kept in bounds only through starvation and the vigilant removal of offshoots (or buried restraint barriers made of steel, cement, or heavy plastic). Groups of shapely copper sedge, *Carex filifera*, need a thorough combing each spring to clear out the dead straws of winter, no easy job on a good-sized plant. What's more, those distinct tussocks will soon blend into a shaggy muddle unless divided and reset every few years. Statuesque giant pampas grass, *Cortaderia selloana*, degenerates quickly from an exciting accent into an oversized haystack that can overwhelm a modest border, and its division demands strength and determination as well as protective eye goggles and serious garden gloves (the stubs and young blades are very sharp indeed). Tidy dwarf mops of the variegated sedge, *Carex conica* 'Hime Kansuge', broaden slowly, in a mannerly fashion, yet in many gardens, they tend to die out in the center while expanding laterally. Since the unsightly brown central tufts can't be cut away without spoiling the look of the plant, which is evergreen and base clumping, frequent hand grooming or biennial division—which keeps the plants small but good looking—is required to keep the plant in good form.

Though the first heat of our passion for grasses is on the wane, certain of them rightfully remain horticultural hot stuff. The glossy red ribbons of blood grass, *Imperata cylindrica*, look stunning in myriad combinations; behind tall sedums like rusty rose 'Autumn Joy' and the molasses tinted 'Honey-song'; amid blue 'Maxi Star' or 'Lavender Chip' junipers; mixed with *Heuchera* 'Palace Purple'. Blood grass is so easy to use well that gardeners across the country count it among their staples. Another blue oat grass, *Helictotrichon sempervirens*, forms a shimmering, perfectly symmetrical mound some two or even three feet across, the color of glacial ice. Its foliage complements any color scheme, while its fine texture sets off the broader leaves of shrubs or perennials nicely. When it blooms, its seed heads dance on slim head high stalks, making an airy scrim through which to view the border interior.

A step up the size scale, feather grass, *Stipa gigantea*, boasts an exceptional catalog of border virtues. Few plants can match its balletic extension of line as its bloom stalks soar above surrounding greenery. Its textures are multiple, but always good; coarse of leaf, fine and wiry of stem, the seeds needlelike. The dry stalks sing in silken, rustling music awakened by any wind. It blooms in a glorious burst of golden rain, glittering seeds dangling from thready stalks. All this in exchange for dividing the creature every third year (I do the job with an axe, before the crown gets too big to handle) seems a most reasonable trade off. Still, for every stellar border grass, there are several dogs, and it can take a few seasons to discover just how each grass is going to behave in your garden. It is well worth restricting all unknown grasses to the nursery bed to learn their proclivities before unleashing them in the borders.

The worst aspect of the hype surrounding grasses was that it misdirected our thinking about how to use them in garden situations. Bold, overstated swaths of purple moor grass, *Molinia arundinacea*, work well with stark modern architecture, yet in front of cozy suburban bungalows they succeed only in throwing off the architectural scale and values. Outsized grasses like *Stipa gigantea* have too strong an impact to fit comfortably into most small garden borders when massed as directed by the grass boosters, but a single plant will rise triumphant be-

Smaller grasses may be considered as garden neutrals, providing contrasts of color, texture, and shape for flurries of border perennials. Blue oat grass, Helictotrichon sempervirens, *is an amiable evergreen which fits comfortably into nearly any color scheme. Photo: Mark Lovejoy*

side a windswept broom, or make a visual crescendo among a cluster of spiky foxgloves or verbascums. In the average border, such stately grasses act as deciduous shrubs, greening up by late spring and rising in midsummer to plumed glory. In a big mixed border, a well-placed series of such giant grasses will lead the eye along in a rhythmic repeat that helps link adjoining areas of the garden.

The midsized and smaller grasses are very much at home in the mixed border, where they contrast handsomely with the foliage of perennial and shrub. Vase shaped, upright or hummocky, delicate or coarse of texture, their leaves may be lax or stiff, wide as ribbons or slim as wires. Unlike lawn grasses, border grasses come in a full spectrum of colors. Beyond a hundred shades of green, one may choose amongst golden grasses of various textures and sizes, of tints from near white through the palest buttery yellows to sunny golds. The recent influx of New Zealand grasses has broadened the palette with tawny oranges, copper and bronze, buff and tan. Fountain grass, *Pennisetum* 'Burgundy Giant', is a lustrous, intense wine-purple in flower, stem, and leaf. Many variegated grasses show tints of pink and

The stiff leaves of Carex comans *'Bronze Form' contrast pleasingly with the softer lines and amorphous shapes of less distinctive plants. Withey/Price garden, Seattle. Photo: Mark Lovejoy*

rose, while blood grass turns a clarion, true red over the summer. There are dozens of blue grasses, a few distinctly grayish ones, and at least one pure black (though mondo grass, *Ophiopogon planiscapus* 'Nigrescens', is not a true grass, it is grassy enough in form and habit to qualify as one in gardener's terms). Certain of the most striking grasses are too tender to survive in the coldest gardens, yet they generally take well to life in pots, and can be wintered over in a sheltered garage or cool greenhouse. A few, like *Pennisetum* 'Burgundy Giant', are worth growing even as annuals, since they size up quickly, performing from early summer well into fall.

Though most of the showiest bloomers don't come into their own until late summer, many ornamental grasses begin their contribution in early spring. Hook sedge, *Uncinia uncinioides*, is a punk orange mophead with racy red highlights, and a stunner coupled with the coppery orange late single tulip 'Princess Irene' and the dwarf spirea 'Goldflame', which boasts early foliage of warm orange and cinnamon bronze. Cheerful strands of Bowles' golden grass, *Milium effusum* 'Aureum', make an exceptional ground cover for jaunty 'Tete-a-tete' narcissus and nodding yellow *Primula veris*. In my garden, diminutive tufts of steel blue fescue, *Festuca glauca* 'Blauglut', punctuate a sprawling mat of *Artemisia stellerana* 'Silver Brocade' beneath the arching, white flowered wands of dwarf *Deutzia gracilis* 'Nikko'. Broad and glossy, the green and cream striped leaves of a little sedge, *Carex morrowii* 'Fisher's Form', spread in graceful swirls beneath viridiflora tulips, 'Spring Green', and a white Spanish broom, *Cytisus multifida*.

In early summer, the pink-streaked, ivory ribbons of manna grass, *Glyceria maxima* 'Variegata', set off the fat pink goblets of late peonies and echo the pale cream of the scented columbine, *Aquilegia fragrans*. Ruddy strands of purple fountain grass, *Pennisetum setaceum atrosanguineum*, gleam behind the somber lace of black bugbane, *Cimicifuga ramosa* 'Atropurpurea', or the dark foliage of a nonclimbing *Clematis recta* 'Pupurea'. A shimmering underplanting of a golden sedge, *Carex elata* 'Knightshayes', brilliantly offsets the curving arms of a dwarf, Irish green border barberry, *Berberis thunbergili* 'Kobold'.

Tall grasses make a considerable impact in modest borders, where they must be placed with care. In the Withey/Price garden, maiden grasses are woven in well-spaced repeats along the double borders, supporting their neighbors without overwhelming them. Photo: Peter Ray

The snowy rush, *Luzula nivea*, makes an understated, elegant ground cover among border shrubs, spreading modestly in neat clumps. Its deep green leaves are edged with long hairs that soften the spare architecture of the plant, and the fluffy white flowers emphasize the pale underskirts of the lavender *Thalictrum delavayi* or the touches of cream in the buttery English rose, 'Windrush'.

In midsummer, a purple moor grass, *Molinia caerulea* 'Variegata', opens an upright fan of gilt-tipped stems above a curving clump of wide green and ivory leaves faintly stained with pink, against

which the dusky *Sedum* 'Vera Jameson' tumbles in a cascade of purple and rose. Irregular horizontal golden stripes run across the jungle green foliage of zebra grass, *Miscanthus sinensis* 'Zebrinus', accentuating the exotic flavor of bold-leaved *Acanthus mollis latifolius* grouped against big, sawtoothed hydrangea foliage. Delicate, airy flowers of fine-textured hair grass, *Deschampsia caespitosa* 'Gold Veil', shroud the back of the border in gentle mystery. A stiff clump of a bronzy brown sedge, *Carex buchananii*, stands sentry straight amid a ruffle of ruddy sedums or between a spreading sea of golden marjoram and sheaves of the spidery golden willow-leaved daisy, *Buphthalmum salicifolium*.

Late summer turns blood grass pure red from tip to toes. Tall fountains of red switch grass, *Panicum virgatum* 'Häense Herms', deepen from rust to ruby. Little blue stem, *Andropogon scoparious*, warms from blue-green to bronze and red. By summer's end, the big grasses come to the fore, their foliage gilded and rustling. It is worth noting that, though most are grown primarily for their stupendous bloom, many of the large ornamental grasses flower shyly or not at all in cool summer areas like the Pacific Northwest. Often these plants are handsome enough in their own right to earn important border positions, bloom or no bloom. Wherever summers are warm, giant feather grass and tall maiden grass, towering giant reed and spuming fountain grasses reach their flowery prime just as the angle of the waning sun becomes properly acute. Autumnal backlighting sets the big grasses aglow with radiant aureoles that elevate them to the supernal. Bowing companies of bright asters spill like stars about them. Fiery chrysanthemums gleam fiercely at their feet, while the gilded, glowing masses of autumnal shrub foliage make a suitably dramatic backdrop for their golden glories.

The chill winds of winter stir the burnished, bleaching seed heads in slumberous susurration. Bent and broken, weathered and worn, the stalks slump to the earth to sleep beneath the blanketing snows. As winter recedes, their shaggy heads are shorn to stubble. The first daffodils arrive with their fresh shoots to celebrate the resurrection of the splendid garden grasses.

COMBINATIONS FOR BORDER GRASSES

Though usually paired with drought tolerant or prairie plants and grown in full sun, quite a few midsized grasses remain mannerly under ordinary border conditions, and many tolerate some degree of shade. In mixed borders, one can match grasses with like minded perennials, tough, hardy plants that prefer benign neglect to cosseting, grouping *Carex elata* 'Bowles' Golden' with swamp spurge, *Euphorbia palustris*, and the red leaved *Lobelia* 'Queen

Grasses with definite character are most effective in combination with equally vivid companions. At Powys Castle, a glowing sedge, Carex elata *'Bowles' Golden', is paired with a hybrid spiderwort (*Tradescantia × andersoniana*). Photo: Peter Ray*

Victoria', all of which like damp feet. In dry shade, snowy wood rush, *Luzula nivea* 'Snow Bird', with its fluffy white flowers, big-belled creamy white *Campanula takesimana*, white columbines, and white splashed *Geranium phaeum* 'Variegatum' will weave a wonderful carpet together.

In the border proper, many ornamental grasses will need division every three or four years, though those grown in less lush areas may grow well for considerably longer before degenerating. Since autumn division often results in significant losses, border grasses are divided in spring. Those which bloom early may be set back a bit, but all will recover faster in spring than when going into winter. For garden-sized plants, slice each crown into halves or quarters, trimming back the leaves on all sides for a more symmetrical appearance. If you want a great sweep of plants, you can cut one big clump into dozens of little two- and three-inch pieces, so long as each has a bit of root as well as crown. Very small divisions may require several seasons of growing in a pot or nursery bed before placement in the border. When you do plant them, remember their ultimate size, and allow enough room for the grasses to achieve their graceful, natural shapes and make their full contribution among perennial companions.

BIG, BOLD BEAUTIES

Giant reed grass, *Arundo donax* (Zone 7). The giant reed can exceed twelve feet tall when well suited. In France, where it is grown as a field crop (its internodes are the source of woodwind instrument reeds), it grows in damp ditches and hot, open fields with equal vigor, but in more crowded border situations, it seldom exceeds eight to ten feet. A noble pillar of muted, bluish gray, with drooping leaves as broad as corn, the giant reed keeps company with outsized perennials like *Rodgersia tabularis* (now properly *Astilboides tabularis*), *Darmera peltatum*, and *Hydrangea villosa*, and holds its own comfortably among larger border shrubs. The lovely variegated form is more tender (southern parts of Zone 8) but is one of the most dramatic border grasses when well grown. Late-blooming sunflowers, like our na-

A plain arborvitae hedge makes a strong, effective frame for the overflowing richesse of the high summer border. Withey/Price garden, Seattle. Photo: Mark Lovejoy

tive *Helianthus salicifolius*, or *Heliopsis* hybrids like 'Morning Star' and 'Summer Sun', make good perennial companions.

Maiden grass, *Miscanthus sinensis* 'Autumn Light' (Zone 4). Late to bloom, its eight- to ten-foot spires of ruddy bronze flowers held over silver-striped foliage illuminate the September garden. Fluffy flowered fothergillas, with their rich late leaf color, or a searing red sumach (*Rhus typhina*) make wonderful shrubby companions, as do twisting ropes of purple, grape-leaved *Vitis coignetiae* or thick wreaths of canary creeper, *Tropaeolum peregrinans*. Several species and many named selections of maiden grass are widely available, offering a range of sizes, textures, and colors. Large achilleas, with their horizontally tiered inflorescence, contrast nicely, as will puffy clouds of baby's breath (*Gypsophila paniculata*) or the similar giant woodruff, *Galium aristatum*, which does better in acid soils.

Ravenna grass, *Erianthus ravennae* (Zone 6). Ravenna grass belongs only in the largest of borders, for a mature plant, some twelve feet tall and accordingly broad in girth, is an imposing sight. A spuming green fountain in summer, it turns bronze and clear gold in fall, and holds its color well into the colder months. Such a plant requires powerful neighbors, large shrubs like an arching red barberry, *Berberis thunbergii* 'Atrosanguinea', or a gold-spotted *Aucuba japonica* 'Variegata' shaded by a lace-leaved Japanese maple. Perennial companions too must be of heroic proportions, such as the towering *Inula magnifica*, with its golden yellow daisy flowers, or a great sheaf of creamy *Artemisia lactiflora*.

Reed feather grass, *Calamagrostis acutiflora stricta* (Zone 5). Stacked tiers of curving foliage give this big, buxom grass a more interesting profile than some of the border giants. This one needs a sunny yet protected site, for wind and rain can wreak havoc with six or seven feet of wet grass. After an especially rough storm, I have succeeded in restoring a large plant to good looks by combing it out with a rubber lawn rake, but this is not something one cares to repeat on a regular basis. It is, however, a stunning border plant when happy, its red-gold flowers according pleasantly with beautyberry (*Callicarpa* species) and the orange-red fruits of mountain ash

(*Sorbus* species). I like it fronted down with wide-leaved daylilies like the huge, creamy yellow 'Happy Beauty' and paler 'Classic Simplicity', for the repeat of form and texture is subtle and pleasing.

Giant feather grass, *Stipa gigantea* (Zones 7 to 9). This needs the company of a large shrub or small tree to balance its presence in the mixed border. The outsized, felt-leaved *Buddleia nivea* or a well grown *Rosa rubrifolia* will do the job nicely. In my garden, it grows sandwiched between them, its untidy base hidden behind a shapely *Daphne retusa*. Its stout flowering stems are laced with tendrils of yellow, lemon scented *Clematis serratifolia* which also scrambles fifteen feet up the buddleia to echo the clear gold of the stipa blooms. A five-foot column of ferny leaved goat's rue, *Galega* × *hartlandii* 'Lady Wilson', blooms nearby, its blue and white flowers a pleasant contrast to the glittery golden grass.

MIDBORDER GRASSES

Dwarf pampas grass, *Cortaderia selloana* 'Sunstripe' (Zone 7 or 8). Comparatively compact, this small pampas grass spreads its golden streamers three to five feet up and out, growing taller and stouter in sunny, well-drained sites. Its sun yellow leaves are striped with cream, a vivid brightener for somber plantings of reds and murky purples, and a cheerful addition to color runs of orange, copper, bronze, and yellow. In my garden, I play up its sunny character, backing this chunky grass with a dwarf golden ninebark, *Physocarpus opulifolius* 'Dart's Gold', and several bushes of evergreen *Euonymus japonicus* 'Gold Spot', and underplanting it with several hundred of the dwarf daffodil 'Tete-a-tete', all laced with clumps of a smaller yellow grass, *Carex elata* 'Knightshayes'. In spring, this corner fairly sparkles, but by midsummer, it has cooled down considerably, and is itself brightened by Cape fuchsia, *Phygelius* × *rectus* 'Salmon Leap', and a tall, almost everblooming orange geum found in older gardens here in the Northwest, its proper name or species unknown. Another dwarf pampas grass, *C.s.* 'Gold Band', taller and rather darker in color than 'Sunstripe', is also somewhat hardier, as is a white-banded form, 'Silver Stripe'.

Blue oat grass, *Helictotrichon sempervirens* (Zones 4 to 8). One of the handsomest of garden grasses, its symmetrical, two- or three-foot-tall hummocks, metallic color, and thready texture make an exciting counterpoint for thickly felted, silvery verbascums or the great, storm cloud leaves of 'Rubine' brussels sprouts. It does best in full sun, and is most symmetrical when not overly crowded by perennial companions. A running thicket of shrubby *Stephanandra incisa* 'Crispa' sets off widely spaced clumps wonderfully, where a good deal of space is to be covered, but in smaller quarters, shrub roses or dwarf spireas like *Spiraea* × *bumalda* 'Limemound' may be preferred.

Pennisetum 'Burgundy Giant' (Zones 8 to 10). Almost cornlike in appearance, this one is outsized in every part, with bold red leaves and murky purple flower brushes that may extend to four feet. A very late bloomer, in cool summer areas it seldom manages to flower before killing frosts arrive. In warm, sunny areas, it will bloom well its first year, and is often treated as an annual, since, though highly susceptible to frost, it is very effective in the garden setting. It makes a handsome backdrop for 'Gold Band' yuccas or smoky salmon *Kniphofia caulescens*, and sets off powdery blue *Geranium pratense* 'Mrs. Kendall Clark' and tussocks of pale yellow *Dianthus knappii*. Several attractive fountain grasses are far hardier, like the tall, graceful *Pennisetum caudatum* (Zone 6), a five to six footer with slimmer, soft green foliage and creamy white flowers, and *P. alopecuroides* (Zone 6), a foot or two shorter, and with pale purple flowers and good autumn foliage color.

Bowles' golden sedge, *Carex elata* 'Bowles' Golden' (Zone 5). E. A. Bowles, a great gardener with a famous eye for a good plant, found this handsome gilded grass growing by a riverside near his home, and it does, indeed, appreciate a good, moist soil. However, even in drier conditions, it may reach three feet, and makes a handsome addition to border groups involving bronze, copper, or dusky reds and purples. It looks especially nice with the rounded, purplish leaves of *Ligularia dentata* 'Desdemona', the gold-variegated columbine, *Aquilegia vulgaris* 'Variegated', and the tall, late-blooming *Primula florindae*, clear yellow and smelling of nutmeg. The leaves of

A number of coppery New Zealand carexes offer unusual colors and textures. The larger one here is Carex comans *'Bronze Form', the smaller* C. filifera, *with blue oat grass at the side and purple fennel behind. Author's garden. Photo: Mark Lovejoy*

'Bowles' Golden' are quite broad, and of a light golden yellow, with a slim green stripe running down each side. Far brighter in tint and holding its color longer is the sun yellow form, *Carex elata* 'Knightshayes'. This sedge is stripeless, its somewhat narrower foliage a warm yellow with a hint of reddish orange in it, but is otherwise very similiar in size and form to 'Bowles' Golden'.

Leather leaf sedge, *Carex buchananii* (Zone 7). Completely different in every respect from *C. elata*, this sturdy New Zealander is spaghetti thin, upright, and rather stiff in form. It may exceed three feet in height, its military bearing softened by the twiddly corkscrewing tips. Though many admire the color—a deep reddish brown with coppery highlights—others feel it merely looks dead all year round. Its spare good looks combine exceptionally well with lusher leaves. It looks wonderful placed between a dwarf cutleaf red maple and the soft, salmony haze of *Heuchera* 'Coral Cloud', for instance, and will pleasantly emphasize the red foliage and blackish stems of *Lobelia* 'Queen Victoria' or the broader, almost hostalike leaves of red plantain, *Plantago major* 'Rubrifolia'.

Hair grass, *Deschampsia flexuosa* (Zone 4). As finely textured as human hair, this two to three

Tawny Asiatic lilies emerge through the glowing strands of Carex elata *'Knightshayes'. Withey/Price garden, Seattle. Photo: Mark Lovejoy*

footer makes soft, silky tumbles midborder, its pale, buffy tan flowers rising another foot or so above the clumps in late summer. Tolerant of light or high shade, this hair grass fits well into mixed border situations, where it provides gentle contrast to glossy *Daphne odora* and the shapely foliage of *Acanthus mollis*. There are quite a few named hair grasses, most of them rather smaller, and all of them suited to grouping with ferns, bulbs, and dwarf shrubs in partially shaded situations.

Snowy wood rush, *Luzula nivea* (Zone 4). An excellent ground-covering grass for dry, rooty shade, in its best forms, such as 'Snow Bird', the snowy wood rush flowers as well as many a perennial. The fluffy white froth appears above the strappy, rather hairy leaves some two feet tall, in late spring or early summer. They remain in beauty for a long time, and like the somewhat similar looking everlastings, can be dried for use in floral arrangements. White-variegated hostas, white violets, and creeping *Lamium maculatum* 'White Nancy' are all good companions, consorting well with dwarf rhododendrons and evergreen viburnums in midborder shrubby islands.

DWARF AND COMPACT GRASSES

The following smaller carexes (properly carices, but I have yet to hear anybody use the correct plural form) are among the best of the border grasses. All are undemanding, reliable performers that adapt well to the mixed border, mingling comfortably with plants of all sorts. Most may be grown for four or five years without division and, in some gardens, may hold their looks far longer.

White sedge, *Carex albula* 'Frosty Curls' (Zone 6). Delicate in texture and almost metallic in color, its narrow leaves look rather like narrow strips of aluminum. Though evergreen, it is frost tender, and the shelter of an overturned pot during the coldest months can prevent the unsightly burning of its leaf tips. This dwarf grass rarely reaches a foot in height, and spread to perhaps fifteen inches. It looks very pretty with the cream-marbled foliage of hardy *Cy-*

clamen hederifolium, or mixed in with a colony of dwarf columbines, *Aquilegia flabellata nana*, and the white-striped foliage of *Iris japonica* 'Variegata'.

Japanese sedge, *Carex morrowii* 'Fisher's Form' (Zone 7). This makes a pleasing swirl of evergreen, variegated leaves some fifteen inches across and under ten inches tall. Broad and glossy, each bears a wide central stripe of cream with vivid green margins. Like most of the smaller carexes, it sends up stiff flower spikes ten to twelve inches high, tipped with little green bottle brushes. Annual hand grooming and division every two or three years keep it in good looks. This mixes marvelously with dwarf border hostas, soft yellow primulas, and fritillaries, and its texture contrasts pleasingly with that

Stiffly upright, the tidy little fans of Stipa arundinacea *make a hazy scrim at the front of the border. The sprawling shrub is the evergreen* Euonymus fortunei *'Silver Queen'. Photo: Mark Lovejoy*

of small deer fern or maidenhair ferns (*Blechnum spicant* and *Adiantum pedatum*, respectively). Its buttery variegation is lifted into prominence by a flat sheet of yellow baby's tears, *Helxine soleirolii* 'Golden Queen'.

Dwarf sedge, *Carex conica* 'Hime Kansuge', also sold as 'Variegata' (Zone 5). This plump little evergreen tussock spreads gently sideways fifteen to eighteen inches while staying relatively flat. The deep, rich green of the leaf blades is set off by neat white margins. In some gardens, it dies out at the core each winter, but division every few years will preserve its attractive appearance. It makes a pretty border edging when underplanted with silver blue or rosy sedums, such as *Sedum spathulifolium* 'Roseum', and can also cover the feet of midborder tea or floribunda roses, perhaps partnered with purple-leaved Labrador violets, *Viola labradorica*.

Blue fescue, *Festuca glauca* 'Blauglut' (Zone 4). The cultivar name translates to 'Blue Glow', and this grass really does have a luminous glow, especially at dusk or when fog fills the garden. In full sun, the foliage is a silvery frost blue, deep sea green at the heart, echoing the similar coloration of 'Jackman's Blue' rue (*Ruta graveolens*), with which it partners very attractively as a carpeting for tall, vividly colored perennials or border shrubs. This subtle coloring also lifts soft, chalky pastels into prominence, pairing beautifully with the palest salmon of *Iris intermedia* 'Hazel's Pink', or creamy yellow wallflowers like *Erysimum* 'Moonlight'.

Golden hair grass, *Deschampsia flexuosa* 'Tatra Gold' (Zone 4 or 5). Needle thin and wiry in texture, this choice little grass builds into a dwarf clump some eight inches tall and ten to twelve inches across. In full sun, it is a clear, lively gold which echoes the glittering stamens at the throat of wine-colored 'Decatur Dictator' daylilies, or makes a lovely underplanting for the yolk yellow English rose, 'Graham Thomas'. In partial or filtered shade, 'Tatra Gold' is muted to green-gold, a handsome partner for the dwarf *Spiraea* × *bumalda* 'Lemon Lime', with its citrus bright foliage. In late winter, this evergreen combines pleasingly with sheets of warm yellow *Crocus ancyrensis*. The grass flowers in midspring, its small spikes rising to perhaps twelve

Broad bladed as a bamboo, Carex siderostica *'Variegata' makes a pleasant swirl of cream at the border's edge. Photo: Peter Ray*

inches and tipped with braided brownish seed heads. Base clumping and fairly slow to spread, it retains vigor best when divided every two or three years.

Greater wood rush, *Luzula sylvatica marginata* (Zone 4). This tidy one footer thrives in dry, rooty shade, making it a useful carpeter in a number of difficult situations. The glossy, cream-edged leaves are evergreen, quite broad, and thickly edged with long white hairs which will echo the white blossoms of the dwarf *Rhododendron* 'Ptarmigan', creamy white violets, and the frosty white-striped leaves of *Lamium maculatum* 'Roseum'. In mixed borders, this rush makes an excellent ground cover, mixed with early bulbs and set beneath dwarf shrubs and evergreen hellebores.

Corkscrew rush, *Juncus effusus* 'Spiralis' (Zones 4 to 9). Difficult to place well in a traditional border, its swirling green spirals look dramatic against an unfussy background such as a thick bed of golden Scotch moss, *Sagina subulata* 'Aurea', or golden sandwort, *Arenaria verna* 'Aurea'. Densely textured dwarf conifers or tightly clipped santolinas make complementary companions for it, as does the tidy foliage of *Euonymus* 'Emerald and Gold'. Well under two feet tall, this rush tosses its tangled, wiry arms in a rough circle some eighteeen inches across. If planted in a clay drainpipe sunk partially into the ground, corkscrew rush gains definition and holds its own among surrounding perennials. A group of five, artfully placed, can have an almost sculptural impact in a mixed border, particularly when given a very plain, pale backdrop against which to writhe.

ANNUAL GRASSES

Annual grasses, fast growing and readily movable, will speedily form sweeping, fine textured curves against the firmer foliar background of the mixed border's shrubs. They are invaluable in young borders, where the inevitable gaps between the immature plants can be visually distracting, but more than a few have a distinction of form that gains them permanent positions in established borders as well. Some of summer's most pleasing juxtapositions owe their strength to annual grasses. The pink and gold feathers of squirrel tails (*Hordeum jubatum*) are an unforgettable partner for hazy blue catmints (*Nepeta* species). The fuzzy caterpillar blossoms of violet fountain grass, *Pennisetum violaceum*, in purple and green, or the looser, longer tassels of *P. longistylum* throw the broader curves of golden yuccas into sharp relief. Chunky, braided seed heads of quaking grass, *Briza maxima*, or whiskery clumps of animated oats, *Avena sterilis*, glimmer in airy contrast to more solid shrubs. In shady borders, Bowles' golden grass, *Milium effusum* 'Aureum', self-sows into cheerful crowds, the bright yellow seedlings proclaiming their parentage from first emergence.

In mixed borders, annual grasses do best in full sun and ordinary, rather than well improved, soil. Given enough elbow room, many readily sow themselves into self-sustaining colonies. This helps give a well furnished and naturalistic appearance to the beds, and if excess seedlings are rooted out in good time, they do no harm even when placed among less robust perennials. Until you are confident of recognizing the various young grasses as seedlings, it is wise to plant a few seeds in a well marked pot and keep it nearby for visual reference. Otherwise, it is all too easy to weed out the whole flock, mistaking them for intruding lawn or meadow grasses. Labels in the border help some, but only if you read them before you pull. With most perennials, and many annuals, a label placed near a large patch of seedlings will provoke caution, and we are likely to check for a nametag before tossing out any unfamiliar young.

To learn more about the textures and types of annual border grasses, it's fun to buy mixed packets, made up for flower arrangers, and grow the plants in a corner of the nursery bed or vegetable garden. The best forms can be transplanted into the borders, even in bloom, where they are likely to reseed. If you don't want to trust to luck, gather the dry seed as soon as it is ripe and save it to sow in situ next spring. Grass seed stores well in any dry, cool place; I usually keep it in labeled envelopes tucked into a canning jar with a small packet of silica gel to keep it dry.

Annual grasses are more commonly grown in cutting borders than mixed ones, and may be less familiar than the perennial sorts. Here is a handful of favorites to better your acquaintance with this useful and easygoing clan.

Animated oats, *Avena sterilis*, to three feet. This good-sized, graceful grass boasts a whiskery, golden seed head which is prized for use in dried arrangements. In mixed borders, it consorts nicely with stiff, upright perennials and lax, tumbling ground covers.

Bowles' golden grass, *Milium effusum* 'Aureum', to two feet. Perennial in many areas (Zones 4 to 9), this willing worker grows quickly enough to be a fine annual where it does not survive the winter. It grows well in dry shade, making it a terrific groundcover grass beneath border trees. It looks especially cheerful in spring, when it weaves bright ribbons of sun into all the shady corners of the garden.

Foxtail grass, *Setaria glauca*, to twenty inches. Wide leaves in rather untidy clumps make this a grass to place at the back of the border front; one wants it close enough to appreciate the flower heads, but not so close that it becomes an eyesore. Fat, fluffy seed heads some six inches long ripen in midsummer, their wheat gold deepening to red-bronze as they mature. Tuck them behind dwarf daylilies or between small border shrubs where they can spill in cheerful cascades come autumn.

Hare's tail grass, *Lagurus ovatus*, to twenty inches. This compact, narrow-bladed grass blooms

At North Hill, tender grasses are grown in pots and placed throughout the garden in a movable feast for the eye. Photo: Cynthia Woodyard

in midsummer, its tidy little tips as soft and fluffy as a bunny's scut. It does not seem to reseed as well as most of the others, but is easily grown from saved seed.

Quaking grass, *Briza maxima*, to 20 inches. Broad, soft foliage in a gentle shade of green makes this a useful blender with dwarf daylilies and tall sedums. Its fat seed heads resemble braided bread loaves, and they, too, are often dried for floral arrangements. A smaller version, *B. minor*, is only a foot tall, and more delicate in every part.

Squirrel tail grass, *Hordeum jubatum*, to twenty-four inches. This broad-bladed grass blooms early, opening into large, flexuous brushes of pinky gold. Its complex coloring partners nicely with ruddy foliage as well as blues and purples, copper and bronze. It flowers in early summer, but if cut back hard after

the first crop begins to fade, it will reliably bloom twice or even three times a season.

Tricholaena rosea, to two feet. This handsome grass requires full sun to do justice to its long, silky flower heads, which open warm pink-and-gold and darken to burgundy. It colors best in dry soils, and thrives in sandy situations, but tolerates heavier soils as long as they are well drained. It repeats most reliably in hot summer areas, but returns well from saved seed elsewhere.

Violet panic grass, *Panicum violaceum*, to three feet. Long, soft panicles of green and purple make this showy grass a favorite with flower arrangers. In mixed border settings, it needs plenty of room and a warm position to flower well, but when pleased, it is a steady, reliable performer over a long season.

Hostas make excellent ground covers in shady borders. Many are extremely hardy and present a grand array of leaf color, size, and form to broaden the border builder's plant palette. Photo: Mark Lovejoy

Chapter Ten

GROUND COVERS
IN THE
MIXED BORDER

Ground covers rank among the most valuable plants in the mixed border. Indeed, they are a cornerstone of contemporary ornamental gardening, whose wholesale introduction into beds and borders in the middle of this century triggered a horticultural revolution. Their labor-saving ways led directly to the development of the mixed border, freeing a generation of English garden makers from the tyranny of professional gardeners. When a couple of world wars and a drastically altered world economy had eliminated not only the ubiquitous head gardener but virtually all well trained, inexpensive garden help, traditional herbaceous borders became decidedly impractical almost overnight. Till that time, ground cover plants, though widely accepted in shrubbery and woodland gardens, had been essentially unknown in ornamental borders. Once allowed in, they opened the garden gate to a new and less labor intensive kind of gardening that nonetheless allowed for grand effects. Needing little routine care themselves, and reducing maintenance by keeping large areas free of weeds, ground covers enable a single gardener to keep up to a couple of acres of mixed border under control.

Maintenance reduction is the usual virtue attributed to ground covers, but there are many more. Dense, carpeting plantings not only suppress unwanted weed seedlings, but also conserve water by acting as a living mulch. In the Mediterranean climate of the maritime Northwest, measurable summer rainfall is rare, yet my thickly planted mixed borders (on heavy acid clay) thrive on a single deep watering each month. On lighter soils, more frequent watering might well be necessary, yet a combination of soil amendments and hydrogels, coupled with appropriate ground covers, can significantly reduce water needs in any climate or situation.

Ground covers are also insulators, shielding companion plants from both summer heat and winter cold. Red leaved lobelia hybrids which wither in hot sun will stand tall when their feet are kept cool by a thick carpet of iron cross sorrel, *Oxalis deppei*. Tender crocosmia like the pint-sized 'Jackanapes' often come through a hard winter unscathed under the fluffy silver feathers of *Tanacetum haradjani*. Ground covers can also keep moisture-sensitive plants wet or dry, according to need. A lush planting of ivory striped *Lamium maculatum* 'Roseum' stays delightfully damp despite heat and drought, encouraging the spread of water lovers like *Primula florindae* by sheltering its seedlings from drought. Bulbs which rot in summer wet can be kept perfectly dry under a sprawling mat of velvety lamb's ears (*Stachys byzantina*).

In mixed borders, we seek to use each plant so that its essential qualities are both appropriate and appreciated. This holds true even for the ground cover plants, which are rarely accorded the thoughtful placement automatically awarded to other border candidates. Since ground covers can make or mar a closely planted mixed border, careful attention to their requirements and abilities will pay a handsome dividend for years to come. When well chosen, even the workhorse ground covers employed at the back of the border, where weed control might seem their most vital role, can have their hour to shine. In November, the arrow straight 'Skyrocket' junipers that punctuate my tapestry hedge seem to wear embroidered slippers where the last of the colchicum pierce a blazing blanket of leadwort, *Ceratostigma plumbaginoides*. This stalwart ground cover has leaves of snapping scarlet, among which a few flowers gleam like bits of cobalt. In December, the dank depths of the rhododendron hedge are illuminated by the marvelously marbled and dappled leaves of various cyclamen species. In late January, the ruffle of evergreen Christmas ferns and hellebores at the base of the tapestry hedge is enlivened by the hellebore's ivory buds and pink tinged blossom. In February, the nodding flower heads of evergreen *Euphorbia robbiae* rise up in triumph, their lemon-lime bracts echoing the cheerful tumbles of scented blossom from the *Corylopsis willmottiae* 'Spring Purple' they surround. Ground covers like these emphasize what strengths the border may boast even during the long, quiet months of cold.

In any season, dark corners may be brightened by sheets of sunny 'Buttercup' ivy or tall ranks of silvery moon weed, *Lunaria annua* 'Variegata'. Evergreen ground covers, or those with special strengths in autumn and early spring, can make dull parts of the garden memorable when combined with late and early blooming bulbs. The shallow beds found at the base of hedges are seldom a garden highlight, yet filled with winter blooming bulbs and a companionable ground cover, they become slim ribbons of brilliance, lighting up their somber background despite cold frosts and leftover snow. The deep bays between large background deciduous shrubs can likewise ignite in a concerted blend of bulbs and ground covers. Shrubs which leaf out late and lose their leaves early, like dogwoods and cory-

Traditionally, ground covers have been considered chiefly as weed suppressants. In mixed borders, their role is expanded; they must perform on several levels, often all year round. At Hidcote, a paperbark maple, Acer griseum, *is encircled with* Vinca minor, *its lustrous foliage interrupted by swaths of seasonal bulbs. Photo: Cynthia Woodyard*

lopsis, can enjoy pre- and post-seasons of glory if you have tucked their underskirts full of 'Sweetheart' ivy, colchicums and tall Dutch crocus.

Evergreen ground covers like *Euphorbia robbiae* or *Helleborus foetidus*, which bloom in late winter, keep the garden looking properly clothed, and play up the quiet beauties of the mixed border's shrubby framework during the colder months. Where snow cover is common, the woody background gives shape and character to the winter garden. Even so, larger evergreen carpeters can make wonderful patterns in the snow itself, and stand ready to surface

Annuals make useful short term ground covers, especially in new borders or where final plantings have not been developed. Forget-me-nots and nasturtiums bloom together from April until hard frosts. Photo: Mark Lovejoy

at the first thaw. Where snow comes late or seldom, the gardener may indulge in wintergreen ground covers like *Geranium tuberosum*, which unfolds leaves like lacy green snowflakes in late autumn or early winter, opens wide sprays of lavender blue flowers in midspring, and is dormant by early summer. Rosettes of *Veronica gentianoides* make glossy, tufted carpets below winter and spring blooming hellebores, and if the pale china blue of its April flowers doesn't agree with its neighbors, those of 'Alba' are sure to. A twice-blooming evergreen candytuft, *Iberis sempervirens* 'Autumn Snow', is an excellent partner for winter jasmine, *Jasminum nudiflorum*, which blows its golden trumpets sporadically from November through March, accompanied at every step by the foamy white candytuft flowers.

Not only do ground covers set off the flowers of various seasons, they also serve to mask dying foliage. Bulb foliage, in particular, is remarkably obtrusive as it fades. Though it cannot be removed without harming the bulbs, it can be carefully trimmed and tucked away from sight. Nestled into a deep carpet of *Ajuga reptans* 'Burgundy Glow' or blue leadwort (*Ceratostigma plumbaginoides*), tatty tulip leaves can ripen in peace without detracting from the appearance of the border. In mixed borders, which are expected to be presentable in every season, seasonal bulbs are always paired either with sequentially developing perennials or with ground covers that can cover up a multitude of visual sins. Though the best of these vary with climate and conditions, they all need to be deep enough to bury a few withering leaves under, flexible enough not to resent handling or manipulation, and mannerly enough to be introduced into mixed company without disgracing themselves. Finding the right combinations of bulbs and ground covers can take some experimenting, but good pairings are so effortlessly rewarding as to make any initial effort seem worthwhile once success is achieved.

Though too much of any one plant is visually boring, endless variety can make a garden feel restless, if not frenetic. In gardens where the passion for plants is stronger than the interest in design, ground covers can be excellent unifiers. Repeated pools of catmint or edgings of vinca will visually link di-

Seasonal bulbs will enliven large patches of ground cover, which serve in turn to mask the browning bulb foliage. The bright-eyed cups of Narcissus poeticus *pick up the creamy yellow markings of* Vinca minor 'Aureo-variegata' *beneath a gnarled old cherry tree. Author's garden. Photo: Mark Lovejoy*

vergent sections of garden, making strong connections for the eye. If that seems too limiting or boring, choosing several ground cover theme plants and using them in varying combinations can smooth awkward transitions between areas with differing characters. Plant collectors can take advantage of their acquisitive habit, using similar looking members of plant families like *Stachys* or *Viola* or *Nepeta* in a similar manner throughout the garden. However it is managed, theme plant ground covers can contribute a vital sense of continuity and coherence within the garden as a whole.

If the aesthetic contribution made by ground covers is minor, it is because they are seldom used with verve or imagination. For the most part, they are intended simply to hold ground against weeds, or to provide a solid mass of a particular color or texture over a large area. To consider ground covers as lacking intrinsic interest or worth is to ignore an opportunity to add polish and depth to mixed borders. Here, ground covers are not mere place holders; their role is to maintain or elevate the visual standard, preferably all through the year. Well chosen ground covers can waken the eye to subtle details in the larger picture of the overall border, echoing the tints of secondary colors in a theme, or providing contrast of form and texture to bolder plants. Ground covers organize and give importance to small vignettes and border details, acting as place markers for bulbs and ephemeral plants as well. Where small patches of delicate ground covers are wanted, all candidates should be good enough to earn their position by their own merits. In larger patches, ground covers should share ground gracefully. If a large mass of a single plant is needed to pull a complex planting together or carpet beneath a wide spreading shrub, the circle of ground cover need not be unbroken; a host of smaller plants may be laced through the leafy carpet to create seasonal interest. A wide pool of *Lamium* 'White Nancy' encircles a plump *Hydrangea macrophylla* 'Madame Emile Mouilliere', a striking sight when the huge white panicles of hydrangea are dangling above those frosty leaves. In other seasons, however, the picture is less complete, and interest must shift to the understory. Then, the silvery foliage becomes a handsome backdrop for plump tufts of green eyed snowdrops in late winter, and sprays of creamy *Tulipa turkestanica* and white *Anemone blanda* in spring. Summer's end could bring tall white goblets of *Colchicum speciosum* 'Album', and tufts of evergreen *Iris foetidissima* 'Variegata', with its clean white stripes, would back up these evanescent charmers all year long.

In mixed borders, the principal plants may be quite large in scale, requiring plenty of expansion space between neighbors. In high summer, the borders will be fully furnished, with no bare soil in sight, but from late winter through midspring, the gaps may be glaring. Ground covers which perform during the off seasons, yet survive the crowded conditions of summer, are invaluable in such situations. Those old standards, vincas and ajugas, offer a fine range of foliage size, color, and plant vigor, as do florists' ivies, many of which are surprisingly hardy. Where evergreen plants are not wanted, perennial weavers and knitters will pour around perennials or clamber over woody stem and branch. These long-armed plants expand with summer, adapting themselves to whatever room is available as the season progresses. In a deep border, the vigorous woody *Clematis* × *jouiniana* 'Praecox' will quickly conceal any bare ground between robust perennials, then scramble decoratively into a larger shrub or small tree before opening its fluffy little flowers of skim milk blue. On a smaller scale, cloud-eyed sprays of *Geranium wallichianum* 'Buxton's Blue' extend on long, angular arms, each plant covering two or three square feet of ground by late summer.

Smaller knitters thread companionably through larger plants without harming their complacent hosts. Pansies and violas make excellent small scale mixers, offering a huge range of colors to work with. 'Black Devil' pansies can unify the front of the border when placed in rhythmic repeats between dwarf shrubs and sprawling evergreen herbs. Pastel yellow *Viola* 'Beshlie' blends colors which might otherwise be at odds. Long blooming 'Clear Crystal' pansies in apricot or slate blue will lend color to plants that have passed their floral prime. The horned viola, *Viola cornuta*, spills in cascades over the border's edge while lacing shoot after flower laden shoot as much as three feet long through taller plants nearby. Diascias, the South African twin-spurs, are equally splendid knitters, worthy of a place even where they must be grown as annuals. Their small, spurred flowers of rose or coral or coppery salmon bring zest to an excess of pastels, and they have a knack for putting themselves into stunning combinations. Two-foot-wide mats of *Diascia* 'Ruby Field' willingly run between great clumps of lavender and spiky globes of blue fescue, *Festuca cinerea* 'Blauglut', some shoots carpeting the soil, others clambering happily to higher vantage points.

Weavers are long-armed ground covers which scramble companionably into their neighbor's arms. In the Withey/Price garden, Caryopteris 'Worcester Gold' *is infiltrated by* Viola cornuta, *an ardent, long-blooming perennial often used in this manner. Photo: Peter Ray*

Its cousin, the annual *Alonsoa warscewiczii*, with its tomato red flowers, will thread in and out of king-sized clumps of 'Six Hills Giant' catmint.

The only rule with weavers is the same as that for climbing plants of all kinds: the guest must never overwhelm the host. We can try to balance these relationships from the start, selecting weavers according to the size of the jobs they must perform and the vigor of the company they keep. No matter how well planned, however, weaving combinations can get out of hand, and the gardener must stand ready to encourage a timid scrambler or control a rambunctious one.

The issue of size is an important one, for it is a common assumption that ground covers are by definition small, low growing plants. Like everything else, ground covers must be appropriate in scale for the border they serve. Great wheels of *Helleborus foetidus*, yard high sword ferns, and broad hostas make splendid ground covers where a birch or California buckeye (*Aesculus californica*) cast significant shade. In a tiny urban mixed border, the lighter shade beneath a diminutive golden dogwood like 'Cherokee Sunset' might be carpeted with club mosses, their plush punctuated by tufts of little hard fern, *Blechnum penna-marina*, and graceful clumps of Bowles' golden grass, *Milium effusum* 'Aureum'.

Only the choicest, slow-growing plants should be considered for the role where space is strictly limited, but elsewhere, ground covering plants may be chosen for a number of attributes beyond size, such as overall form, leaf color, and texture. Prostrate ground covers should certainly be used, but not necessarily at the front of the border. Placed in midborder, perhaps encircling a small tree or shrub group, flat carpeters can create interesting garden topography. Groups of taller plants at the border's front will veil the interior vignette, which is seen in fascinating glimpses rather than left open to view. Nearby, a mature rhododendron may be under-

Certain plants are too lusty for small gardens, but may be invaluable where there is a lot of ground to cover. Lamium galeobdolon *'Variegata' has clambered into the lower reaches of an old willow, yet does not swamp the Northwest native* Dicentra formosa, *an equally determined colonizer. Author's garden. Photo: Mark Lovejoy*

planted with mats of a creeping comfrey, *Symphytum grandiflorum* 'Hidcote Blue', which reach two feet in heavy, moist soils, and the yard-tall *Euphorbia robbiae* might romp between the tapestry hedge and the back of the border proper. In bigger borders, and in transition areas where the garden changes from relatively formal to more naturalistic plantings, ground covers may be very large indeed. Relentless thugs like *Lamium galeobdolon* 'Variegata' (now considered, though seldom sold as, *Galeobdolon luteum* 'Variegatum'), which almost immediately outgrow their welcome in a well regulated garden, can work miracles in wild gardens, where the naturalistic borders meld into genuine woods. There, those implacable arms (which in my garden clamber three or four feet into the arms of a native willow, *Salix schooleri*) are invaluable weed suppressors. Their foliage, though coarse, is very beautiful, and though we often say "silver" when we mean white or cream, these leaves seem licked with metallic paint, a lovely foil for their pastel yellow flowers.

Ground covers are often assumed to be undistinguished, only worthy of admittance to the border in a subsidiary role. Though ground covers rarely take center stage, it is usually their treatment that is commonplace, not the plants themselves. Even pachysandra, that overused cliché, reveals unexpected beauties to the observant. A single fat clump of silver edged pachysandra, placed in a bed of a thick moss or white flowered Corsican sandwort (*Arenaria balearica*), is as striking as many a hosta. It is also a dramatic reminder that less can indeed be more. The lesson is twofold; first, artful gardeners must assess all plants with fresh eyes. Secondly, few plants are at their best en masse. Even in a small border, great glops of any single kind of plant create an ambience more parklike than gardenly.

Where good ground covers succeed, it is always tempting to allow them to work all too well. How many gardens are marred by relentless sweeps of ivy or creeping St. John's wort (*Hypericum calycinum*)? I recently visited a garden where a large border section in the deep shade of a magnificent, high limbed fir was filled entirely with tall, vase shaped lady ferns (*Athyrium filix-femina*). These are strong plants, yet all their character was lost in this sea of self. The effect was curiously sterile as well, especially in contrast with the naturalistic, woody plantings at either hand. A few big clumps of the huge gray hosta, 'Krossa Regal', with a shimmering underplanting of the mannerly *Lamium maculatum* 'Shell Pink', would heighten both drama and intimacy while linking the area more effectively to the surrounding borders.

Choosing the right plants for our specific needs may seem a bewildering task, yet it becomes easier when we broaden our definition of "ground cover" to include any plant that keeps the ground free of weeds and unwanted seedlings. Indeed, in a closely planted mixed border, the distinction between ground cover and border plant may become blurred. Varied in height and size, ornamental in their own right, interplanted in complementary combinations, mixed border ground covers do not fit the standard concept except in function. Here, as anywhere else, their primary purpose is to frustrate weeds, yet their decorative contribution and company manners are of almost equal importance. Most candidates will spread readily, either by overground runner or creeping rootstock. Not a few will self-sow, and some may use all the above methods to procreate. Clearly, willingness to reproduce is a mixed blessing, and the ideal border ground cover is eager to grow, yet easy to control by hand pulling.

Ground covers make excellent servants but horrible masters. Before you unleash these powerful creatures in your borders, look at other gardens in your area and talk with local gardeners. Some widely recommended plants that worked nicely in Massachusetts or Ohio or Colorado have proven relentless thugs in my present garden in Washington State. The satiny gray carpeter *Cerastium tomentosum* that made such satifactory tussocks in Denver romped through my Seattle garden in a single season, and five years of vigilant removal was not enough to eradicate it. Low mats of the same sweet woodruff which was charmingly demure in Ohio took on alarming proportions in the heavy, acid clay of our West Coast garden; here it exceeds two feet in height and expands with incredible rapidity while strangling everything in its wake. Sometimes it works the other way as well; a large, coppery red oxalis (species unknown) which effortlessly carpets

A handful of ground covers are implacable thugs, fit only for the roughest company. Bishop's weed, Aegopodium podagraria, *does not belong in the border, but its adaptability makes it a good choice for difficult situations. Here, it flows around* Crocosmia masoniorum, *itself a relentless multiplier, in a well-matched combination. Garden of Daphne Stewart, Bainbridge Island, Washington. Photo: Mark Lovejoy*

gardens in North Carolina (Zone 8) grows sparse and sullen in the maritime gardens of the Pacific Northwest (also Zone 8). An especially good form of woolly thyme that carpets shell lined paths in a sandy seaside garden a mere mile away dwindles in my heavier soil, and often dies out all together after a cold winter. A plant highly recommended by a Colorado gardener may turn nasty in New Jersey or fail to survive in North Carolina. Such changeable behavior does not mean that anybody was misleading us, or that others are wrong in their assessments. It only points out the fact that plants react to many, many environmental factors. No matter how much research you do, it is not always possible to predict accurately how a given plant will behave in your own garden.

Nursery beds were invented for just these reasons, and a good rule of thumb is to give all unfamiliar ground cover candidates a year of trial before introducing them to the border proper. Ground covers can reduce the gardener's workload, or make more trouble than they save; whether they work for or against us depends on our making thoughtful and informed choices, then hedging our bets. This is not to say that vigorous plants are never the right choice, but only that they are better used deliberately than by accident. Aggressive carpeters like symphytums, vincas, and ajugas may be necessary to make an adequate impact in an outsized or half-natural border, and may be the only plants that can survive beneath a large spruce or beech. In the average garden, such plants could be used with care, but preference might be given to their less rampant varieties or forms, like the relatively slow and decorous *Symphytum ibericum* 'Goldsmith', an Eric Smith selection with soft golden markings, the slow-growing *Ajuga pyramidalis* 'Metallica Crispa', or the dainty *Vinca minor* 'Miss Jekyll's White'. Tiny gardens have no room for rowdy plants and there we might look to choice rock garden plants of many kinds for ground covers of the proper scale which demonstrate acceptable manners.

We tend to ask a good deal from our ground covers, poking them slapdash into bad soil, and leaving them to get on as best they can with little or no help. The very toughest will establish and serve our needs faster if we give them a good start, and the more mannerly among them may perish if faced with utterly adverse circumstances. All ground covers deserve the same soil preparation as any border plant, and all will need adequate watering throughout their first season. Where dry or rooty soils make establishment challenging, digging a layer of hydrated hydrophilic polymer in, along with some compost and coarse grit, will give a tremendous boost to your plants. The polymer continues to act

One of my favorite ground covers is a weed, an annual Oxalis *(species unknown) shown surrounding* Hosta *'Sun Power'. This wild sorrel carpets the garden freely, accepting shade and drought as readily as sun and, since it does not run, it is easily controlled. In another country, my weed might well be a valued garden plant. Author's garden. Photo: Mark Lovejoy*

as a reservoir for years, but both it and the soil itself will need replenishing periodically. How soon depends on many factors, but when ground covers begin to dwindle rather than spread, or look tired and tatty before their time, they have probably become congested and are ready for renewal. Usually, it is enough to pull out a good quarter of the plants, filling their places with fresh compost and polymer. Sometimes, however, the entire colony starts to fail, which may mean that there is a deficiency of nutrients. Where evergreen primulas have grown for many years, a soil sickness can develop, making it all but impossible to grow primulas or their relatives in that spot despite improvements and amendments of all kinds. This is considered by some to be an indication of a mineral or trace element deficiency, though nobody seems clear about which or what to add. In any case, if one kind of plant stops working for you, feed the soil, improve the drainage, and switch to plants from an unrelated family. Persistently difficult ground may be contaminated with residual herbicide or have other problems, and samples should be sent to your county extension service lab for testing.

GROUND COVERS FOR SHADE

Mixed borders, with their full complement of shrubs and small trees, sooner or later develop a significant amount of shaded ground. These areas require judicious and generous planting if they are to remain in visual balance with the sunnier, more luxuriant parts of the borders. In such situations, ground covers can give a well furnished look to mixed plantings that may otherwise look meager in comparison with the rest of the border. Where shade is produced by large, woody plants, the soil is often both dry and infiltrated with roots. Here, it is not enough to prepare or renew the ground before planting, for those greedy, thirsty roots are a serious menace to your plantings. You can't just hack away at them without harming the tree or shrub that produced them, but you can dig out as much old soil as possible, then put down horticultural barrier cloth before amending and replacing the soil. You can also put down the cloth directly on the ground, piling fresh soil on top to a depth of eight or ten inches, so long as the crown of any woody plant is left uncovered. If neither approach proves practical, you might find a solution among the tougher ground covers, many of which are amazingly tolerant of drought and shade, once established.

The snowy wood rush, *Luzula nivea*, and Bowles' golden grass, *Milium effusum* 'Aureum', both do well in dry shade, as do many other attractive grasses. *Lamiastrum galeobdolon* 'Herman's Pride', an upright, silver flecked dead nettle, is an outstanding performer under trees. Though itself deciduous, it consorts pleasantly with evergreen companions like green flowered *Helleborus foetidus* and the red wood spurge, *Euphorbia amygdaloides* 'Rubra'. Another evergreen, the tall, dark leaved *E. robbiae*, is also an efficient carpeter in dry shade, associating well with the white form of *Geranium sylvaticum*, which sows itself among the spurge's glossy shoots. Nearly all of the bugle weeds (*Ajuga* species) tolerate considerable shade as well as sun. Those with light or variegated leaves, like *Ajuga* 'Grey Lady', with pewtery foliage and light blue flowers, or 'Silver Beauty', brushed with cream and silver, show to better advantage in shade than the dark-leaved sorts like 'Purple Brocade'. However, the mottled, beet red form called 'Burgundy Glow' pales to lovely tints of pink and cream and sage in shade, where it makes a pretty underskirt for small border hydrangeas like 'Preziosa' and 'Lanarth White'. Vinca, too, offers many attractive variegated forms, both gold and silver, which lighten dark corners admirably. In both cases, an extreme willingness to travel is tempered as much by the weakness often inherent in variegated forms as by dry soil.

Where shaded ground remains damp or outright wet all summer, tall, whorled Japanese primulas will colonize freely, carpeting thickly as they begin to seed in. Umbrella plant, *Darmera peltata*, spreads quite quickly from its thick, tangled roots, which cover the ground so completely that there is no room for weeds even before the huge, rounded leaves appear in the wake of its tall umbels of frizzy pink flowers. A number of early blooming ground covers thrive in damp shade, notably the lungworts (nearly all hardy to Zone 3). *Pulmonaria rubra* (Zone 5), with salmon-red flowers held above rough-textured leaves, may begin to bloom in December, carrying on through March. *Pulmonaria saccharata* has wonderfully spotted leaves and clusters of pink-and-blue flowers, while a fine form selected by Vita Sackville-West, 'Sissinghurst White', has chalk white flowers above white-spotted leaves. *Pulmonaria villarsae* 'Margery Fish' (probably Zone 5), a striking Italian, has hairy, narrower leaves strongly spattered with silver, its flowers very red in bud, but opening celeste blue. *Pulmonaria longifolia* 'Bertram Anderson' has narrow, straplike leaves, heavily dotted with white, and flowers of summer sky blue, while its offspring, 'Roy Davidson', is somewhat neater in habit, and offers powder blue blossoms. Blue-eyed Mary, *Omphalodes verna* (Zone 7), spreads in tidy, low mats, its evergreen, matte leaves and small sprays of blue flowers (white, in the form 'Alba'), lovely from late winter through spring. However, by midsummer, all of these can rapidly lose their looks, often succumbing to mildew as well. To combat this, they can be trimmed back to a small rosette of new growth in early summer, then treated to a dose of compost and manure tea. The resulting new growth will be compact and remain handsome through the summer.

EVERGREEN GROUND COVERS

Evergreen ground covers present the gardener with a great variety of options, both in form and degree; some technically qualify as evergreen, yet look decidedly less prepossessing in winter. Some will act deciduous in a hard winter, leafing out again in early spring. Others come into their own during the colder months, which makes them especially valuable in mild winter areas where they may be expected to pull considerable weight during the off seasons. Certain plants like *Geranium tuberosum* are winter green but summer dormant, making them most valuable in mild winter areas. Any ground cover's winter appearance obviously matters most where snowfall is late, light, or rare. However, even where snow obscures the ground from November through March, evergreen ground covers may be of considerable value, keeping bulbs clean in mud sea-

son, providing some measure of insulation during thaws, minimizing frost heaves, and acting as a thermal blanket to bring borderline hardy companions through harsh winters.

Reliable bugle weed, *Ajuga reptans* (Zones 3 to 4), is a variable species with many colorful forms. Among the best are 'Burgundy Glow', a warm reddish pink marbled with cream; the oversized, wine red 'Jungle Beauty'; and the silvery 'Variegata'. Slower to spread, but highly dramatic in appearance are the elegant, crinkled clusters of *A. pyramidalis* 'Metallica Crispa' (Zone 6), their new leaves almost black, the flowers deep blue on four-inch spikes. A lovely hybrid, 'Purple Brocade', seems to combine the foliage type of 'Metallica Crispa' with the size and coloration of *A. reptans* 'Atropurpurea', and is among the easiest plants to use well.

Although bergenias (Zones 3 to 6) have been sadly unfashionable in recent years, their solid virtues earn them a valued place in mixed borders. Especially fine are *Bergenia cordifolia* 'Purpurea' (Zone 3), whose big, round leaves take on murky tints of maroon in winter, and *B. ciliata* forma *ligulata* (Zones 4 to 5), a hardy Himalayan that makes tidy, cabbagelike rosettes of freshest green, tinged in the cold months with bronze and copper. Hybrids like 'Bressingham White' (white flowers) and 'Rotblum' (dark magenta red flowers) are hardy to Zone 3, but may be less evergreen in the coldest regions. Bergenias are moderate but dependable spreaders, though their appearance may suffer in dry, exposed positions.

An old cottage garden favorite, *Campanula poscharskyana* (Zone 3), will pour in pools and rivulets through larger border plants. Its flowers—Wedgwood blue in the species, white, pale pink, lavender, or clear blue in various forms—are produced from midsummer well into autumn, and its leaves remain presentable all year round. This fast worker must be watched in small gardens, though an annual shovel pruning holds it in check.

The dark green, lustrous ruffles of little *Cardamine trifolia* (Zone 6) set off small border treasures without smothering anything, and its own frilly white flowers lighten shady spots in spring. It will also grow in sun, where its dense foliage provides winter insulation for half hardy bulbs like the refined *Crocosmia* 'Citronella'.

Strange little *Chiastophyllum oppositifolium* (Zones 5 to 6, to eight inches) is a charming creeper with leathery, succulent-looking scalloped leaves. In a hard winter, it will act deciduous, the leaves returning with the first crocus. Its curious chains of yellow florets, looking much like miniature laburnums, arrive in late spring and persist through early summer, making a wonderful partner for fried egg flower, *Limnanthes douglasii*. This tough little creature spreads fastest in moist shade, but is very drought tolerant, enough so to accept a dry wall position in rock gardens.

Mrs. Robb's spurge, *Euphorbia robbiae* (Zone 7), is a vigorous, upright species with rapidly running rootstock. The eighteen-inch stems carry dark, rounded leaves in neat whorls, topped by loose flowering heads of limey green which are very long-lasting in bloom. Tolerant of almost any condition, it performs extremely well in dry shade, though it has a distinct tendency to abandon the original point of introduction. This is eaily remedied by resetting wandering plants to fill the bare spots every few years. Not for small gardens full of choice treasures, this is nonetheless an invaluable plant, and its errant offshoots, along with their ropey roots, are easily removed by hand pulling in early spring when the ground is soft.

There are any number of excellent evergreen border ferns, in a tremendous variety of forms and sizes. Some, like the Japanese autumn fern, *Dryopteris erythrosora* (Zone 5), have unusual coloration which suggests all sorts of fascinating combinations. In spring, the new fronds are a metallic, copper-pink, a color readily matched with Julian primroses. Its rich summer green emphasizes the firm, crisp texture of its shapely fronds, which will cover fading daffodil or tulip foliage handily. Cool weather tinges the mature leaves with red and bronze, calling up color echoes in red spurges like *Euphorbia amygdaloides* 'Rubra' and *E. martinii*. Autumn fern makes a mannerly, slowly spreading ground cover in shade. Christmas ferns, *Polystichum acrostichoides*, native to the Southeast, hardy to Zone 3, make compact, neatly furnished clumps some two feet high, and

adapt readily to the shady depths of the mixed border. On a larger scale, the western sword fern, *P. munitum* (Zone 4) builds into majestic clumps of lustrous, dark green, at their best in full shade but able to take considerable sun in stride if the soil remains moist. A handful of hydrophilic polymer in its root zone makes most any fern tolerant of drier soils, and keeps evergreens looking fresh all year round.

If *Geranium oxonianum* 'Rose Clair' (Zone 5) did not seed quite so enthusiastically, I might consider it a perfect ground cover for medium and large scale plantings. In winter, its resting rosette of glossy, hand sized leaves is perhaps a foot across and equally high. By spring, it has doubled in bulk like rising bread, and the first of its countless clear rose (thus the name) flowers appear. At midsummer, it forms an unbroken half circle a yard across and two or three feet high. Any which begin to flag or flop are sheared back, and will be neatly refurnished, recovering within days. Where I want more compact summer plants, I cut them back quite hard in midspring. All of them get sheared hard in late summer, so they present a trim appearance during the winter. Our orchard trees are all encircled with a ruff of 'Rose Clair', which protects the trunks from the whirring mower, taking weekly mowing of its own outer leaves cheerfully.

Winter roses, the hellebore clan, are perhaps the best known of the cold season bloomers. *Helleborus foetidus* (Zone 6) is among the handsomest during the off season. This striking plant colonizes rapidly by seed in shade or sun, and is notably drought tolerant. Its massive leaves and strong silhouette earn it top marks as a tall ground cover beneath mature trees, where it associates beautifully with silver-leaved lamiums and Christmas ferns.

Ivy (Zones 5 to 7) is more versatile than is generally recognized, and where hardy, its dozens of attractive forms broaden the garden's ground-cover palette considerably. 'Little Diamond', green and silver; 'Goldheart', green splashed gold; and 'Buttercup', soft, clear yellow, are excellent border candidates, climbing walls or carpeting with good will, as will unmarked forms such as 'Sweetheart' and 'Green Ripple'. Many florists' and houseplant ivies that offer an exciting range of form and foliage

Shady borders may be carpeted with ferns, both evergreen and deciduous, in partnership with hostas, of which there are literally hundreds of hybrids available to be mingled in mutually enhancing combinations. Photo: Peter Ray

texture are hardy to Zones 5 to 6, and are well worth a try in a sheltered spot even in colder gardens.

Dead nettles—the lamiums—are rightfully popular border ground covers, for they are both efficient and attractive. The family includes some thugs, especially *Lamium galeobdolon* (now officially *Galeobdolon luteum*), but most of the named forms are willing but manageable. A few, like *L. maculatum* 'Shell Pink', are rather slow to spread, and may need initial cosseting in unprepossessing sites. Though nominally evergreen, the lamiums tend to look ratty rather than natty during the colder months. A rejuvenating trim to two or three inches, and a dose of manure tea or mild fertilizer given during late summer when the autumnal cleanup begins will re-furbish the plants within a few days, and the new leaves hold their freshness through the winter. *Lamium maculatum* (Zone 3, to twelve inches) is more vigorous and less appealing than its forms 'White Nancy', silver of leaf and white of flower, and 'Roseum', with a feather of white on each leaf and chalk pink blossoms. The closely related *Lamiastrum galeobdolon* 'Herman's Pride' (currently lumped into *Galeobdolon luteum*, Zone 4) is an upright, close carpeter, its tidy foliage flecked with white tweed, against which the soft yellow flowers look especially handsome. It is a slow starter in deep, dry shade, but once established, it performs very well. The ex-lamiastrums are only evergreen during mild winters, but releaf in time to accompany early bulbs.

Saxifrages of many sorts may be used as ground covers. The many mossy ones like *Saxifraga rosacea* (Zone 6) can be set to run between clumps of dwarf iris at the border front, especially in lighter soils. Among the most reliable on heavy soil in shade is *S. stolonifera* (Zone 6, to ten inches) the houseplant familiar as mother of thousands. It has rounded, hairy leaves of very dark green veined in reddish black, their undersides flushed clear red. It makes an excellent ground cover for colonies of the native bowman's root, *Gillenia trifoliata* (Zone 4, to three feet), for both produce sprays of starry cream-colored flowers, reddish in the bud, at midsummer, and both take on extra tints of red in autumn. Mother of thousands may act deciduous in colder winters, but reappears faithfully come spring. London pride, *Saxifraga umbrosa* (Zone 6), is a traditional ground cover beneath shrub roses, but its foamy flowers, more pale red than pink, and scalloped, glossy green leaves are an excellent foil for arching *Buddleia davidii* 'Burgundy' or the tiered branches of white-flowered *Viburnum plicatum* 'Mariesii'.

Symphytum grandiflorum (now considered *S. ibericum*, Zone 3, to two feet), is as determined as any other comfrey, yet few other plants will carpet so well among large rhododendrons or under spreading firs. Several selected forms are available, among them 'Hidcote Pink' and 'Hidcote Blue', their creamy bells tipped in sugar pink or china blue, and 'Goldsmith' with gold-variegated foliage. The

In sun or shade, good soil or dry, Lamium maculatum *'White Nancy' is a trouper with lasting good looks. In winter, it is fitfully evergreen and low growing, but its tall summer growth will hide the flopping foliage of* Colchicum speciosum *'Album' effortlessly. Author's garden. Photo: Mark Lovejoy*

named forms are larger than the plain species, and all are fine ground-cover plants for larger or more naturalistic mixed borders.

Periwinkle or vinca is planted in tremendous quantities, yet rarely well used. The dwarf myrtle, *Vinca minor* (Zone 5) offers over a dozen named forms with variously colored leaves and flowers, all of them fine border ground covers so long as their inherent vigor (which is relative) is considered before planting. Vincas are lacy intertwiners that root as they run, making them splendid cover for bulbs and early blooming wildflowers. They tolerate drought better in shade than in sun, and an annual shearing keeps them fresh in appearance and moderate in behavior. The mannerly little 'Miss Jekyll's White', nearly prostrate, is an outstanding performer in light shade, where it remains very airy and open, making excellent cover for tiny bulbs that coarser companions might smother. In more sun, it is denser in habit, filling in wonderfully after species tulips have ripened off. Where a more complete carpet is wanted, the vigorous *V. m.* 'Bowles' Variety' will spread in thick pools, its broad, shiny leaves an effective weed barrier which can nonetheless be penetrated by scillas and colchicums in their seasons. Deep, summer sky blue flowers are especially large in this form, as in *V. alpina purpurea*, with soft green leaves and deep burgundy red flowers.

Woolly lamb's ears, Stachys byzantina *'Cotton Boll', is an ideal ground-cover plant for mixed border work, covering ground freely yet easily controlled. At night, the leaves reflect headlights effectively, so I use it along the driveway; it keeps cars on track, and if anybody miscalculates, the lamb's ears recover in a matter of days. Author's garden. Photo: Mark Lovejoy*

DECIDUOUS GROUND COVERS

Deciduous ground covers are legion, and may include almost any perennial, as well as a number of bulbous plants, grasses, and even shrubs. Following are a few outstanding performers for mixed border situations, but this must be considered a very partial listing, and in no way exhaustive. Every region has its own natives, its own specialties, its own planting styles and manners, all of which will be reflected in the most imaginative ground cover plantings as well as in commonplace treatments. The rule of thumb here is that the ground-cover plant echo, support, or supplement the main players as well as perform the more routine functions of the job.

Lady's mantle, *Alchemilla mollis* (Zone 3), has a small resting rosette, from which its pleated, fanlike foliage expands in late spring and early summer. It makes a fine cover for species crocus and minor bulbs, which bloom outside the circle of its crown, then ripen and wither in the shelter of its extensive arms. A prolific self-sower and efficient smotherer of weeds, it can take a couple of years for alchemilla to settle in, but once established, it is in the garden for good. The fluffy, feathery sprays of chartreuse flowers dry well, and are very popular with wreath makers and flower arrangers. Blooming well in partial shade or full sun, the matte, sage green of its leaves blends nicely with nearly any color scheme, and offers considerable foliar interest once its flopsy flowers have been removed (do this as soon as color begins to fade, before it has time to seed itself everywhere).

Mouse plant, *Arisarum proboscideum* (Zones 5 to 6), sends up its glossy, arrow-shaped leaves in late winter. By early spring, they are full of fascinating flowers, like fat brown and white mice with extraordinarily long tails that stick up provocatively above the thick leaves. It grows well in damp shade, and is a charming carpeter among clumps of *Iris foetidissima* and lacy ferns.

Blue leadwort, *Ceratostigma plumbaginoides* (Zone 4), is perhaps the best of all companions for minor bulbs and species tulips; during their glory, it is all but invisible, yet it rises handily to shield their fall from beauty. Pleasant but unremarkable in spring, blue leadwort gains distinction as summer ripens. By early autumn, it is brilliant both in flower and foliage. Its coppery red leaves and lucid blue flowers make an excellent understory for bronzed chrysanthemums and rose or purple asters and sets off lavender colchicums attractively.

The delicate foliage of *Corydalis lutea* (Zone 5) spreads in lacy mounds throughout the garden. An irrepressible self-sower, it often places itself very cleverly, and since the extra seedlings are very easily pulled, they are not a nuisance. Tolerant of drought in shade or sun, it responds to good border conditions with unflagging vitality, producing hundreds of birdlike, warm yellow blossoms through the summer. Its sage green, teardrop foliage, rather like that of a maidenhair fern, lightens the heavier leaves of most perennials. In the form 'Alba' the flowers are creamy white and the leaves a frosty blue. It is evergreen during mild winters.

Hardy geraniums like the ardent runner *Geranium macrorrhizum* (Zone 4) can cover a great deal of ground in a season, suppressing even territorial ruffians like creeping buttercups and witch grass. Though implacable in pursuit of pests, *G. macror-*

rhizum itself is quite easy to control simply by pulling errant pieces. Its big, felty leaves are attractive until you accidentally crush one and release its acrid, most unpleasant smell. (The foliage is sometimes described as "apple scented," but they must mean rotten apples.) The species blooms a clear magenta pink, softened to sugar pink in the form 'Ingwerson's Variety', and very pale pastel pink in the form 'Album'. Many other color forms are available in the nursery trade. An unusual clump former, *G. wlassowianum* (Zone 5) opens new leaves like ruby stained glass, turning coppery green by early spring. The lovely summer foliage is spangled with big, periwinkle blue flowers, and in autumn, the whole plant turns bronze and gold with reddish highlights. *Geranium himalayense* (Zone 3) builds slowly into

Golden creeping Jenny, Lysimachia nummularia 'Aurea', spills out from hedge and pot in the Withey/Price herb garden. Both this yellow form and the plain green-leaved one accept sun or shade, and are tolerant of moderate drought once established. Photo: Mark Lovejoy

On a warm day, this scented thyme bank is alive with bees. Thymes and other Mediterranean herbs grow well in poor soils and exposed positions, wanting only plenty of sun and good drainage to perform well. Stecher garden, Seattle, designed by Carrie Becker. Photo: Lynne Harrison

broad mounds of finely cut foliage, above which its violet-blue flowers cluster all summer long. The family offers a very large range of colors, habits and sizes from which to choose.

Creeping Jenny, *Lysimachia nummularia* (Zone 3), will thread its way through perennial or woody companions without harm, and also makes good cover for small bulbs. The golden form, 'Aurea', lightens dark corners charmingly, and is neat enough for the border's front. Though a very quick worker, it is readily controlled by an annual shovel pruning session, and young shoots may be hand pulled.

Border catmints are mostly forms of *Nepeta* × *faassenii* (Zone 3), a sterile interspecies cross that does not self-sow. It spreads in fully clothed clumps of sage green, and in most forms is eighteen to twenty-four inches tall. *Nepeta* × *faassenii* 'Blue Wonder' has larger, greener leaves than most, and the flowers are extra large and very clear blue. 'White Wonder' has very soft white flowers, and blooms a few days later. The plant called 'Blue Beauty' in this country is known as 'Souvenir d'Andre Chaudron' in Europe and England, a robust plant with takeover tendencies that make its vivid blue flowers less enticing. A better form for mixed borders is *N.* × *f.* 'Dropmore', with bright blue flowers produced over a long period. 'Six Hills Giant' is a hybrid with lots of energy, making it a terrific plant for big borders with room for three or four feet of catmint at a whack. All benefit from an early trimming to keep them from splaying open in late spring, and all should be cut back a bit after blooming, to promote second and even third crops of flowers.

Prostrate and semi-shrubby thymes may escape the herb bed or kitchen garden to creep their way into the border. Myriad color forms, from the splashy little shrublets of lemon thyme, *Thymus* × *citriodorus* (Zone 5), either silver or gold variegated, may spread in sunny, warm spots to cover two square feet in a single season, making them well worth growing even as annuals. The mat formers like *T. pseudolanuginosus* (Zone 6), woolly gray and pungent of leaf, clothe the front of the border or carpet beneath standard roses or tall sheaves of Siberian iris. Collectors enjoy amassing the numerous named forms of garden thymes, but marvelous calico carpets can be woven simply by combining plants of mother of thyme, *T. serpyllum*, (Zone 3)

in all the shades between red and white, including the lilacs and lavenders.

The large and cheerful violet family includes many good ground covers. Tiny charmers like *Viola tricolor* 'Bowles' Black' (Zone 4), an ardent self-sower with coal black flowers held amid minute, dusky purple leaves, and the rugged little spreader, *V. labradorica* 'Purpurea' (Zone 5), both tolerate sun or shade as well as drought, and their shallow roots make them noncompetitive with bulbs and delicate perennials. The horned pansy, *V. cornuta* (Zone 5), offers a wide palette of tint and tone, and its long, loose-jointed arms clamber willingly into neighboring plants. It is a splendid border knitter, and each plant will cover up to two square feet of bare ground in good soil. Investigation will reveal many more delightful options awaiting our discovery.

Books for Further Reading

ollowing are a number of books that will prove most useful to the mixed border builder. Some, like Barbara Barton's *Gardening by Mail*, are worth a whole bookshelf in themselves. Others, like Penelope Hobhouse's *Color in Your Garden*, are very specialized, yet still of general interest. They are not all in print, but are worth prowling for in used bookstores or ordering through book-searching services. Regional knowledge is always invaluable to the gardener, and it is well worth checking regional libraries and local universities as well as county extension services for good sources of specific, regionally appropriate information.

Capability's Books carries the largest selection of in-print garden books in the country. For a catalog, call 1-800-247-8154.

Booknoll Farm, started by the late Elizabeth Woodburn, carries a large selection of new and used garden and horticulture books. For a list, write to: Booknoll Farm, Hopewell, New Jersey 08525.

Armitage, Allen. *Herbaceous Perennial Plants*. Athens, GA: Varsity Press, 1989.

Balston, Michael. *The Well-Furnished Garden*. New York: Simon & Schuster, 1986.

Barton, Barbara. *Gardening by Mail*. Boston: Houghton Mifflin, 1990.

Bean, W. J. *Trees & Shrubs Hardy in the British Isles, 8th Edition* (5 volumes). Portland, OR: Timber Press, 1988.

Beckett, Kenneth. *Growing Hardy Perennials*. Portland, OR: Timber Press, 1982.

Boisset, Caroline. *Gardening in Time*. New York: Prentice Hall, 1990.

Brookes, John. *A Book of Garden Design*. New York: Macmillan Publishing Co., 1991.

———. *The Small Garden*. New York: Crown Publishers, 1989.

———, Beckett, Kenneth and Everett, Thomas. *The Gardener's Index of Plants and Flowers*. New York: Collier Books, 1987.

Chatto, Beth. *The Green Tapestry*. New York: Simon & Schuster, 1988.

———. *The Damp Garden*. London: J. M. Dent & Sons, Ltd., 1982.

———. *The Dry Garden*. London: J. M. Dent & Sons, Ltd., 1978.

Coombes, Allen J. *Dictionary of Plant Names.* Portland, OR: Timber Press, 1985.

Druse, Ken. *The Natural Garden.* New York: Clarkson N. Potter, 1989.

Ferguson, Nicola. *Right Plant, Right Place.* New York: Summit Books, 1984.

Fish, Margery. *A Flower Every Day.* London: Faber & Faber, 1981.

———. *Cottage Garden Flowers.* London: Faber & Faber, 1981.

———. *Gardening in the Shade.* London: Faber & Faber, 1981.

———. *Ground Cover Plants.* London: Faber & Faber, 1981.

Harper, Pamela. *Designing With Perennials.* New York: Macmillan Publishing Co., 1991.

———, and McGourty, Frederick. *Perennials: How to Select, Grow and Enjoy.* Los Angeles: Price Stern Sloan, 1985.

Hillier Color Dictionary of Trees and Shrubs. London: David & Charles, 1984.

Hobhouse, Penelope. *Color in Your Garden.* Boston: Little, Brown, 1985.

———. *Flower Gardens.* Boston: Little, Brown, 1991.

———. *Garden Style.* Boston: Little Brown, 1988.

Jellito, Leo, and Schacht, Wilhelm. *Hardy Herbaceous Perennials* (2 volumes). Portland, OR: Timber Press, 1990.

Keen, Mary, *The Garden Border Book.* Deer Park, WI: Capability's Books, 1987.

Lacey, Stephen. *Scent in Your Garden.* Boston: Little, Brown, 1991.

———. *The Startling Jungle.* Boston: David R. Godine, Inc., 1990.

Lacy, Allen. *The Garden in Autumn.* New York: Atlantic Monthly Press, 1990.

Lawrence, Elizabeth. *Gardens in Winter.* Baton Rouge: Claitor's Publishing Division, 1977.

———. *The Little Bulbs.* Chapel Hill, N.C.: Duke University Press, 1986.

———. *A Southern Garden.* Chapel Hill, N.C.: Duke University Press, 1991.

Lima, Patrick. *The Harrowsmith Perennial Garden.* Camden East, Ontario: Camden House, 1987.

Lloyd, Christopoher. *The Adventurous Gardener.* New York: Random House, 1983.

———. *Foliage Plants.* New York: Random House, 1973.

———. *The Well-Chosen Garden.* New York: Harper & Row, 1984.

———. *The Well-Tempered Garden.* New York: Random House, 1985.

Malitz, Jerome. *Personal Landscapes.* Portland, OR: Timber Press, 1989.

Nuese, Josephine. *The Country Garden.* New York: Collier Books, 1989.

Osler, Mirabel. *A Gentle Plea for Chaos.* New York: Simon & Schuster, 1989.

Phillips, Roger, and Rix, Martyn. *The Random House Book of Bulbs.* New York: Random House, 1989.

———. *Perennials* (2 volumes). New York: Random House, 1991.

———. *Roses.* New York: Random House, 1988.

———. *Shrubs.* New York: Random House, 1989.

Rice, Graham. *Plants for Problem Places.* Portland, OR: Timber Press, 1988.

Sabuco, John. *The Best of the Hardiest.* Flossmore, IL: Plantsmen's Publications, 1990.

Sackville-West, Vita. *Vita Sackville-West's Garden Book.* New York: Atheneum, 1983.

Schenk, George. *The Complete Shade Gardener.* Boston: Houghton Mifflin, 1984.

Thomas, Graham Stuart. *The Art of Planting*. Boston: David R. Godine, Inc., 1984.

——. *Perennial Garden Plants*. Portland, OR: Timber Press, 1990.

——. *Plants for Ground Cover*. London: J. M. Dent and Sons, Ltd., 1984.

Verey, Rosemary. *The Art of Planting*. Boston: Little, Brown, 1990.

——. *The Garden in Winter*. Boston: Little, Brown, 1988.

Whitehead, Jeffrey. *The Hedge Book*. Pownal, VT: Storey Communications, Garden Way Publishing, 1991.

Whiten, Faith and Geoff. *Creating a New Garden*. New York: W. W. Norton and Co., 1986.

Wilder, Louise Beebe. *Adventures With Hardy Bulbs*. New York: Collier Books, 1990.

Wright, Michael. *The Complete Handbook of Garden Plants*. New York: Facts on File, 1984.

Wyman, Donald. *Wyman's Gardening Encyclopedia*. New York: Macmillan Publishing Co., 1986.

Index

Note: Page numbers in *italics* refer to illustrations.